The Mythical Battle

Battle

HASTINGS 1066

The Mythical Battle

HASTINGS 1066

Ashley Hern

ROBERT HALE

First published in 2017 by Robert Hale, an imprint
of The Crowood Press Ltd, Ramsbury, Marlborough
Wiltshire SN8 2HR

www. crowood.com

British Library Cataloguing-in-Publication Data
A catalogue record for this book is available from the
British Library.

ISBN 978 0 7198 2475 3

Typeset by Jean Cussons Typesetting, Diss, Norfolk

Printed and bound in India by Parksons Graphics

Contents

Acknowledgements

My sincere thanks go to Dr Glenn Foard of the University of Huddersfield, for generously sharing with me his research on his excavations at Hastings and his extensive experience of battlefield archaeology. Alan Larsen shared his enthusiasm for the battle and his unique insights into the culture of the Hastings re-enactments. Jack Edwards of University College, Oxford, kindly allowed me to look at his thesis on Danish settlement. The staff at the Battle of Bosworth Visitor Centre responded helpfully to my many enquiries. My colleagues in the History Department at the Manchester Grammar School have tolerated my distraction and mental absences while writing this book with their customary grace – particular thanks go to Simon Orth for reading some of the chapters. Alexander Stilwell has been a patient and supportive editor, and his perceptive comments have greatly improved the book.

This book would not have been possible without several years of teaching the Battle of Hastings to Sixth-formers at Manchester Grammar School, each of whom have subjected me to that idiosyncratic mixture of cynicism and curiosity that the British education system seems to provoke in later adolescence.

In many ways this book is also a testament to the inspirational history teaching of John Croasdell and Bill Reed, who eschewed modern teaching methods and instead used enthusiasm and an emphasis on knowledge and set me on the path to spending the majority of my life contemplating the past.

Above all else, I am grateful to Anne, Felix and Rufus for their love and encouragement.

List of Illustrations

Map of England in 1066 with key locations mentioned in the book.

Introduction

BEING FACTUAL

'What is a fact?' This is a question I often ask any Sixth-form student if they tell me that they want to study history at university. A look of bemusement on the student's face usually results, an expression that seems to appear with increasing frequency as the years pass. 'We know what a fact is, sir,' they reply. 'It's what you always demand we put more of in our essays. Are you finally losing it, sir? We have had our suspicions for some time!'

After some cautious discussion, I can usually persuade them to humour me and we then collectively attempt to take an empirical approach to the matter.

'What about the Battle of Hastings?'

There are nods of agreement. Like most school pupils in England, they studied this particular battle when they began their history education at secondary school. Some studied the battle at primary school; a few studied it again in their Sixth-form studies. Nor is this a parochial concern: teaching about the Battle of Hastings is a national phenomenon. History teachers, just like King Harold II, will never escape the battle unless they leave the classroom and ascend to greater things, like Duke William of Normandy.

Below is a composite version of a classroom exchange on this issue in the form of a dialogue (with apologies to Plato).

ME: Where did the battle take place?

PUPILS: Hastings, of course, sir!

ME: Did it?

PUPILS: Well, alright. It took place at Battle – but that's near Hastings.

ME: So, why do we call it the Battle of Hastings then? One could argue that by the standards of modern warfare, it would not be considered a battle at all – it lasted a day and we can't be sure how many people were fighting on both sides. The Battle of the Somme in 1916 involved millions of soldiers, resulted in hundreds of thousands of casualties and lasted for four months. Would it not be better to refer to what happened in 1066 as 'a skirmish in Sussex'? Skirmishes can have devastating political consequences, after all. Look at Prince Llewellyn ap Gruffudd, whose death in a skirmish at Builth in 1282 heralded the conquest of Wales by Edward I of England.

PUPILS: But the battle led to the conquest of England. You can't dismiss it as just a skirmish. We should call it the Battle of Hastings as that's what people have always called it. It's traditional. People know what you are referring to.

ME: Who decided this tradition? When did it begin?

PUPILS: We don't know! Ask us another one.

ME: OK, so when was the Battle of Hastings actually fought?

PUPILS: 1066!

ME: What date?

ONE VERY BRIGHT PUPIL: Fourteenth of October? It was the anniversary a few months ago! [This conversation usually occurs in January]

ME: Officially – but that was according to the old Julian calendar. When this was revised and Britain was brought into line with the Gregorian calendar in 1752, the anniversary of the battle officially became the twenty-fifth of October. OK, what about the year 1066 – what dating system does this use?

PUPILS: The Christian dating system.

ME: Doesn't this reflect one cultural perspective? According to the Islamic dating system, the year the battle took place was AH 459. In the Jewish calendar, the year was 4827. In the Mayan Long Count, the date was 0.12.0.0.18 ....

I will allow the rest of the scene to unfold in your imagination.

Confusion and irritation are the two principal emotions this conversation provokes amongst my pupils, but before being accused of semantic pedantry and postmodern flippancy, there is a serious point to be made as part of a wider attempt to make my pupils think more critically about the information that they think they know. We believe that the Battle of Hastings is an important event because of the way our understanding of the past has been organized. The famous 'Whig' interpretation of history, which emerged in the eighteenth century, remained a standard view amongst professional historians well into the twentieth century. 'Whig' is the term given to a loose affiliation of individuals with common political beliefs that developed in support, amongst other things, of constitutional monarchy, the Hanoverian succession and parliamentary sovereignty. This viewpoint saw the Norman Conquest as the end of a 'Golden Age' in which native English customs of freedom and equality were destroyed by the oppressive rule of foreigners. For writers such as Thomas Macaulay and his successors, English history after 1066 consisted of a series of struggles to regain these lost freedoms, through Magna Carta, the Reformation, the Civil War and the Glorious Revolution of 1689.

This is, of course, nonsense. Anglo-Saxon England was not a paragon of proto-parliamentary sovereignty and freedom. According to Domesday Book, slaves made up between a tenth and a quarter of the rural population. The English law codes from the earliest surviving examples of the seventh century to those of Edward the Confessor all made it clear that status was the most important principle in assessing justice, not a universal conception of human rights. A landowner's word was worth more than the word of someone of humbler origin, and the value in blood money compensation correlated to one's social status. There was no equality before the law. Nevertheless, these romantic notions of the past are extremely potent because tradition is one of the most powerful means of legitimizing political ideas.

It is easy to spot when authoritarian regimes manipulate history to justify their rule. In modern China, the ruling Communist Party manipulates the history of the Sino-Japanese War (1937–45), which the party claims to have won for China, and keeps alive the memory of very real Japanese atrocities to stoke up nationalist feelings that distract popular anger from the corruption and scandal that dogs party rule. In 2016, the Russian President Vladimir Putin was acting very deliberately when, in Moscow, he unveiled a giant statue of another Vladimir, the prince of the Kievan Rus' who adopted Orthodox Christianity (ruled 980–1015) and who is seen as the father of modern Russia; this Vladimir is also regarded by Ukrainians as the founder of

Ukraine. Hence, unveiling a statue of the prince was a strong message explaining and justifying Russia's determination to prevent Ukraine moving away from Russian influence on the grounds of their shared historical development.

We are less able to see when our own society behaves in a similar way. Interpreting the past through the lens of contemporary concerns is a universal aspect of human behaviour when we form complex societies. Contemporary debates about how society should change, or not, are reflections of what we believe about the past, whether those beliefs are positive or negative. Discussions over the future of the NHS reflect views towards its founding principles of the 1940s and whether they are relevant today. One's position on Britain's relationship with the European Union depends on one's view of Britain's record as a nation-state: is this something to be proud of or are supra-national institutions the future for human government? The Battle of Hastings is not an axiom. How it has been understood has been shaped and altered by the generations that followed.

The Battle of Hastings, 1066, remains a key date in British collective memory and an important part of the shared understanding of British history. It has been drummed into school-children as an easily memorable phrase and a major turning point in the story of Britain ever since a national education system was created in the late nineteenth century. This was, in turn, a product of the creation of university history courses, which primarily focused on the history and evolution of the British constitution. It was the earlier Whig belief that the Battle of Hastings had introduced important changes by paving the way for the subsequent Norman Conquest that was refined and documented in a more systematic way by the likes of Bishop Stubbs. Stubbs' *Constitutional History of England* (3 vols, 1874–78) was one of the foundational texts of the History School at the University of Oxford that has shaped subsequent debate, whether through acceptance or rejection. The battle has never failed to find an audience from the medieval period through to the 900th anniversary, which was marked by a series of celebrations across England and a new wave of television documentaries, heritage events, newspaper columns, and reprinted editions of numerous academic and more popular history books that have been written in the past few decades. However, the question remains: what do we actually *know* about the battle itself? Is our knowledge of it entirely derived from the concerns of the present?

We tend to think of history as events that have happened in the past, but the more one attempts to study these events, the more one realizes how elusive the key details are. Human history is never preserved intact, but is reflected through a series of individual experiences, which are recorded directly or indirectly through written and oral records. An historian has to sift through this mass of confusing, and often contradictory, information in an attempt to reconstruct what they believe to be the most feasible interpretation, taking into account the more obvious attempts by those who would prefer a certain interpretation favoured. The Battle of Hastings was one of those events where an official version became imperative. Our most detailed source, the Norman author William of Poitiers, can be considered to have been writing what would today be recognized as propaganda. There are many problems with the use of that word for the eleventh century, but whatever the size of the reading public then, it seems clear to me that authors such as William of Poitiers were writing with posterity firmly in their sights. William had studied the classics and was impressed that he could know of the deeds of Julius Caesar a millennium after they occurred; he was determined that a similar fate should befall his patron, Duke William of Normandy – and in many ways William of Poitiers succeeded.

The other key word in this book's title is 'mythical', from 'myth'. 'Myth' is often misused in historical writing as a simple synonym for 'false' or 'untruth'; sometimes even a 'lie'. While the aphorism that 'the first casualty of war is truth' is a useful corrective when dealing with official accounts of conflict, one has to be careful not to base one's entire epistemology upon such a phrase. 'Myth' is a polymeme – a word with multiple meanings. Theorists have disagreed over the word's precise meaning ever since the subject became grounds for intellectual investigation in the nineteenth century. At this point, the focus, led by pioneers such as J.G. Frazer, was on the physical world and myths were believed to function as a way of explaining this. Myth was thus the counterpart to modern science and had no place in modernity. In the twentieth century, anthropologists and other social scientists began to broaden the term beyond the limitations set by this narrow definition, and increasingly read it symbolically as a way to understand how society functioned or human psychology. My definition is to see a myth as the way that an event is remembered and adapted to place the differences and similarities of the past, and understand it through immediate human experience. This transforms a single episode into a narrative that becomes a credo or cherished conviction. The idea of 'rags to riches' in the United States of America is a myth, which exists independently of any particular story or reality. Nevertheless, it is a myth that many Americans believe in, even if its validity is challenged. The story can be true or false, but it must have

13

a powerful hold over its adherents. As we will see, our understanding of the Battle of Hastings has been deeply shaped by its ever-evolving mythical nature.

This book is, therefore, more than merely another attempt to reconstruct a narrative about what happened at Hastings that day in October in 1066. This has already been done supremely well by several other authors. Instead, this book is an attempt to highlight two issues: how little we actually know for certain about the battle, and how the popular understanding of the battle has been shaped by the debates and concerns of later periods. This is important as there are certain debates about the Battle of Hastings that are perennial, reoccurring regularly in the modern media when the topic is discussed: how did Harold die and why did the English lose?[1] There are a variety of possible answers to these questions, but while assessing the interpretation that best suits the evidence is fundamental, it is also crucial to examine the context for the alternative answers that have been proposed.

The other issues that will be discussed in this book include the diplomatic significance of Duke William of Normandy's claim to the throne of England and the Norman attempt to secure papal support for this claim. The major issue here is the way that William – to use a term with contemporary resonance – created a 'dodgy dossier' to bolster his military support and how that shaped Norman representations of the battle. Another issue is the extent to which the Norman and Anglo-Saxon armies represented diametrically opposed military systems. The usual view is that the battle represented a conflict between cavalry and infantry, heralding three centuries of the dominance of the horseman over the foot-soldier that would only end in the fourteenth century. Finally, the book will examine the way in which the battle has become woven into the established narrative of British history, and the changing role it has played as a perceived turning point in the national story.

That this can be claimed to be a 'British' story is problematic. I grew up in Scotland and it was attending primary school when I first came across the story of Hastings. The vagaries of memory make reliance on such anecdotes difficult, but I seem to remember a teacher consciously drawing out the contrasting significance of the battle for those of English descent in the class as opposed to those whose families had their origins in Scotland. This can be seen in the reactions of contemporary authors. The Welsh Chronicles of the eleventh century make little of the events of 1066: they are dealt with in one sentence by the Brut chronicler of West Wales. A contemporary, the Irish author of the Annals of Innisfallen, does not mention it at all. For both authors, the year 1093 was far more significant, for in that year the Normans killed Rhys ap Tewdwr, king of Deheubarth (or South Wales), while in the north of Britain Malcolm Canmore, king of the Scots, died with his eldest son, Edward, in an ambush by Robert de Mowbray, the Norman earl of Northumbria. Some Scottish historians agree there was a 'Norman Conquest', but interpret this as a peaceful assimilation of northern French aristocrats by the Scottish monarchy in the twelfth century as part of a strategy to maintain a degree of political autonomy from England.[2] This academic scepticism is also reflected in popular opinion. A recent survey showed that only 64 per cent of respondents in Scotland felt the Norman Conquest was significant as opposed to 83 per cent in England.[3] While clearly there is variation, the acknowledgement of over two-thirds of respondents shows that the Battle of Hastings still plays a part in the country's collective memory. The main problem is that most people have little contextual knowledge of what came before and only slightly more awareness of what came afterwards.

Even the notion of 'Englishness' is not straightforward. We use the short-hand terms of 'English' and 'Norman' to describe the main political units involved in the story, but fail to appreciate how problematic these terms are. Both terms were used by the priests and monks who wrote our history to convey a sense of a distinctive people who probably did not exist in reality. R.H.C. Davis' famous book *The Normans and their Myth*, published in 1976, represented a devastating assault on the nation of a distinctive 'Norman' contribution to European history. Harold Godwinson is often referred to as the 'last English king', but this idea depends on a rather selective view of 'Englishness'. Harold was not part of the royal house of Wessex, which had ruled a kingdom 'of the English people' since the ninth century, and which arguably was really a Greater Wessex rather than England as we understand it today. This was Edward the Confessor, who had spent most of his adult life in Normandy and probably spoke French as his first language. Harold had a Danish mother and a Danish name, having been part of a family that rose to power under the dynasty created by Cnut, the king of Denmark who conquered England in 1016. When Duke William of Normandy became king of England after the battle, this event is usually portrayed as a rupture in the chronology of the English monarchy; in fact, it was in itself nothing extraordinary. The notion of Englishness itself evolved after the Conquest, and within a generation the descendants of the Norman conquerors identified more with the territory they had taken over than with the land their families came from. The term 'Anglo-Saxon' is itself a relatively modern coinage and would have meant little to anyone standing in the vicinity of the battle in October 1066.

Thus, the most illuminating thing we can learn from the Battle of Hastings is what it tells us about the evolution of our collective identity and the relationship of England – and, more broadly, Britain – in relation to Europe and the wider world. It has been suggested that the battle is merely a footnote in British history and plays quite a different role from other battles, such as the Battle of Kosovo in 1389, which has played such a central part in Serbian identity, to the extent that it has fundamentally shaken the geopolitics of the Balkans since the late 1980s by facilitating the rise of Slobodan Milosevic. While it is certainly true that the Battle of Hastings has not produced a comparable reaction of such visceral intensity, I will suggest that the difference is not as great as it first appears.

THE SOURCES

We possess more information about the Battle of Hastings than almost any other medieval battle, but our sources are not straightforward and their interpretation has been subject to considerable debate. Medieval history writing came in a range of different forms, from those written in careful Latin using classical models taken from Roman historiography, to vernacular poems using strings of staccato sentences that barely use any grammatical rules. While much of the work strictly contemporary to 1066 was written by monks, the cloister lost its monopoly during the twelfth century and secular clergy (i.e. priests) became increasingly involved in producing historical writing on behalf of aristocratic patrons who were interested in their families' past. When discussing the medieval world, we often use the term 'chronicler' to be synonymous with 'historian', though there was a formal difference. The monastic historian Gervase of Canterbury, writing c. 1200, made a famous distinction between the two: chroniclers compiled a chronologically correct order of events while historians were there to 'instruct truthfully concerning the deeds, manners and the life which he describes'. Gervase had to admit, however, that in practice, 'the intention of each was the same, for each seeks the truth'.

As with the modern professional study of history, medieval writers were very concerned with presenting the truth about the events they described. The modern understanding of truth is conformity to fact, by which we mean exactitude, precision, correct chronology, accurate names, dates and places. This was something that historians living in the Middle Ages also strived for. Usually, they would outline their qualifications for writing in a prologue. In the introduction to his 'Deeds of the Norman Dukes', the eleventh-century Norman historian William of Jumièges explained that he had gathered material:

> partly related by many persons trustworthy on account equally of their age and their experience, and partly based on ... what I have witnessed myself.

However, history in the medieval world did not exist simply to preserve information; history possessed a moral function and was a didactic tool. There were certain deeper 'universal truths' that could be deduced from every event in the past and which were just as important to elucidate as simply list a dry factual account. This is a particular issue when it comes to battles. Medieval chroniclers undoubtedly were keen to present 'facts' about the different engagements they described, in terms of number, principal manoeuvres, tactical decisions and casualties, yet most accounts in surviving texts are very similar.[4] Victorious armies always maintain good discipline as they approach the battlefield and arrive in order under a unified and purposeful command, which maintains strict discipline, devoutly subjecting themselves to the arbitration of God. At the last minute, a rousing speech by the leader will prepare the men for the ordeal ahead. In contrast, the defeated armies are always ill-disciplined in the run-up to the battle, and arrive in confusion due to the divisions and uncertainties of their commanders, whose quarrelling or irresolution undermines any advantages they originally had. It is clear, therefore, that medieval authors followed a formula that allowed them to reveal deeper, universal truths about battles and the way that men *ought* to approach them and how they *ought* to conduct themselves. A battle was not just an event to be described, but an exemplar for emulation by others.

The most famous evidence that survives for Hastings is primarily visual: the Bayeux Tapestry. This 70-metre long embroidery was produced soon after the battle, possibly being associated with the dedication of Bayeux Cathedral in 1077, though much about its production is obscure. It plays a key role in any understanding of the Battle of Hastings, as the second part of the tapestry's narrative is dedicated to the campaign and its denouement at Battle. As such a rich and unique source, full of images rarely accessible to the medieval historian, it has been the subject of exhaustive study, which can be seen in the enormous bibliography that accompanies any study. Even in the last decade, at least three large collected volumes of essays have been produced on the basis of conferences dedicated to the Bayeux Tapestry.[5] There is still no consensus on who produced it and what its message actually was. The traditional belief was that it had been commissioned by William's wife Matilda, but more recently some historians favour William's half-brother, Odo of Bayeux, due to his very prominent role in the narrative; and, again, others have suggested Eustace of Boulogne may have been responsible. The location of its production is also disputed, with candidates including Bayeux in Normandy and Canterbury in England. The usual argument is that the source reflects an interpretation that is favourable to the Normans, given that it supports the story of Harold's journey to Normandy and the swearing of an oath to William that is found in contemporary Norman accounts and not in Anglo-Saxon sources. On the other hand, it is possible to argue that Harold is portrayed in a sympathetic light as a heroic figure, which reflects certain aspects of his claim to legitimacy, such as receiving Edward's deathbed approval and his acclamation by the Anglo-Saxon council or Witan in Harold's coronation scene. Establishing anything certain about the tapestry is very difficult.

The best English source that reproduces views contemporary to the battle is the *Anglo-Saxon Chronicle*. This work is of crucial importance for English history as it provides a chronological framework for the Anglo-Saxon period that we would otherwise lack. The title is misleading as it is not one text but a series of annals that were constantly read, edited and updated well into the twelfth century. There are seven different manuscripts – assigned the letters 'A' to 'G' by scholars – but these only represent a small proportion of those that would have existed. They originate with a chronicle produced in the 890s, probably produced by the Wessex court of Alfred the Great and then sent to different religious houses for copying. The relationship between the different versions is complex and the subject of much scholarly argument.

There are three recensions that deal with the events of 1066: the 'C', 'D' and 'E' versions. Version C dates to the mid-eleventh century and contains entries relating to the monastery at Abingdon, though establishing that this was where it was written is very difficult. Both Versions D and E derive important information from a text that is concerned with the history of Northumbria, the so-called 'northern recension', but we cannot be sure that the text was actually composed in the north. This reflects the attempts of the southern-based English kings to extend their control into the north in the late tenth century onwards. Version D was produced either at York or Worcester, probably during the episcopate of Ealdred, who held both offices in plurality. It has strongly been argued by several scholars to have been composed very soon after 1066, though several later events were later interpolated into it. The final version ('E') was written in Peterborough from 1121 to 1154, but the main text was composed at St Augustine's monastery in Canterbury around 1066. These laconic accounts are invaluable as a corrective to the florid Norman versions, but have their own problems of interpretation as they often describe events in a cryptic manner, which suggests wider circumstances that would be understood by contemporaries but which have been lost to us. Their different regional perspectives are invaluable as they reflect the political debates of the period rather than presenting a monolithic view of the past. This can be seen most particularly in the years 1035–66 where Version C shows marked preferences for the family of Earl Leofric of Mercia while Version E favours Earl Godwin of Wessex and his family.

We have two Norman sources written within a decade of the battle. The first of these, *Gesta Normannorum Ducum* ('Deeds of the Dukes of Normandy'), was finished in 1060 by the monk William of Jumièges. This was an update of an earlier work on the origins of the Norman duchy by Dudo of St Quentin (965–1026). Unlike Dudo, who had composed his work at the request of Duke Richard the Good (996–1026), there is no evidence that William of Jumièges wrote his work at the direct command of Duke William, though we know that it was in response to a ducal request that he extended his account to cover events leading up to 1070, and includes his account of the Battle of Hastings. This implies that the purpose of the *Gesta Normannorum Ducum* was the legitimization of the ruling duke, which strongly affects the reliability of its narrative.

A second source, *Gesta Guilelmi ducis Normannorum et regis Anglorum* ('Deeds of William, Duke of the Normans and King of the English'), was finished *c*. 1071 by William of Poitiers, who originally trained as a knight and served Duke William as a chaplain before entering a monastery. William of Poitiers' military experience has been used to suggest that his account of the Battle of Hastings – the most detailed contemporary version we possess and the source of most of the details used by historians – is realistic. His account is clearly written with the aim of magnifying William's achievements, and its heavy use of classical models from the Latin literature of imperial Rome means that there is a fundamental question over whether his account is actually an attempt to compare William with ancient heroes such as Julius Caesar. John Gillingham has famously characterized the work as being 'nauseatingly sycophantic' in its treatment of Duke William. It is such an important source that most scholars are willing to accept its fundamental reliability, but this is a dangerous assumption. While both accounts do portray William in different ways, ultimately these authors need to be treated with considerable caution given that they are deeply entwined with William's diplomatic initiatives and attempts to bolster his image as the divinely sanctioned, legitimate ruler of England.

A third detailed narrative that survives is the *Carmen de Hastingae Proelio* ('the Song of the Battle of Hastings'). This work has been subject to intense debate. R.H.C. Davis famously rejected the *Carmen* in the late 1970s, arguing that it is a literary exercise from one of the schools of northern France or southern Flanders and written between 1125 and 1140. Its champions have argued that it is a contemporary account written by Bishop Guy of Amiens around 1068. Frank Barlow has recently argued strongly in favour of its authenticity and that it was a source for William of Poitiers, while L.J. Engels has pointed out that the poem addresses Duke William as a living person, thus implying that the work is contemporary. The debate remains deadlocked. What is useful about the *Carmen* is that it is not a straightforward account from a Norman perspective and so provides a corrective to the views of William of Poitiers and William of Jumièges. This is best illustrated in the different treatment of Eustace of Boulogne, who is portrayed as the hero of the *Carmen*, whereas in William of Poitiers he is portrayed as a coward.

There are other sources that date from the late eleventh and twelfth centuries that we will use – sources such as the accounts of John of Worcester, Eadmer of Canterbury, Orderic Vitalis, William of Malmesbury, Henry of Huntingdon, Gaimar and Master Wace, but these are all written later and essentially use the sources we have already discussed for the bulk of their material. Thus, they are far more useful as evidence for how the battle was perceived in subsequent decades rather than as evidence for the battle itself, and we shall focus on this, particularly in the second half of the book.

CHAPTER 1

Defending the Church

BEING AWARE OF BIAS

A particular vice of some historians of the pre-modern world is their use of the word 'propaganda' when discussing the presentation of information that reflects an attempt to present events in a way that is politically advantageous. Some modern authors have even argued that monastic chroniclers can be seen as 'spin doctors' and their abbots were, therefore, the 'press barons' of the period.[6] Framing the past in a way we can understand is perfectly commendable, and our contemporary world constantly witnesses information being shaped to fit narratives for political, commercial or cultural purposes that, as good citizens, we must be conscious of. But our world is also very different as it operates in a context of mass literacy and an instantly accessible mass media, which was certainly not the case in the eleventh century. Our language reflects the way we classify the world and reflects our specific cultural viewpoint (e.g. the UK in the early twenty-first century). It would, therefore, be both misleading and arrogant to transpose this viewpoint onto other cultures rather than attempt to appreciate those cultures on their own terms. Carelessness causes misunderstanding. Reading Ian Sharman's attempts to present medieval popes as the Rupert Murdoch of their day would appear to reflect the transient concerns with the political and media culture of the first New Labour government (1997–2001) more than it helps us to understand a remote past.[7]

The term 'propaganda' is a modern Latin word derived from the verb *propogare*, which means 'to spread, to disseminate'. It was first used in the context of the Catholic Counter-Reformation of the seventeenth century with the *Congregatio de Propaganda Fide* ('Congregation for Propagating the Faith'), which was founded for the propagation of the newly revitalized Roman Catholic faith. 'Propaganda' only began to have secular connotations from 1790 during the French Revolution. The emergence of an informed and politically engaged 'public sphere' made up of typically middle-class people voluntarily associating with each other as a means of influencing state decisions through rational argument, first appeared in any real sense in the eighteenth and nineteenth centuries (as famously argued by the German sociologist Jürgen Habermas).[8] The consequence of this was that political elites needed to shape this new opinion by providing cogent interpretations of events through the mass media. Using the word 'propaganda' to describe a time before the printing press, where literacy was limited and manuscripts were copied by hand, is problematic, if not anachronistic.

Many historians do use the word with caution to analyse earlier periods. Imperial societies are more typically prone to having the term applied to them, probably because the relative power of the state and the number of politically active and educated individuals was typically higher than in less complex states.[9] The term increasingly appears in studies of the later medieval period rather than in the earlier period, but its working definition can appear to be a crude synonym for 'falsehood'.[10] As we have said earlier, the main problem for using the term in the eleventh century is not only the lack of developed systems of political theory (that only emerged with the development of universities in the twelfth and thirteenth centuries), but the small numbers of people that could read the texts that were being produced.[11] Felice Lifshitz makes this point strongly when discussing the intriguing text *Encomium Emmae Reginae* ('In Praise of Queen Emma'), which was written between 1040 and 1042.[12] The text focuses on Emma of Normandy, the controversial mother of Edward the Confessor and a kinswoman of Duke William. Emma had married first Æthelred II (also known as Æthelred the Unready), then his conqueror and successor, the Danish king, Cnut (also known as Canute).

Noting the absence of any mention of her marriage to Æthelred II, Edward's father, scholars have debated the text's political background and whether it was written to support the royal claim of Harthacnut, Emma's son with Cnut, over those of his older half-brother. Eric John says the suppression of any mention of Æthelred cannot be a guide to the main purpose of the work as the English audience would have been aware of the events it was describing, and so the text should be read as a polemic in favour of Emma as the carrier of royal legitimacy, against the rival claims of the Godwin family and the other enemies of the established order in England. As Lifshitz points out, this debate assumes that the text was a political pamphlet designed to change public opinion in England by making them favour one candidate for the throne over another during an extended succession crisis. He argues that it is anachronistic to draw parallels from texts from the eleventh century with the politicized writing cultures of the English

Reformation in the sixteenth century or the English Civil War of the seventeenth century, never mind the 'spin' and public relations management techniques of the twentieth and twenty-first centuries. Lifshitz makes the further point that, 'the very concept of public opinion is anachronistic for that time,' and given that only four manuscripts have survived, of which three were early modern copies,

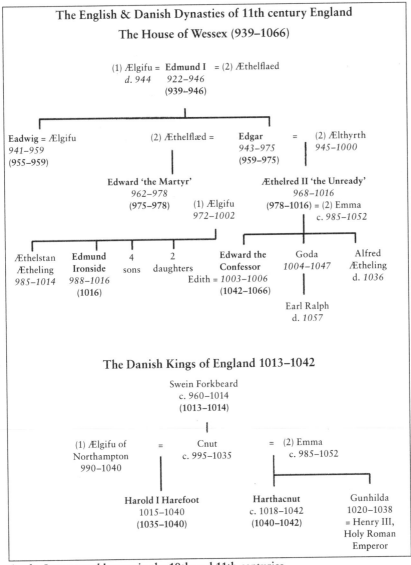

The English & Danish Dynasties of 11th century England

The House of Wessex (939–1066)

(1) Ælgifu = Edmund I = (2) Æthelflaed
d. 944   922–946
(939–946)

Eadwig = Ælgifu
941–959
(955–959)

(2) Æthelflæd =   Edgar   =   (2) Ælthyrth
943–975   945–1000
(959–975)

Edward 'the Martyr'
962–978
(975–978)   (1) Ælgifu
972–1002

Æthelred II 'the Unready'
968–1016
(978–1016) = (2) Emma
c. 985–1052

Æthelstan   Edmund   4   2   Edward the   Goda   Alfred
Ætheling   Ironside   sons   daughters   Confessor   1004–1047   Ætheling
985–1014   988–1016   Edith = 1003–1006   d. 1036
(1016)   (1042–1066)

Earl Ralph
d. 1057

The Danish Kings of England 1013–1042

Swein Forkbeard
c. 960–1014
(1013–1014)

(1) Ælgifu of   =   Cnut   =   (2) Emma
Northampton   c. 995–1035   c. 985–1052
990–1040

Harold I Harefoot   Harthacnut   Gunhilda
1015–1040   c. 1018–1042   1020–1038
(1035–1040)   (1040–1042)   = Henry III,
Holy Roman
Emperor

Anglo-Saxon royal houses in the 10th and 11th centuries.

one can argue that the readership for these documents was very small. Lifshitz believes that the text was written to persuade the count of Flanders to aid Emma. This explains why they can be so cavalier with the evidence: it was unlikely that the count knew much better.

However, using such a specific, structural definition of propaganda is limiting as it is possible to ignore the fact that propaganda in its broadest sense can be understood as a form of communication and persuasion that seeks to shape behaviour and attitudes, often through a voluntary response, and help consolidate group identity.[13] The earliest writing systems that human societies evolved quickly sought to use the technology to defend the current political system as legitimate, as we can see most clearly in the famous Sumerian King List produced in Mesopotamia around 2000BC, which used to be treated as an historical outline, but is now seen as promulgating a political vision or doctrine that the pattern of kingship or hegemony in Mesopotamia could only be exercised by one city at a given time and for a limited period.[14] The Greek city states of the ancient world developed the technique of rhetoric, which became highly desired as it trained the practitioner to persuade fellow citizens of a particular course of action. This was transmitted down to the medieval world via the Romans. While the issue of 'public opinion' is a complex one, we should not throw the proverbial infant out with the bathwater.

Our information for the Battle of Hastings confronts us with the same problem of evaluating material that has clearly been written to present a particular perspective on events. While the issue of the competing claims to the English throne in 1066 is usually just a background issue to the battle itself, I would argue that we must appreciate how far our information is intimately shaped by the justifications made in support of William's claim. The two accounts of William of Jumièges and William of Poitiers, in particular, lay the foundation for what is recognized as an officially sanctioned Norman version of events. As we have already discussed, both Williams had strong connections with the court of Duke William, and their histories are clearly designed to reflect the duke's version of the truth. Their versions show that the Norman court had four clear arguments for William's legitimacy.

THE CASE FOR WILLIAM

Edward the Confessor had been in exile in Normandy since 1014 after his father, King Æthelred II, fled England as a result of the invasion of King Sweyn of Denmark. Æthelred's marriage to Emma, the daughter

24

of Duke Richard I of Normandy, in 1002 had probably been arranged to secure Norman aid against the threat of the Danes, who had been resurgent since the early 990s. With the final triumph of Cnut in 1016 over Edmund Ironside, the surviving members of the Wessex dynasty were to spend the next two decades in exile. Meanwhile, Emma – remarkably to modern eyes – abandoned her sons and married Cnut. With the death of Cnut, there was a chance for the restoration of the House of Wessex and Alfred, the brother of Edward the Confessor, landed in England with a Norman force to see what he could achieve. However, the English elite rejected his claims, and their support swung behind Harold Harefoot, Cnut's elder son. Earl Godwin had initially supported Cnut's younger son by Emma, Harthacnut, who was back in Denmark. With Harold's victory imminent, Godwin swapped sides and, to prove his loyalty, he ensured that Alfred's threat was neutralized. His followers were killed, mutilated or sold into slavery, while Alfred himself was blinded and confined to the monastery in Ely, where he died from his wounds. Both William of Jumièges and William of Poitiers give detailed accounts of this incident when the 'most noble prince Alfred was done to death without justice'. Although William of Jumièges acknowledges the prime role of Harold Harefoot in the decision, it was Godwin who is accused of behaving like 'Judas', having given Alfred 'the kiss of peace and eaten with him' before his act of betrayal. William of Poitiers explicitly refers to Godwin's responsibility and how the 'most noble duke' would avenge Alfred's death on Godwin's son, Harold.

The second claim was that William had arranged Edward's restoration to the English throne. With the death of Harold Harefoot in 1041, Edward the Confessor returned to England, and the Norman sources claimed that he was only able to do this because of Norman aid. William of Poitiers claims that Edward was restored due to Norman diplomatic and military pressure on the English, underwritten by the military reputation of Duke William, which is difficult to take too seriously given that the young duke was in his early teens at the time! The account makes it clear that Edward was hugely in debt to William and the Normans, and states that Edward was 'determined as a matter of honour to repay him in equal measure'. This reconstruction of events is not fully supported by our other sources, and it is much more probable that Edward had returned to the country on the death of Harefoot. The *Encomium Emmae Reginae*, published *c.* 1041–2, shows that Edward had been invited back by his half-brother. The work presents Harthacnut ruling with the aid of his half-brother Edward: 'Emma and her two sons, among whom there is true loyalty, share the revenues of the kingdom between them'. The earliest manuscript that survives may be the original and shows Emma receiving the work from a monk watched by two bearded figures, presumably Harthacnut and Edward. Quite why Harthacnut invited Edward back is unclear: perhaps Emma and Harthacnut were unpopular and so wished to boost their legitimacy by associating themselves with the older ruling dynasty, or perhaps they did not want another round of civil strife with an alternative claimant.[15] It would suggest that the reality of a peaceful negotiation at either Edward or Harthacnut's initiative has been changed by William of Poitiers to reflect his own agenda in rearranging events to stress the Norman rights to succession.

The third part of the claim was the Norman argument that Edward the Confessor had chosen William as his heir. William of Jumièges and William of Poitiers both clearly state that Edward appointed Duke William as his successor. William of Jumièges says this was done through the agency of Archbishop Robert of Jumièges, one of the Normans who had accompanied Edward to England in the 1040s and who had been appointed bishop of London before being translated to Canterbury in 1051. William notes that Robert was archbishop when he came to Normandy 'to nominate him [Duke William] as the heir to the kingdom which God had given him'. The opportunity for this would have been during the Godwin family's exile from England between 1051 and 1052 after their conflict with Edward. William of Poitiers confirms this story, adding for good measure that Edward had secured the support of the English nobility in this matter and had also sent Harold's brother and nephew, Wulfnoth and Hakon, to Normandy as hostages. The only other contemporary assessments we have are the different versions of the *Anglo-Saxon Chronicle* of which only one gives any details relating to this incident. Version D confirms that Archbishop Robert of Jumièges had travelled to Rome to receive his *pallium* from the pope in 1051 and that Count William came across the English Channel 'with a great force of Frenchmen, and the king received him and as many of his companions as suited him, and let him go again.'[16] There has been extensive discussion over whether William did, in fact, visit England, which some have argued is hard to believe given that he was campaigning in Domfort and Alençon at the time, though this is disputed.[17] The question of whether he was actually ever promised the throne by Edward the Confessor is probably unresolvable with the current state of evidence.[18]

The final plank in William's case that is presented in the sources is Harold's infamous voyage to Normandy, where he swore an oath on relics to William promising to help him gain the throne on Edward's death. This is traditionally dated to 1064 or 1065, at the latest. William of Jumièges reports that Edward:

> sent the duke Harold, the greatest of all the earls in his dominions
> in riches, honour and power, that he should swear fealty to him
> [William] concerning Edward's crown and confirm it with Christian
> oaths.

On crossing the English Channel, Harold was captured by Guy of Ponthieu, before William lobbied for his release. Harold then spent time with William before he 'swore fealty concerning the kingdom with many oaths'. William of Poitiers' account agrees in outline, but gives a far more elaborate account, commenting, for instance, that Edward's move was:

> prudent, for his power and authority might be expected to
> contain the dissent of the entire English people if in their faithless
> inconstancy they were moved in any way to rebel.

William of Poitiers also emphasizes the duke's generous treatment of Harold and the hospitality Harold was shown at Rouen before he swore the oath to Duke William. According to William of Poitiers, Harold swore this oath of his own free will (according to 'notable men of utter integrity who were present at the time') and, on his own initiative, Harold promised to actively help Duke William succeed. He also promised to hand over Dover castle and any other castles that would be erected when the Normans constructed them. In return for being accepted as William's vassal by oath, Harold was granted all his lands and powers. Following this, Harold accompanied William on an expedition to Brittany.

The outline of this story is shown in the first part of the Bayeux Tapestry, though there are a few differences from the account of William of Poitiers, notably in the order of events. Contrary to William of Poitiers, the expedition to Brittany and Harold's knighting comes *before* the oath ceremony in the tapestry narrative. Generally, though, there is a consensus in the contemporary Norman sources about Harold swearing an oath to Duke William. The three versions of the *Anglo-Saxon Chronicle* that cover the period say nothing about this incident: in fact, for 1064 they literally mention nothing! Was this embarrassment on their part? The author of the *Vita Ædwardi*, writing just after the Conquest, makes an aside that Harold 'was too free with his oaths, alas!', which certainly suggests that the story was widely known. The story of Harold's journey across the English Channel has incited more interest amongst historians than whether Edward actually ever nominated William as his heir because it is so inherently mysterious. What on earth was Harold doing? Some have suggested that it was a fishing voyage that went wrong. The Norman story does have an internal logic to it, but that is due to the purpose of the narrative, which assumes that Edward wanted William to succeed him, for which there is no independent evidence. It is just as likely that if Edward had made any offer to William, this was purely tactical on his part, to be used in an attempt to negotiate a stronger position for himself domestically. Edward's problem in ruling England was that he inherited a system created by Cnut, where three great earls – Godwin, Leofric and Siward – dominated. Cnut had the forces of Denmark and Norway to call on if they caused him trouble, whereas Edward had no such independent power base. Was the Norman alliance Edward's wildcard that would underwrite a much stronger position for him in a new, post-Godwin order? There were plenty of alternative candidates who had stronger claims to the throne than William. The sources would just as easily suggest that after the death of Edward's nephew Edward the Exile, father of Edgar Ætheling, who had been brought back from Hungary in 1057 and who had died shortly after his arrival, Edward abdicated any further interest in the succession.[19]

Even if Edward had wanted Harold to travel to Normandy and renounce all claims that he and his family had to a lord with a list of grievances against them, by 1064 Harold had a very firm grip on government, to the extent that he is referred to as *subregulus* ('vice-king').[20] Although there is no evidence that Harold failed to comply with royal commands, it seems very unlikely that Edward would be able to compel Harold to do anything. This is vividly illustrated in 1065 during the Northumbrian revolt against Harold's younger brother Tostig. Harold negotiated with the rebels and agreed a deal that, according to the *Vita Ædwardi*, Edward disagreed with but could only rage about impotently. There is independent evidence that Harold visited Flanders in 1056, where he is described as a *dux* while witnessing a charter; this may have been the occasion for his meeting with William that our sources are discussing.[21]

Eadmer, a monk at Canterbury who was writing in the early twelfth century, recorded another version of the story that sounds more plausible. The hostages Wulfnoth and Hakon mentioned by William of Poitiers had been given to Edward by Godwin as a guarantee of his good behaviour in the deal of 1052 that saw his family's restoration, and then Edward sent these hostages to Normandy for safekeeping. Ten years later, with his family still chafing in exile, Harold went to Edward to ask permission to reclaim them, but Eadmer says that the king wanted nothing to do with the scheme due to his premonitions of future misfortune. Harold went anyway, and Edward's warnings came true: 'I have a feeling that you will only succeed in bringing misfortune on yourself and the whole Kingdom.' While the use of hindsight to make Edward's prophetic words give the story a moral quality renders the account suspect as a reliable guide to events, the basic premise, that Harold was on a rescue mission that went wrong, is certainly plausible. This more sympathetic reading of Harold's actions is certainly possible when looking at the Bayeux Tapestry, given that Edward does not look particularly pleased when Harold reports his adventures.

The Norman accounts reflect a carefully thought out, almost legally minded case (again, one would prefer not to use anachronistic language) in support of William's claim to the English throne. To make matters worse, according to these accounts, Harold had also committed perjury. They present Harold as a usurper who seized what was, by right, William's crown. Thus, the duke could argue that his dispute was not a private feud, but of sufficient magnitude to conform to the tradition of public war (*bellum publicum*). St Augustine, the great late Roman theologian whose work mediated many Roman imperial legal principles to medieval churchmen, elucidated the famous discussion of a just war. For Augustine, a war fought for private gain was sinful, whereas a war resulting from legitimate public authorities defending a community's rights and interests, despite being the result of a fallen world, was acceptable.

The situation is described in almost hysterical language: William of Jumièges said that Harold had caused 'the whole English people also to be faithless to the duke'. William of Poitiers writes of the shock that met Duke William when he learned that Harold was wearing the crown.

> Not for this insane Englishman the decision of a public choice, but
> ... he seized the royal throne with the plaudits of certain iniquitous
> supporters and thereby perjured himself.

Thus, William's military enterprise – an invasion – was an entirely legitimate exercise in attempting to reclaim his lands from rebels who had broken with the established social order. The usual response is to see these accounts as 'propaganda' appealing for public support.

As we have already pointed out, there was no 'public space' in the eleventh century for this information to be debated. These accounts were all written down several years after the events of 1066, which begs the question of why they were so keen to present the Norman claim in such detail after it was of no practical use, beyond a wish for consistency. There is no doubt that the presentation of the 'facts' was produced by William and his advisers to boost his claims, but one still needs to explain why he put so much effort into this when his main selling point for recruitment was the acquisition of new territory. Northern France was busy exporting its surplus of land hungry, expansionist elites at this period all across Europe – most notably in southern Italy and Spain, where military skills were in high demand.

GAINING THE SUPPORT OF THE CHURCH

For most historians, the explanation for this carefully presented version of events relates to William's attempts to gain ecclesiastical sanction for his invasion. William is usually described as having fought with the backing of the Church, symbolized in the form of the papal banner (*vexillum sancti petri*), which had been granted by Pope Alexander II and which William's army carried into battle[22]. The ability to present his invasion as divine punishment for Harold's usurpation and himself fighting a holy war, often glossed by authors as a 'crusade', has been argued to have played a crucial role in allowing William to recruit the necessary military and political support necessary for his high-risk enterprise to succeed.[23] The broad context for this argument is certainly sound. It is hard to underestimate how pious the northern French aristocracy was, despite the cynical modern tendency to see this form of religion as disingenuous and self-interested. The military aristocracies of the eleventh century expressed their individual devotion through material goods: precious items for the churches, for the construction of which they donated stone and mortar (though brick was used on a few occasions, given its association with the imperial Roman past).[24] The building of churches and the subscriptions for religious communities were investments on behalf of warriors and their families, ensuring them a safe place of burial where their souls would be prayed for by those with a full-time religious vocation and whose liturgies were seen as being particularly efficacious in reaching a divine hearing. The effort William put into gaining ecclesiastical approval most likely demonstrated concern about how far the attraction of plunder and land would appeal to a sufficiently broad range of contemporary warriors' interests.

There can be no doubt that William was a deeply pious man who was genuinely committed to the Church. Such commitment operated on both a personal and an institutional level. William of Poitiers creates an image of him as being conscientious in his devotion to the sacramental rituals of the Church, such as attending Mass every day; Orderic Vitalis similarly describes William as behaving with humility and respect in the presence of holy men. William's concern for his own soul is clear in the construction of the Abbey of St-Étienne (Stephen) of Caen, in which he was buried, as penance for his marriage to his cousin Matilda, which was prohibited according to the Church's rule on consanguinity (blood relationship) in marriage. The well-preserved charters for the abbey show a generous donation of land, as well as William's continued concern for the well-being of his institution. He initiated efforts to find suitable relics of saints to boost the abbey's spiritual prestige, such as when he purchased an arm of St Stephen from Besançon in eastern France, along with a phial of the saint's blood.

The other aspect of religious observance that affected a secular ruler in the eleventh century was the need to protect and reform the Church to ensure the safety and well-being of those he ruled – an increasingly conventional notion of politics as a moral obligation, which had been practised across Western Europe since its development by the Carolingian rulers, Charlemagne and his son Louis the Pious, in the late eighth and ninth centuries. William was very active in bringing the Norman church into line with the latest ideas emanating from key religious centres in Western Europe at this period, religious centres such as the monastery of Cluny, which was calling for a reinvigorated Church, free of the 'corruptions' that were afflicting it. The Monastic Reform movement of the eleventh century is a fascinating and notoriously complex phenomenon to understand, but should be seen as a series of responses to the breakdown in centralized royal power during the tenth century. The collapse of the Carolingian imperial system and the invasion of Christian Europe by pagan Vikings in the north, Magyars in the East and Saracens in the south had created a vacuum from which emerged local warlords, such as the dukes of Normandy, who were originally Viking raiders granted land on the Seine coast to protect the richer inlands from their compatriots. The levels of insecurity this caused saw increased levels of violence, with churches and peasants being particularly vulnerable as local bandit-chiefs erected castles (of the motte and bailey type in this period) and raided each other's territory with impunity. At this time, the Carolingian successors were so weak that they were barely able to control the land around Paris.

Alongside the more destructive aspects of these changes, the foundations were being laid for the creation of a European civilization as peasants were being brought under much tighter control, settled in villages ruled by the local castellan so their labour could be better managed. The subsequent increase in agricultural productivity stimulated a sustained period of economic and population growth that funded – for the top echelons of society, at least – an exponential growth in their resources. Stone buildings, elaborate cultural forms and a much more stratified society in which the warrior elite became a distinctive higher social class were all products of the social and economic changes that left local rulers like Duke William capable, if they had the strength of character, of seizing the opportunity to consolidate their power and bring their populations under much tighter control. They were best able to do this in alliance with churchmen who, influenced by the monks of institutions like the abbey of Cluny, were also looking to rebuild society on a stable basis, which, they believed, needed God's favour to return. One of the first attempts at 'Reform' was, in fact, nothing to do with the papacy, but was a 'grass-roots' movement called the 'Peace of God', which was declared in south-west France in the late tenth century when local clerics collectively prohibited attacks on clergy and peasants. This developed in the 1020s into the 'Truce of God' when 'private' violence was prohibited on certain days. William declared the Truce in Normandy in 1047 after his great victory at Val-ès-Dunes over his rivals for the duchy, with an exemption for his own army to ensure he kept the peace.

The other key demand that emerged amongst many reforming clergy was the ending of practices that had emerged due to the close intertwining of the secular elites and their local church establishments. Campaigns were launched against simony (the purchase of church offices) and demands were made for a well-educated and full-time specialist clergy who could carry out the Church's soteriological ministry through the issuing of a standardized range of sacraments. To ensure that these demands for change were not opposed by local special interests, William brought in respected and pious clergymen from outside Normandy, the most famous being the leading Italian theologian and lawyer Lanfranc, who retired to become a monk and taught at the monastery of Bec in the 1040s. At William's prompting, Lanfranc returned to the public sphere to attend the famous papal reform council of 1049 in Rheims. He then became William's key religious adviser and was undoubtedly the main figure behind ecclesiastical councils held at Lisieux in 1054 and 1064 and at Rouen in 1063, where the Norman Church was brought into line under William's presiding authority. Although there is no evidence for either the anointing or the crowning of the duke before 1066, there is a suggestion that the evolution of ceremonial rituals to accompany a coronation ceremony in the form of litanies sung at Charlemagne's coronation was developed in William's reign to make him a ruler of ecclesiastical sanction without peer amongst his fellow aristocrats in France.[25]

Crucially, like all rulers of the day, William appointed his bishops and leading clergymen on the basis of trust and competence. This explains why he placed his half-brother Odo as bishop of Bayeux, and why so many of his personal royal chaplains ended up in senior ecclesiastical positions. William's piety and sympathy for the Monastic Reform movement did not mean sentimentality about the Church. There was plenty of room within the Reform mind-set that recognized the powers of responsible secular rulers. He expelled at least one abbot for disobedience before 1066, and seized land from the monastery of Mont-Saint-Michel after their support for his rivals at the battle of Val-ès-Dunes. He was obsessed first and foremost with loyalty, which is perhaps understandable given the traumas of his youth, when factions competing to control him murdered his guardian, his tutor and his steward, leaving him in fear of his own life. While William of Poitiers presents the fall of Archbishop Malger of Rouen in 1054 as a result of the archbishop's impiety and hostility to the papacy, Orderic Vitalis presents a rather different view in the earlier chapters of his *Historia Ecclesiastica* ('Ecclesiastical History'). His later account of William in volumes five and six relies heavily on the account of William of Poitiers, but in his earlier writings, before he becomes concerned with constructing a sympathetic view of William, Orderic suggests that the duke behaved vindictively and took the advice of the wrong men in his treatment of Malger. Whichever way one looks at it, William's piety contained a strong element of pragmatism and he would insist on his own rights to demand obedience from the Church establishment.

In this context, it makes sense to take William's piety at face value and argue that his claim to the throne of England has to be seen within the context of his excellent relationship with the Church in Normandy. It was probably his belief in divine providence that underlies his conviction that he was the rightful heir of Edward the Confessor. Although we can never be entirely certain what William really thought and whether he was simply disguising his opportunism with lofty rhetoric, it is hard to escape the conclusion that he genuinely believed that he had been denied his rightful claim. He undoubtedly ensured this was burnished and cogently recorded by his loyal ecclesiastics. This approach finds parallels in the development of public discourse in the conflicts created by the Reform movement in the late eleventh century. The best evidence can be seen in the period just after 1066 in the pontificate of Gregory VII (1073–85).

Gregory's agenda was to pursue the Church's complete freedom from secular control. This may not have been a new tactic, but the energy with which he pursued it and the lengths he was prepared to go were. His complete refusal to ground his beliefs in any notion of compromise or respect for local custom made his papacy particularly disruptive to Latin Christian society. His dispute with the Holy Roman Emperor, Henry IV, in the Investiture Contest literally tore Europe apart and inaugurated decades of war, both civil and less civil. Gregory began to equate dedication to the Church with obedience to papal commands: it was no longer enough to believe, one had to act. 'Rarely have the forces of heaven been summoned so directly and confidently to influence the minds and behaviour of men as they were by Gregory VII.'[26] Almost anything, even innovation – the great enemy of the pre-modern world – was legitimate in the fight for divine justice that Gregory believed was symbolized by papal authority; boycotts, agitation and even violence were acceptable. Most of all, though, was the importance of publicity, as can be seen through the great number of polemical pamphlets produced at this time, which attempted to debate issues at a much wider level than a few educated clergymen.[27]

Karl Leyser argued that the Investiture Contest created a new culture of political literacy where both sides threw everything they had at each other and, unlike earlier debates amongst the *literati*, there was no restraint or respect for institutions or reputations. The fury and aggressiveness that was channelled by authors using scripture, history and canon law to hammer out their views and demonize their opponents was creating something new. Even Emperor Henry IV's mistresses were named and shamed. This could be argued to have created the beginnings of a public sphere, which Jürgen Habermas has denied could have existed in the Middle Ages. Perhaps, rather than bowing to the dictates of Enlightenment snobbery about the 'barbaric' simplicity of what came before, if we try to understand that such an entity could exist on its own terms, we might see that there is some merit in using 'propaganda' in its broadest sense to understand what our Norman sources are doing?

This is not to argue that William's attempts to proclaim his legitimacy as king of England were part of the polemical culture that surrounded the Investiture Contest as Gregory's disputes with secular authority began in the decade after 1075. His pontificate has tended to dominate the historiography at the expense of his predecessors and to marginalize earlier developments. Gregory did not invent the Reform Movement and his polemical strategy developed an inheritance of several decades of 'rational' discourse between competing visions of what the Church should look like. William's clergymen, given their connection with the wider European Reform Movement, would have themselves been shaped by this development of a 'public' discourse. William of Jumièges and William of Poitiers both reflect a broad, polemical purpose, which was a key part of eleventh century rhetorical culture that derived from William's attempt to gain the diplomatic support of other western rulers and the papacy for his invasion. In the aftermath of Hastings, with the turmoil in Europe and persistent threats from abroad, William's claim needed to be re-stated. This is why these claims were never marginalized: if anything, his claims became more pronounced.

It is also important to remember that Western Europe sat at a threshold moment where it was beginning the process of being transformed from a predominantly oral to a written culture. We often ignore the likelihood that William's claim would have been presented in forms other than manuscripts in written Latin. William's version of events would be passed on to his subjects and potential recruits through liturgy, pageantry, the visual arts and other forms of symbolic communication, allowing its distribution to move beyond the literate elite. The Bayeux Tapestry is probably a good example of the wider cultural investment that William would have encouraged to boost his political programme. The very transient nature of so much of this material means little such evidence has survived. The Latin sources we read would not necessarily have reflected a *Pravda*-style media operation by William, either. It would have been very clear what his version of events would have been, and the author's eternal quest for approval and favour would have done the rest. The immense stress William placed on loyalty amongst his servants undoubtedly meant an atypical sense of unity within those whose careers depended on him.

It was perfectly logical, given his close relationship with the Church, for William to look to it for aid in his struggle to reclaim what he believed was rightfully his. This is the best context we have for the elaborate creation of his claims to the throne and the construction of the 'perfidious' Harold. The main evidence we possess for William's appeal to Pope Alexander II in Rome comes again from William of Poitiers, who reports:

At this time there sat upon St Peter's chair at Rome Pope Alexander, a man full worthy to be obeyed and consulted by the entire Church, for he gave good advice and just decisions ... The duke begged the support of this pontiff, informing him of his undertaking and received of his benevolence a standard as a sign of the approval of St Peter, behind which he might advance more confidently and securely against his enemy.

Orderic Vitalis fills in the name of the cleric sent to negotiate the deal: Gilbert, archdeacon of St Lisieux. Apart from this, though, the evidence is rather limited, which is rather strange given that it would appear to have been so important. There is some circumstantial evidence that makes this scenario plausible. Lanfranc had connections with the papacy as he had worked with Hildebrand (the future Gregory VII) in the debates with Berengar of Tours over the nature of the Eucharist in the 1060s. Lanfranc's school at Bec also attracted notable pupils who went onto high-ranking careers, though the claims that he educated the young Alexander II are probably inaccurate.

William's ability to secure a banner from Pope Alexander II (a *vexillum sancti petri*, as Orderic calls it), which was believed to grant the remission of sins for all its followers who died in battle, would mark the ultimate reward for the duke's cultivation of the Church.[28] The evidence for its existence, though, is less clear and some doubt has been expressed over whether this banner ever existed.[29] The Bayeux Tapestry depicts a scene in which William tips back his helmet to show his face; nearby, a character, usually assumed to be Count Eustace of Boulogne, bears a banner that has been interpreted as being the banner granted by the papacy.[30] The design is white, with a rudimentary yellow cross between four roundels whose colour is either dark blue or black. However, the symbol also appears on the coins of Eustace's son, which makes the banner appear more like a comital symbol. Other scholars have argued that it is the plain cross that appears on the masthead of one of the ships arriving at Pevensey.[31] It is just as likely that the banner does not appear at all: the tapestry makes no direct reference to the religious context of the campaign, though it may appear more subtly in the symbolism of its imagery.[32]

None of this is especially conclusive, and Catherine Morton has expressed considerable doubts over whether the banner actually existed.[33] She points out that most of written sources from the eleventh century, namely William of Jumièges, Guy of Amiens and Baudri of Bourgueil, fail to mention the banner at all. While the bishop of Amiens' dispute with the papacy would explain the lack of mention in the *Carmen*, one would expect the two other sources being directed at William and his daughter, Adela, Countess of Blois, to emphasize the Church's support, given how important this was to William, as argued above. Most of the twelfth century accounts, apart from Orderic, who was relying extensively on William of Poitiers, do not mention the aid from Pope Alexander II at all. William of Malmesbury mentions a discussion in his *Gesta Regum* between William and Harold to send the whole issue to Rome for resolution, but then does not mention the matter in his other works, the *Gesta Pontificum Anglorum* or the *Vita Wulfstani*.

The context of the donation of the banner is also problematic. The 'Reform' papacy period is traditionally believed to have begun with the pontificate of the German Leo IX (1049–54), which heralded a more assertive papacy than had been usual in previous centuries. Apart from championing reformist causes, such as the abolition of simony, and improving the moral standards of the clergy, the papacy recognized the need for a degree of territorial control and government that could provide the stable social conditions necessary for the Church to thrive and improve. This belief in the need to create a just and peaceful society (which had originally led to the 'Peace' and 'Truce of God' movements) drove Pope Leo IX in 1053 to lead an army of local Italian troops and German mercenaries in person against the Normans in southern Italy in an attempt to curb their expansionist behaviour, which was causing chaos. The calamitous defeat of his army at Civitate led to a reversal in policy, and by 1059 the papacy was allied to the Normans, whose leader Robert Guiscard was given a title 'by the Grace of God and St Peter' against the Roman aristocracy, who sought to seize back control of the papal office from the reformers. This increased possibility in using violence as a means of achieving the interests of the Church was soon developed in the context of the holy wars against the Muslims. In Spain, where the *Reconquista* was making a stuttering start against the remnants of the Umayyad caliphate, the arrival of knights from France triggered papal interventions in 1064 and 1073, with legates being sent to defend papal interests. It was in the context of the Norman expansion into Sicily that Pope Alexander II granted a papal banner (*vexillum sancti petri*) to Count Roger in 1061.

However, it is certainly not straightforward that the papacy would have granted a banner to approve war against fellow Christians in the 1060s. In a letter to his ally the Byzantine emperor, Leo IX described the Christian Normans as behaving with pagan godlessness on account of their attacks on churches. Morton contends that the main context for the granting of papal banners was either wars against Muslims or dealing with rebellions against the Holy See, as was the case when a banner was sent in 1066 to Erlembald, the secular figure involved in an ecclesiastical civil war in Milan, at the time the largest city in Western Europe. A small group of clerics, supported by a large faction amongst the lay community (the Patarines) were attempting to force the rest of the clergy and the local church leadership, including the archbishop, to adopt much stricter codes of behaviour, such as outlawing clerical marriage. The papacy sporadically sided with the Patarines in their struggle, as the Patarines had a shared interest in tightening the boundaries between the clergy and laity, hence the banner was granted.[34] William's situation did not fit easily with either of these precedents. The granting of papal banners was accompanied, from the evidence of Civitate and Roger of Sicily, with the absolution of sins, a solemn papal blessing and an assurance that all those who fell would be martyrs of the Church. Leo IX had promoted a cult of the fallen German knights, revering them as martyrs. Given that the papacy insisted that Duke William's army had to do penance after the Battle at Hastings before he was recognized as king does not suggest that these spiritual privileges had been granted with the banner.

The usual explanation why the Normans were able to secure papal support is that they proposed themselves as the champions for the reform of a backwards province whose church was irredeemably corrupt.[35] This view of the English Church certainly became the official view in the twelfth century. The Anglo-Saxon Archbishop of Canterbury, Stigand, was the main target on account of his uncanonical consecration by a pope who reformers believed was improperly elected, as well as being a pluralist who held two bishoprics simultaneously. A classic example of a worldly cleric, Stigand had close links to five kings and he was enormously wealthy, which may have made him amenable to the king and secular lords. Stigand's status as a valid clergyman appears to be attacked by Norman propaganda, given his appearance in the Bayeux Tapestry as the cleric who oversees Harold's 'unholy consecration'. The surviving *Anglo-Saxon Chronicle* versions do not mention who carried out the consecration of Harold – another telling silence – but John of Worcester, a monk writing in the first half of the twelfth century, records that it was Archbishop Eadred of York who crowned Harold. This would suggest that the English sources were aware of the arguments put forward by the Normans and were responding to them. There appears to have been no similar association with the 'liberation of Christendom' message that Leo IX had justified his actions.

Edward the Confessor, who appointed numerous European clerics and introduced the Romanesque style into England with his rebuilding of Westminster Abbey, does not seem to have objected to Stigand. William maintained him in office until 1070, when he made a clean break with most of the *ancien regime*. This is often explained away as being due to William's concerns with stability and continuity of government, given the importance of senior clergy in such matters, but Stigand consecrated Remigius as bishop of Dorchester in 1067 and witnessed the charter granting land to St Denis in 1069, signing straight after the royal family, which implies his involvement was not merely nominal. He is often portrayed as being a creature of the Godwin family, but this is not based on any positive evidence. Stigand did not share Godwin's exile, for instance. While the religious houses that contributed to his wealth did not always see him in a favourable light, he had a good reputation with several houses, including the Old Minster Winchester, St Augustine's Canterbury and Ely to whom Stigand gave expensive crosses and other liturgical gifts and where his name and day of death were inscribed on their necrologies.[36] He was buried honourably in Winchester, where his body lies. His reputation only suffered a major decline after his death when the scramble by clergy to retain land by royal assent after the Conquest meant that religious houses distanced themselves from Stigand. As we have already noted, William's reign resulted in a comprehensive re-writing of history, which presented the English Church as a nest of corruption, though in the second generation after the Conquest this narrative was re-shaped and English Church history became a series of peaks and troughs between periods of reform and decadence.

There can be no doubt that the papacy was involved in William's campaign in some form, but the precise details are unclear and obscured by our sources, and re-written in the aftermath of the Conquest. The case for William's invasion being seen as a 'crusade' for the reform of the Church, an idea that appears in several authors, would appear to be a casual use of the word. William believed that his cause was a holy war, but the evidence suggests that papal support was ambivalent at best, as it did not comply with any ecclesiastical traditions. Pope Gregory VII sent William a letter in 1080 asking the king to swear an oath of fealty to him and acknowledge him as his feudal overlord. In the letter, he expressed his disappointment at William as:

> even before I rose to the supreme height of the papacy, what effective concern I have always shown in your affairs and ... with what zeal I laboured that you might rise to the dignity of kingship.

Contrary to suggestions otherwise, Catherine Morton argues that the letter does not prove that William had secured papal support at all. Compared with Gregory's other letters to monarchs, as pope his demands and claims are very modest, and the 'zeal' with which he laboured for William is in contrast to his earlier statement on his efficacy (*efficax*), which suggests he did not actually manage to achieve anything concrete. The lack of reference to his predecessor, Alexander II, and the papal bull is also significant in the wider context of Gregory's correspondence, where he was usually quite happy to list in detail what the papacy had done for rulers in the past.

The problem with treating in isolation examples of papal support for the holy wars of the eleventh century is that this ignores the paradox inherent in the Church's attitude to violence. The Beatitudes of St Matthew's Gospel ('Blessed are the peacemakers ...') were hardly compatible with the medieval knight's way of life. Gregory's letter alludes to criticism he received for supporting William from those in the Church who felt encouragement of violence was theologically suspect. Gregory himself when meditating on the nature of true penance in 1078 came to the conclusion that knighthood could scarcely be performed 'without sin'. He did acknowledge that this could be overcome if the knight subjected himself to the direction of bishops, before he modified his views later in his career when he came into conflict with Holy Roman Emperor Henry IV. 'Gregory the man of action outran Gregory the man of ideas,' as his biographer H.E.J. Cowdrey put it.[37] This ambiguity may well explain the reticence of many clerical authors to discuss the matter. Pope Leo IX similarly presented his military expedition against the Normans in several sources as an attempt to make the Normans comply by intimidation rather than a wish for bloodshed.[38]

It is also worth acknowledging that the lay piety of the knights already discussed above was perfectly capable of creating its own theological justification for their actions. The Christianization of war had been a process that had begun in the Late Roman Empire of the fourth century after the conversion of Emperor Constantine, and had been particularly intensified under the Carolingians and their successors, as we can see most particularly in the works of King Alfred in Wessex. Given that most of our sources are written by clergymen, we can easily fall into the trap of seeing clerical patterns of thought as dominant, when they most certainly were not. As R.W. Southern wrote:

> The theories and mechanisms of secular society also developed. The world did not stand still while the clerical ideal was realised.[39]

Duke William, no doubt under advice from his loyal clergy, probably shaped his own religious paradigm to allow him to square his conscience with his planned expedition.

The issue appears to be that we are being presented with a version of events that fits a narrative aimed at concealing the ambiguities of William's case and the extent to which he had papal backing. His ultimate success allowed him to present the past in a much neater way than messy reality. As is clear in the way William was presented in the sources, he took every negative omen, from falling over on the beach at Pevensey or being handed a hauberk the wrong way round, and turned this into a positive sign. This retrospective shaping of the past in the light of God's revealed plans is very common in the medieval period and can be seen most clearly in the copious writings on the First Crusade (1096–99) in the twelfth century, which are shaped by the knowledge of the fall of Jerusalem in July 1099. These were literary constructions deeply concerned with creating an understanding amongst the audience for what the First Crusade said about God's providential plan for mankind. These accounts, therefore, reflect what the literate classes in Europe wanted to believe had happened more than the reality they purport to describe.[40] This is of enormous significance for the Norman sources that we use to reconstruct the Battle of Hastings, as they were written with the same mind-set.

It is worth noting the relative success of these diplomatic endeavours: the view in Europe that has survived through contemporary authors indicates that most people were very impressed with William's military efforts. The Italian Normans, themselves backed by the pope, were quite happy to give their moral approval of the duke's actions, as were William's French contemporaries. Elsewhere, the feelings were more ambiguous with the Scandinavians angry and regretful about the failure of the Anglo-Danish union, while the Flemish, who had long-standing links with the English, were particularly strident in their condemnation of William's aggression.[41]

A final illustration of how the framing of William's claim distorts how our sources present the battle is the issue of the winds that kept William's fleets on the coast of Normandy for three months. The inability of William to cross until late September ultimately proved to be a decisive factor in his victory, as the huge force that Harold had mobilized to oppose the landing had returned home, and the king was himself marching north to confront Harold Hardrada and Harold's brother Tostig at Stamford Bridge, allowing William to land on the English coast unopposed. For the Normans, this was a sign of divine favour; for modern authors, an enormous stroke of luck. The most extensive account we have is recorded in William of Poitiers:

> Presently, the whole fleet, equipped with such great foresight, was blown from the mouth of the Dives and the neighbouring ports, where they had long waited for a south wind to carry them across, as driven by the breath of the west wind to moorings in Saint-Valery. There too the leader, whom neither the delay and the contrary wind, nor the terrible shipwrecks nor the craven flight of many who had pledged their faith to him, could shake committed himself with the utmost confidence by prayers, gifts and vows, to the protection of Heaven. Indeed, meeting adversity with good counsel, he concealed (as far as he could) the loss of those who drowned, by burying them in secret, and by daily increasing the supplies, he alleviated want. By many encouragements he retained the terrified and put heart into the fearful. He strove with holy prayers to such a point that he had the body of Valery, a confessor most acceptable to God, carried out of the basilica to quell the contrary wind and bring a favourable one; all the assembled men-at-arms who were to set out with him shared in taking up the same arms of humility. At length, the expected wind blows ....

Support for the story from the other sources is inconsistent. The *Anglo-Saxon Chronicle* refers to a storm battering Harold's fleet as it left the south coast for London in September, while William of Jumièges only says that a favourable wind was William's reason for leaving St-Valery and does not mention the delay. This story was subject to increasing scrutiny in the 1980s and 1990s with more historians questioning its authenticity.[42] Stephen Morillo has recently made a spirited defence of the story, citing meteorological evidence of the Channel wind patterns to show that, given the nature of Norman ships, it was quite feasible for a crossing of this magnitude to be considerably delayed by the conditions.[43] Ultimately, though, while the wind was undoubtedly a consideration in the crossing, it was only one of many: William would only have one opportunity at a landing, and needed to wait for the right moment. Undoubtedly, William believed that such an opportunity would present itself, but this must be seen as a product of calculation, which was subsequently presented as another example of divine support for William's cause. Contrary to the modern view of the English Channel as a moat, isolating the British Isles from Europe, the sea has facilitated intense communications since the end of the last Ice Age, which makes it inconceivable that William did not have a very good idea about what was happening. There is no convincing evidence that he co-ordinated his actions with those of Tostig and Harald Hardrada, but this is a more plausible explanation than the 'divine wind' theory.

What should now be clear is that the contemporary Norman accounts for the Battle of Hastings have to be read in the context of their composition, as part of William's legalistic campaign to persuade the leading figures of Europe, both secular and ecclesiastical, that his cause had divine favour and that his conquest was legitimate. His success gave this claim credibility, but his invasion remained controversial, and this would explain why the chroniclers who were associated with his court emphasized the rights of his claim long after it was no longer necessary to do so. This all occurred in the context of the swirling contemporary debates about morality, power and authority that were transforming the cultural world of Western Europe. William's insistence that God's support was crucial to every aspect of his campaign, and his desire to credibly claim papal support, showed a capacity to exploit this fluidity in ecclesiastical thinking for his own advantage, which would probably not have been possible in subsequent decades as the theology of holy war coalesced more firmly around the ideas that became the First Crusade in 1095–9 and which led to a more systematic approach to clerically approved violence. We should, therefore, be very careful when using these accounts to construct explanations for Norman success and not simply pick out details that fit into a narrative that is attractive to the modern, rationalist perspective that sees military victories as a result of strategic coherence, suitable tactics and luck.

CHAPTER 2

There'll always be an England

CHALLENGING THE VIEW OF TRADITION

The Battle of Hastings is often framed as part of a narrative continuity that runs through English history – the threat of invasion from across the Channel. Colonel Lemmon reflects the mid-twentieth century English perspective, with two world wars fresh in mind, in his enthusiastic study, *The Field of Hastings*, written in 1956: 'During the summer of 1066 England, as again in 1588, 1804 and 1940, lay under threat of invasion.' This tradition goes back to Edward Augustus Freeman's monumental study of the Norman Conquest, against which the clean-limbed English were fighting, in vain, to save 'a free and pure Teutonic England'. But one can question the extent to which Harold's army at Hastings really was an 'English' army at all. Indeed, before we can answer the question of how significant Hastings was to English history, we must first answer an even more fundamental question: to what extent did 'England' actually exist in 1066?

The problem of casting the Battle of Hastings as a conflict between 'English' and 'French' is that these terms are anachronistic: products of nineteenth-century Romantic writers such as Walter Scott, who carelessly transposed contemporary notions of national identity onto a past where such ideas would have been confusing, to say the least. Ideas about nations and race formulated in the eighteenth and nineteenth centuries were believed to have been immutable and to extend deep into the past; they laid the foundations for modern historical study. This increasingly scientific interest in the past was no accident. It is by shaping a people's collective memory and their understanding of the past that a sense of nationhood is consolidated: creating a notion that the *status quo* has been determined by providence and validated by tradition. This period saw history curricula emerge in universities and, most crucially, in the school curriculum for just this purpose, as universal education systems were introduced across much of the industrializing world. Arguably, these ideas also helped lay the foundation for many of the atrocities carried out in the first half of the twentieth century in the name of patriotism or national destiny. The reaction against the horrors of total war since 1945 has contributed to a re-evaluation of these discredited ideas and, as a result, a series of important intellectual currents have deeply affected social science research. The idea of the nation, once seen as being biologically determined, is now largely understood as a response by different communities to an array of social, economic and political forces acting upon them. England and France, as they exist today, are not products of manifest destiny, but a result of a series of historical contingencies and accidents.

Such a critical position is representative of the Modernist critique of national identity. Benedict Anderson's *Imagined Communities* is one of the most influential texts supporting this sceptical view of national identity.[44] For Anderson, capitalist printing and mass literacy unleashed the cultural and political movements of the eighteenth and nineteenth centuries, which undermined traditional elitist beliefs, such as the divine right of kings and the dominance of elite languages, that had maintained earlier hierarchical social structures. These were replaced by notions of national identity, produced by the emergence of vernacular literacy and increasing administrative standardization. The Industrial Revolution was the catalyst that laid the foundations for a sense of comradeship and common bonds between people who had never met each other: literally an 'imagined community'. Ernest Gellner, another leading theorist, takes this further by arguing that 'nationalism is not the awakening of nations to self-consciousness: it invents nations where they do not exist.'[45] However, both share the view that national identity is a product of the modern world and is thus not an appropriate way to understand medieval kingdoms.

It would be wrong to imply that the views of Anderson and Gellner hold the field unchallenged. There have been challenges to the consensus that national identities are simply an example of false consciousness. Primordialists argue that, *contra* Anderson and Gellner, nations (or at least some aspects of national identity) have deep historical origins. Place of birth, ethnicity and religious affiliations are all seen as the basis of attachments that cannot simply be dismissed as being 'constructed'. Azar Gat has staged a more recent re-statement of these ideas in his book, *Nations*.[46] He criticizes the Modernist rejection of the capacity of earlier societies to build a collective consciousness that could begin the process of consolidation of a nation state. He suggests that they have been too quick to use examples that lack a history of national independence, for instance, northern European peoples such as the Finns and Estonians, who are the exception rather than the rule. Anderson's work was based on his experiences in south-east Asia, which arguably limits its universality. Gat rejects the argument that the fluidity of ethnicity and the shaping of political and social factors must deny its authenticity. As events have shown in the three decades since the end of the Cold War, when a new world liberal order was predicted by some commentators, nationalism is by no means a diminishing force in global politics.[47]

ENGLAND AND *ANGELCYNN*

It is within the parameters of this wider debate that the evolution of the idea of England and Englishness has fascinated historians. The English kingdom's apparent precociousness in the wider context of the far more fragmented and 'anarchic' Western Europe of the tenth and eleventh centuries, where central authority had almost completely collapsed in the aftermath of the Carolingian Empire, provides an excellent case study to assess the relative merits of each position. The Domesday Book provides a compendious testimony of an *Anglia* that had a uniform administration system based on the territorial units of shires, which would suggest by 1086, that it was a distinctive territory with a particular identity. The idea of an 'English people' existed before there was an *Engla-land*, which would strongly support the 'primordialist' case. In the centuries following the end of Roman rule in Britain in the early fifth century, a distinctive series of cultures emerged amongst the inhabitants of the southern and eastern parts of the British Isles, an area we would now recognize as England. The idea that they were all part of the same people can be traced to the Northumbrian monastic scholar Bede. In his *Ecclesiastical History of the English People*, Bede wrote of a *gens anglorum* ('English people') who were united by a common language and were distinct from other ethnic groups that resided in the British Isles (i.e. the Britons, Picts and Irish). When Bede wrote, the English had recently acquired the Roman tradition of the Christian faith, which was different to other, insular forms of Christianity (often misleadingly called 'Celtic' Christianity), which had developed in the fifth and sixth centuries AD. For Bede, this commitment to orthodoxy over the 'corrupt' faith of the British was a key aspect of this divinely formed national identity.

A Modernist critique of Bede would argue that his idea of 'Englishness' was an ecclesiastical, rather than ethnic, concept.[48] This is contradicted by Bede's persistent identification with, and celebration of, earlier English rulers, such as Æthelfrith the Northumbrian (c. 593–616), who were not Christian, yet who happily slaughtered Britons who were.[49] From this perspective, Bede's notion of identity seems primarily ethnic. Bede's labels were also not simply invented, as they were used by other insular authors as well as those on the Continent. However, Bede simplified the varied traditions he had inherited to create something distinctive. His ideas of Englishness were undoubtedly influenced by his conception of the superiority of the Roman Christian tradition in its arguments with the champions of indigenous traditions, so the ecclesiastical context cannot be ignored.

Bede's startling innovation of emphasizing a common English identity for the peoples of southern and eastern Britain had very few practical consequences when he was writing in the early eighth century. What we now call England was constituted of many different, competing kingdoms. A process of political consolidation can be traced in the written records from 600 onwards with smaller tribal units of peoples being consolidated into larger groupings, either through voluntary or involuntary amalgamation. The Tribal Hidage, a famous document probably from the seventh century, lists the names of 35 tribes, kingdoms and administrative areas that, by 800, had merged into four larger kingdoms – Wessex, Northumbria, Mercia and East Anglia – whose inhabitants had their own distinctive traditions and affiliations. Northumbria, Mercia and Wessex had each consecutively exerted a period of hegemony over the others, reflected in the title *Bretwalda* ('British ruler'). It would be misleading to suggest these developments would inevitably result in a single, unitary kingdom. How far this process created an 'English' identity that had a tangible existence beyond the writings of monastic idealists like Bede is also far from clear.

Angelcynn, the Old English word that is used to express the idea of 'English', appears in a charter from Mercian Worcester, which was produced in the 850s and used to distinguish between those of local (Mercian) origin and those who were from elsewhere.[50] As far as the evidence permits us to see, the key identity concerns for the majority of the population was regional. They were interested in who exerted authority over them locally and, sporadically, the distant ruler, who on occasion would visit to consume their taxes, in the form of food obligations. The clerical elite could conceive notions of a broader community more easily as they were already part of a 'supranational' institution that transcended local ties. The Latin Church saw secular political boundaries as nothing more than temporary arrangements, secondary to its soteriological mission. Then again, this worked better in theory than in practice. While they could dispute control of land with their secular counterparts, many of the church hierarchy were from similar aristocratic families who saw no necessary conflict between ecclesiastical and local dynastic interests. Such intersection of loyalties was being roundly condemned by Bede back in the early eighth century, which indicates how fundamental they were.

If Bede created a cultural notion of 'Englishness', its development as a political idea, it has been argued, belongs to the reign of Alfred the Great. The Viking era in Britain began in the 790s with a series of raids that, by the 860s had evolved into invasion by armies bent on conquest. Between AD865 and 871, East Anglia and Northumbria were brought under the control of the 'Great Heathen Army', Mercia's independence was eclipsed and Wessex's survival was hanging by

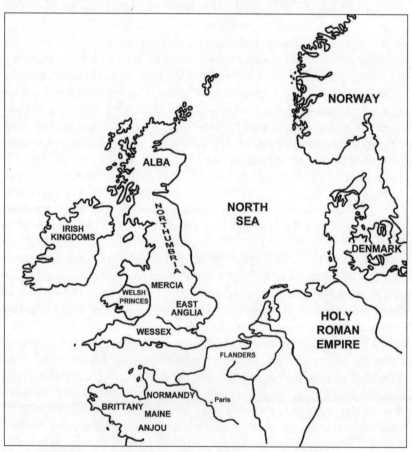

The English kingdoms of the Anglo-Saxon period, *c.* AD 800–1066.

a thread. After halting the Viking advance at Ashdown in 871, Alfred resisted several further offensives, famously emerging from the Aethelney marshes in Somerset to achieve, in 878, a decisive victory over the Scandinavian warlord Guthrum at Edington. Alfred established a *modus vivendi* with the Viking elite after they converted to Christianity, sealed with the Treaty of Wedmore. Alfred controlled Wessex, Kent and western Mercia while a frontier was established along the old Roman road of Watling Street. The 'Danelaw' was established in these northern and eastern regions, dominating Essex, East Anglia and eastern Mercia. Alfred's achievement laid the foundations for the future English kingdom, but his policies over the following two decades shows no complacency. He understood how close Wessex had come to destruction and, following an inquest, sought to ensure that this would never happen again. Watling Street would remain an important geopolitical fault line for much longer.

Alfred's reforms are well known. He constructed a network of fortified urban sites (*burhs*) and re-organized the military system (*fyrd*) to ensure there was an effective army and navy in place to fight off future attacks. But while these practical responses helped to make Wessex into one of the most formidable kingdoms of the tenth century, Alfred believed that the mind was just as important a location as the battlefield for achieving long-term political stability, and this explains the programme of religious and cultural renewal he inaugurated. We know from his own writings that he believed the root causes of English weakness were spiritual and cultural in origin: by neglecting correct forms of worship and study, by becoming obsessed by lust and other matters of the world, the Anglo-Saxon kingdoms had become decadent. Alfred put himself at the heart of this renaissance by personally translating a series of works into Old English such as Pope Gregory the Great's Pastoral Care and Boethius' *Consolation of Philosophy*. These texts were to form the basis of a curriculum for the education not just of the clergy, but the secular aristocracy, too.

As Sarah Foot has demonstrated, this programme saw considerable intellectual energy expended on formulating new notions of identity. Alfred and his advisers adapted Bede's concept of the *gens anglorum* to formulate a collective national idea of a single people – *Angelcynn*. This was used to unite those not under Danish rule.[51] This notion of being 'English' was, therefore, a situational construct, a social identity based on the notion of unifying peoples who were not Scandinavian, who became the 'other'. This process also required re-writing history so Alfred could argue that he was reviving an English identity that existed before the Viking conquest. The *Anglo-*

Saxon Chronicle, produced by Alfred's court in the 890s, presented a narrative showing how Wessex, possessing the sole remaining indigenous English royal house, had risen to pre-eminence. The work had a deeper purpose than mere dynastic propaganda. It sought to weave together a shared history for all those peoples under Alfred's rule. It was also crucially written in the vernacular (Old English) as opposed to Latin. Promoting a common language (*Englisc*) was a particularly powerful tool in creating a notion of 'Englishness'. In most other parts of Europe, this literary tradition only occurred from the thirteenth century onwards, evidence of how precocious much of this was in its immediate geographical context.

The notion of 'Englishness' created by Bede and Alfred was an instrumental identity, created as part of the two men's cultural–political programmes. Alfred's conception of *Angelcynn* reflected the specific interests of Wessex, and of his dynasty in particular. The royal succession was streamlined to ensure that only his immediate family could succeed, excluding his wider kin, a decision that was not accepted passively: his nephew Æthelwold rebelled when Alfred's son Edward the Elder succeeded in 899; Æthelwold sought aid from the Danes and Northumbria to reclaim Wessex from his cousin. The Midlands was conquered by Alfred's successors Edward the Elder (899–924), Æthelflæd (911–18) and Æthelstan (927–39). This was achieved through a combination of military expedition, diplomatic initiative and the construction of fortifications, which allowed their conquests to be controlled quickly and effectively. The high-point in this process came under Æthelstan, who defeated a coalition of British monarchs (Welsh, Scots and Scandinavian) at the Battle of Brunanburh in 937 to leave him as the dominant figure across the whole British archipelago. The author of the *Anglo-Saxon Chronicle* could claim of Æthelstan that 'He brought under his rule all the kings who were in this island'. This may be hyperbole, but it heralded centuries of attempts by the southern polity to dominate the north.

That this process was presented as 'liberation' of the 'English' people by the kings of Wessex can be seen in the *Anglo-Saxon Chronicle*'s description of the consequence of the capture of London from Danish control in 886: 'All the English people who were not under subjection to the Danes submitted to him'. In fact, this was less an accurate reflection of how the 'liberated' felt than a development of Alfred's narrative tradition, which re-wrote history to suggest that the Northmen had taken lands that had previously been 'English'. Such a teleological view of history has been seductive for many later readers. Wessex expansionism is often described as a process of 'unification' or a 'reconquest'.[52] This is misleading as it presents the formation of the kingdom of England as an inevitable and natural state of affairs when, in fact, it was a contingent process reliant on decisions taken by rulers of the Wessex dynasty and, as always in history, accidental. This is not to crudely deny, just because something is invented or imagined, that a notion of 'Englishness' had no tangible essence and existed merely as a slogan in a vacuum. The kingdom of the English was a reality by the late tenth century. In 1017, after a series of intense conflicts within the native Wessex dynasty, the *Anglo-Saxon Chronicle* could say that 'King Cnut succeeded to all the kingdom of England'. Cnut described himself as *ealles Engla landes cyning* ('king of all England'). It was the person of the king that gave the kingdom unity rather than a broad notion of 'Englishness'. Loyalty to the king had to compete with a myriad other regional identities and local obligations, which meant that both the English kingdom and the notion of being English was inherently unstable.

Assessing the extent to which the Wessex kings established a common identity of 'Englishness' amongst the people it controlled is not straightforward, due to the sparseness of our evidence. There is strong evidence that many of the northern and eastern parts of the kingdom remained distinctive in their ethnicity and culture, particularly those areas inhabited by descendants of the Vikings. Trying to understand what was so practically distinctive about the 'Danelaw' is difficult to grasp. There are some variations in the names of administrative terms, such as the 'wapentake', which appears to have been the equivalent of the hundred, a territorial sub-unit of the shire. Many scholars deny there is anything inherently Scandinavian about these variations and suggest they represent the continuation of distinctive local practices originating long before the Vikings appeared. There is also considerable debate over the extent of Scandinavian settlement in the areas that fell under their political control in the tenth century. Some argue that were there large numbers of Scandinavian peasants who came in the aftermath of the Viking armies, while others argue that it was quite small scale and involved a takeover by a small military elite.[53]

The debate is too intricate to do more than outline here, but the main evidence is the extensive number of Scandinavian place names across northern and eastern Britain. Places ending with Danish words such as '-thorpe' (e.g. Scunthorpe) or '-by' (e.g. Ingelby) are common in the Danelaw while the Cumbrian landscape has a distinctive Norse nomenclature with '–thwaites' (Rosthwaite) and '-dales' (Borrowdale) interspersed with 'ghylls' (mountain streams). Local elite figures appear with names such as 'Ulf' and 'Grim', names that dominate in areas such as Lincolnshire and Yorkshire in the Domesday Book. Ascertaining what these names signify is more difficult than acknowledging that they exist. Name changes are consistent with both models of settlement. If a new Scandinavian lord controlled an estate, then he would presumably name it in his mother tongue and the indigenous inhabitants would have to adapt. Language change could also accompany a replacement of the existing population by outsiders. The development of DNA evidence in the last three decades had promised a revolution of our understanding of the extent of migration, but the results have been ambiguous. This is partly due to an inability to distinguish between different northern European groups such as Saxons or Danes. Linking shifts in genetic patterns to chronology is also difficult, meaning that isolating data from the Viking era is very difficult. The most recent studies have tended to suggest that the genetic impact was limited.[54]

The Scandinavian impact is better understood not as a numbers game, but as a catalyst for new re-configurations of identities and social structures in the vacuum created by the destruction of the earlier Northumbrian, Mercian and East Anglian polities. A series of 'successor states' emerged in tenth century Northumbria: the kingdoms of York and Cumbria, the 'liberty' of the Community of St Cuthbert and the earldom of Bamburgh. These entities were all relatively short-lived, however. Although we do not know a huge amount about these kingdoms, they were perfectly capable of developing their own local cultural and political identities. An example of this is the sculptured monument known as the 'hogback' found in certain concentrations across these regions. These recumbent tomb covers are strongly associated with groups with a Scandinavian affinity, though they represent an entirely new insular tradition that evolved in Britain. Jim Lang suggested that most of these were constructed within a single generation in the second quarter of the tenth century.[55] The communities who developed the practice were probably using their heritage as a way of differentiating themselves from other local groupings. The innovative appearance of images of armed men on stone sculpture in ecclesiastical contexts such as that at Middleton in the Vale of Pickering is also an innovation, representing a significant change from the well-documented artistic patterns of the eighth century and ninth century.

The centuries that followed the end of the Roman Empire in the west was a similar period of ethnic re-configuration. This process is known as 'ethnogenesis' and shadowing the arguments of Gellner and Gat, historians disagree over how far this required a pre-existing ethnic reality. Members of a heterogeneous group would create a new identity that allowed them to insert themselves into their new territories as a political and military elite. Then, over time the local population would begin to adopt these identities themselves and the elite would assimilate to some degree. This is what explains the emergence of a 'Danish' identity in the tenth century: it did not simply apply to those of Danish origin, but reflects those locals who became more closely affiliated to their new neighbours than they did to their distant southern 'cousins'. The appearance of Scandinavian names across the whole of England (and especially the north and east) is, therefore, not a reliable guide to ethnicity. Locals would adopt them for their families if it was socially advantageous for them to do so. Earl Godwin famously named his children with Scandinavian names (Swein, Harold and Tostig).

The southern expansion of Wessex in the tenth century, therefore, encountered regions with distinctive identities who were not simply awaiting incorporation into an English state. A summary of the evolving relationship between the elites of Northumbria and the kings of the English based in the southern part of Northumbria underline how complex this is. The sporadic nature of royal interventions in the north under successive kings indicates that Northumbria was largely left to its own devices, except when some strategic threat emerged. The alliance of northern rulers that Æthelstan encountered at Brunanburh in 937, or the choice of an autonomous Norse king in York in 948, which led to an intervention by Eadred (r.946–955), are the exceptions rather than the rule. Æthelstan was the first southern ruler to be acknowledged as ruler of the Northumbrians, and lavished considerable attention on the cult of St Cuthbert, which had been based at Chester-le-Street since 882 after leaving Lindisfarne. Æthelstan's coins are found in large numbers in Northumbria, which is evidence of his influence. On Æthelstan's death, Wessex's authority lapsed until after the death of the last king of York, Eric Bloodaxe, in 954. After this, there were no rival royal powers in Northumbria, and the southern kings began to appoint ealdormen to maintain order and wield authority on their behalf. Crucially, though, the dominant family was the local earls of Bamburgh, who had controlled the northern section of Northumbria (Bernicia) since the end of the independent monarchy in 867. They maintained an unbroken line of hereditary succession to the earldom through to the eleventh century, which would suggest the extent that the king had to recognize the autonomy of local families.

To further complicate things, Northumbria itself was not an indivisible whole. It had its origins in the seventh century as two distinct territories: Bernicia in the north and Deira in the south. For a time (966–1006), the Deira earldom passed under the control of other individuals (Oslac, Thored and Ælfhelm) about whom there is little information save that they appear to be royal appointments attempting to limit local autonomy. Oslac's regular witnessing of the charters of King Edgar (959–75) indicates that he was closely associated with the southern government. His successor Thored's name indicates he

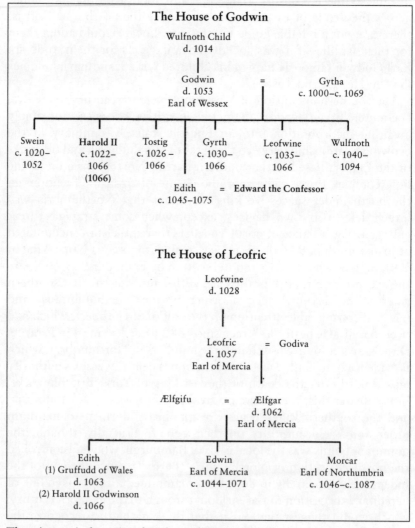

The aristocratic dynasties of Godwin of Wessex and Leofric of Murcia.

54

may have been of Scandinavian origin, which suggests that he was from the local elite. His daughter married the new king, Æthelred II (978–1016) and so he was strongly linked to the royal court. Ælfhelm, appointed by King Æthelred II to replace Thored, was from Mercia and is first found witnessing documents as the ealdorman in 994. The fates that befell the Deira ealdormen indicate that the English kings had managed to integrate them into a national political scene to some extent. It has been speculated that both Eadwulf and Oslac were swept away in the succession crisis (975–8) that followed Edgar's death and culminated in his son Edward's murder, while Thored disappears after a defeat by a Danish army in 992: whether through death in battle or disgrace at the outcome, it is not known. Ælfhelm became a victim of the factional politics of Æthelred's reign in 1006, when he was killed and his sons blinded.

Attempts by the southern royal court to extend its influence in the north are also strongly suggested by the selection of candidates for the major ecclesiastical appointments in the north, especially the archbishopric of York. After the death of Archbishop Wulfstan in 956, all the appointments to this key ecclesiastical position were of men from Mercia. Wulfstan's career had been spent navigating the complex political changes in York and he was apparently a key figure in either supporting or undermining those who held power in the city in the decades before Eric Bloodaxe's final defeat. The territorial, administrative and ideological powers held by the archbishops meant that the kings of the English could not afford for the post to become the tool for local interests. For the next century, the archbishop also usually held the bishopric of Worcester in plurality with York. This was irregular, according to ecclesiastical rules, so was clearly driven by pragmatic imperatives. By appointing their own men who were dependent on external support in the absence of local affiliations, these archbishops would become champions of the king's interests in a strategically vital position. Oswald, archbishop from 972 to 992, was a leading champion of Benedictine Monastic Reform, which was eagerly supported by kings as it not only reaped spiritual benefits but helped to undermine local secular influences in monastic houses. Reform in practical terms usually saw the current hierarchy removed (who were often kin to the local secular aristocracy) and replaced with outside leadership, thus helping to support royal control. Oswald's successor Wulfstan (1002–23) was not only a reformer who tried to bring York into line with practices in the south, but also a leading intellectual and statesman for both Æthelred and Cnut and thus intimately involved in drafting royal legislation.

James Campbell and Patrick Wormald have both written eloquently that the Anglo-Saxon 'state' was a fully formed national entity, the like of which was unique for tenth century Europe.[56] This 'maximalist' view suggests that English kings could wield unprecedented levels of control over the population through the institutions that developed under their aegis, first in Wessex and then extended into the conquered regions. A particularly powerful method of control was the division of land into local administrative units (shires) overseen by reeves, royal officials we know as sheriffs. The royal monopoly on coinage is a powerful example used to emphasize the precocious influence of Anglo-Saxon royal power. Along with the king's name and image, other didactic symbols, such as the Hand of God found on coins of Æthelred II, made powerful ideological statements. Anglo-Saxon monarchs issued written instructions and law codes. They gave themselves grand imperial titles such as *Basileius* (the Greek for 'king' used by Byzantine emperors) and created an elaborate coronation ceremony (first used in 973 and a direct ancestor of today's service) to reflect their conception of a new, exalted status. The enormous sums raised by Æthelred II's government to pay the Danegeld that bought off Viking armies between 991 and 1018 are very impressive.

Rather than being the direct product of the policies of Alfred and his successors, George Molyneux has recently revised this argument to suggest that the tenth century kingdom was run more as an informal lordship and the administrative structure and territoriality of the eleventh-century kingdom was a product of changes introduced by King Edgar in the 970s.[57] Molyneux also rejects the view that the Old English state was necessarily more precocious than the rest of Western Europe. Much of what was happening on this side of the Channel can be paralleled with developments on the other side. The apparent differences are largely semantic. There is also the problem with the word 'state', which, like 'nation' and 'propaganda', has emerged in the battle between modern and medieval historians over whether the Middle Ages were just a precursor and background to the really important periods of human history. In their attempt to move beyond crude stereotypes, medievalists have triumphantly appropriated the concepts of social science analysis to demonstrate the complexity and intrinsic worth of their periods.[58]

It is possible, therefore, to take a more sceptical position. The 'maximalist' position often relies on arguments from silence, as so much of our evidence about the administration system is missing. It also takes the perspective of sources such as the *Anglo-Saxon Chronicle* at face value. One could just as easily argue they give us the perspective of the royal court, which aimed at legitimizing an untraditional, centralized system of rule by Wessex-based kings over a recalcitrant population who wished to preserve their local customs. Law codes, coinage, written charters and the other elements of this apparatus of autocracy, which have so impressed scholars, is only evidence of the government's intentions, not its achievements. It would almost be like judging a political party's record in government by its manifesto promises, rather than by how they deliver them. The so-called 'minimalist' position emphasizes that the grandiose claims of these early English kings were an attempt to conceal the yawning gap between the ideal and reality. What really counted when a king wanted to get his way in matters of policy was building a consensus with his leading subjects, not the imposition of royal will through force. Informal powers of persuasion and negotiation with local elites were probably more central to the way that the kingdom of England functioned.

Well-established local identities remained deeply entrenched within society, as we have outlined from the history of Northumbria. Northumbria and Wessex are both extremes, and we should see Mercia and East Anglia as being on a spectrum in between. Kent has significant evidence of distinctive local custom in land management and inheritance patterns. Its men maintained the right to fight in the vanguard of royal armies, as they apparently did at Hastings. It was never subject to Forest Law under the Normans. A recent study has emphasized how long it took English kings to establish any authority in East Anglia.[59] Regional elites ultimately had to balance the rewards and obligations that came with allying themselves to the royal court, and the need to maintain their position as leaders and champions of their own peoples' interests.

The 'minimalist' view is more compatible with what we can see when we reverse the telescope and look at the south from the northern perspective. During the eleventh century, Northumbria came more firmly within the orbit of the English monarchy, but still retained a strong separatist tradition. By the late tenth century, the earldom of Bamburgh had returned to Oswulf's family with the appointment of his son Waltheof. Uhtred, the son of Waltheof, defeated a Scots invasion in 1006 and, as a result, brought the whole of Northumbria, with the addition of Deira, under his family's sway. He achieved this by forging a successful relationship with the regime of Æthelred II *Unraed*: his first wife was Ecgfrida, the daughter of Aldhun, the first bishop of Durham, and his last wife was Ælfgifu, Æthelred's own daughter. Uhtred had strong local connections, as can be seen by his

role in helping to found a new site for St Cuthbert's shrine at Durham.
Uhtred was unfortunate to live at a time of unprecedented crisis as
England had been subject to thirty years of increasingly persistent
raids from the re-invigorated Viking fleets. Æthelred's government
managed to resist or buy off Danish armies with more success than he
is usually credited with, but the enemy they faced was more organized
and formidable than that which Alfred had resisted.

In 1013, however, Sweyn Forkbeard, the king of Denmark, brought
an army to Gainsborough in Lincolnshire and proceeded to take the
submission of the main towns and earldoms in the north-eastern half
of England, including from Earl Uhtred. Many of those who had
been alienated from Æthelred's court, especially those close to the late
Earldorman Æflhelm, flocked to join Sweyn and pledge allegiance to
him. Sweyn's son Cnut may have married Ælfhelm's daughter Ælgifu
at this point to consolidate the alliance between the Danes and the
dissident English nobility. Æthelred fled to Normandy with his family,
but Sweyn's death in early 1014 saw another mass of defections from
his English supporters and, on condition that he promised to rule
more consensually ('reform all the things that they [his subjects]
hated') than he had before, Æthelred was invited back to England.
However, Æthelred's return saw little goodwill. The Mercian thegn
Sigeferth and his brother Morcar were killed at an assembly at Oxford,
apparently by Eadric Streona, earldorman of Mercia, and the king
seized their property. This policy of murdering dissident noblemen
shows how fragile royal control was in the area north and east of
Watling Street. With the continuation of the factional conflicts from
before his exile, Æthelred's second reign collapsed in chaos with his
son Edmund Ironside in rebellion against him and Sweyn's son Cnut
leading a new fleet back in 1015 to finish what his father had started.

Cnut's conquest of England was almost accidental, as his rivals –
Æthelred and his sons, Æthelstan and Edmund – all managed to die
within a very short space of time. Having brought a fleet to ravage
the kingdom, Cnut suddenly received the support of Eadric, who was
probably desperate to preserve his position with the imminent death
of Æthelred and the threat of a hostile Edmund Ironside. Eadric also
brought Wessex over to his side, probably without any real enthusiasm
on its part. With Æthelred's death, Edmund managed to unify much
of the kingdom behind him and engaged in a series of clashes with
Cnut that culminated in the Battle of Ashingdon (*Assandun*) on
18 October 1016. This was followed by a division of the country,
with Edmund taking Wessex and Cnut, Mercia. Edmund died soon
afterwards, probably from his wounds, and Cnut was left as sole ruler.

Cnut divided the country up into four parts, appointing those who had fought for him. He assigned East Anglia to Thorkell, a Viking warlord who had fought for Æthelred; Mercia to Eadric; and Northumbria to a Norwegian supporter, Eric Bloodaxe.

The Battle of Maldon is one of the most celebrated Old English epic poems detailing the death of the Ealdorman Brythnoth while trying to fight off a Viking army in 991. It appears to be a strong statement of how invasion helped crystallize a notion of common identity in the face of an enemy attack. The earl shouts to the Viking fleet that he is 'ready to guard this realm, the home of Æthelred my lord, people and land'. When Brythnoth fell, his men bravely continued to resist, and several allude to their different origins. Ælfwine states that he was 'born in Mercia of a great race', while a Northumbrian hostage Æscferth 'Did not flinch in the war-play but urged forth the dart unceasingly'. Here, the notion of the strengthening bonds of common interest and loyalty between the different regions is clearly being pushed to its limits, but one has to be very careful reading a work that follows poetic licence.

The poem has often been seen as a challenge to Æthelred's policy of buying off the Vikings while championing a more aggressive response, but given that the poem has lost its beginning and end, it would be rash to look too deeply for contemporary resonance. The date of the poem has been subject to considerable debate, but there is a strong argument (largely based on the use of the term 'earl' for Brythnoth, which only comes into standard use under Cnut) that it was written in the 1020s and is part of a re-writing of Æthelred's reign, which can also be seen in the *Anglo-Saxon Chronicle*. However one analyses it, the picture the poem gives of an 'English' resistance must be seen as reflecting contemporary arguments and debate, and not a simple reflection of reality. The men fighting at Maldon were an Essex force, not an English one. The *Anglo-Saxon Chronicle*'s condemnation of the 'treachery' of the English earldormen and thegns that joined Sweyn Forkbeard and Cnut reflect regional, not national, perspectives.

To further complicate regional traditions, we must consider the continuation of intrusive ethnic identities in the tenth and eleventh centuries. A 'Danish' identity in England is referred to in our sources on several occasions. The most spectacular example was the St Brice's Day Massacre in November 1002, when Æthelred ordered that all the 'Danes' in the country be killed owing to their potential disloyalty. This has sparked intense debate: if it was all those of Scandinavian descent, it would certainly be testimony for the English kingdom possessing unprecedented power. A sensible reading would be that it was referring to those who had arrived in England recently, and it is, in fact, only documented as occurring in Oxford. The law codes of the late tenth century of Edgar and Æthelred both acknowledge separate 'Danish' legal customs in the East Midlands and Northumbria. Such separate identities only appear in our sources in the context of conflict. Historians now see this situation as regional interests placing limits on royal authority rather than newcomers living under separate traditions. There was no political 'Danish' identity after the death of Eric Bloodaxe. The accession of Cnut changed matters again, re-introducing Danish lordship across the country.

Cnut established his rulership by removing those local elites he felt he could not trust, purging the sons of leading earldormen of the previous regime. Most significantly, he disposed of Uhtred of Northumbria. Having submitted to Sweyn, and then probably being involved in the decision to invite Æthelred back from exile, Uhtred then abandoned his father-in-law to fight alongside his brother-in-law Edmund Ironside in his struggle against his father and then with Cnut. Edmund's death forced Uhtred to make terms with the new monarch, and it was while making his submission to Cnut that he was murdered, with forty of his retainers, in Cnut's hall at *Wichele* by his local rival Thurbrand in 1016.[60] There was no way that the new ruler could have trusted Uhtred, given his record, but he contracted the killing out, exploiting a local feud. Eadric did not last long, either, being killed the same year. Cnut's Earl Eric of Hlathir was, in turn, replaced by another Scandinavian, Siward, at some point between 1023 and 1033 (it is impossible to be any more precise). Bamburgh, however, stayed in the hands of Uhtred's family. His brother Eadwulf Cudel (Eadwulf II of Northumbria) was succeeded in turn by Uhtred's son Ealdred before passing on the office to Ealdred's brother Eadwulf III. Siward married into Uhtred's family by marrying Ealdred's daughter Ælfflaed and, after killing Eadwulf III in 1041 on behalf of Harald Harefoot, he emerged as the earl of the whole of Northumbria for the first time since Uhtred's death.

Cnut's reign is notable for the infusion of another wave of Scandinavian settlers into the country. Cnut demobilized the army that had conquered the kingdom for him in 1018 using the vast tribute of £82,500 he had been able to extract from the country to pay him off. There was no replication of what would happen after 1066, with the mass replacement of the elite landholders, and so the Danes increasingly intruded themselves into localities of England by patronage rather than by appropriation. The significant numbers of Scandinavian names that can be found within Domesday Book across the south-west of England are probably best explained by settlement of those who came to the country with Cnut, given the lack of evidence for earlier settlements. This is best seen in Worcestershire, where Bishop Lyfing addressed all the thegns 'both English and Danish' in a charter of 1042. However, once again this was no simple colonial implantation; rather, it was a fusion of an elite drawing on local English and Scandinavian traditions to create something new. Cnut portrayed himself in the traditions of Christian English kingship through his patronage towards churches and law codes, while in Denmark being portrayed as a heroic Viking warrior who listened to skaldic poetry.

While only a few Englishmen survived amongst the ealdormen in Cnut's earlier reign, it is clear that below the elite social strata, large numbers of indigenous administrators remained in position to continue the work of government, and that there was more continuity than at first appears. By the 1030s, this situation had been reversed and a series of Anglo-Saxon earls had emerged as the leading figures of his regime. These were 'new men' from landowning families who had not been members of the upper echelons of the elite in earlier periods. Much of Cnut's reign was spent abroad following his interests in Scandinavia, including a visit to Rome in 1027 to attend the crowning of the Holy Roman Emperor Conrad II. It was these expeditions that allowed Godwin, the son of Wulfnoth, a thegn from Sussex, to rise in royal favour. Having been one of the earliest Englishmen to join Cnut at some point between 1015 and 1018, he had married one of Cnut's kinswomen, Gytha. He was soon appointed earl of Wessex and became Cnut's effective regent. With Leofric of Mercia and Siward in Northumbria, England was dominated by powerful regional magnates. All of these men adopted the new fashions and culture of lordship that developed under Cnut, which is usually described as Anglo-Danish.

The events of the reigns of Æthelred and Cnut show how, after the attempts by the earlier monarchs to create a unified kingdom, four distinctive regions remained: Northumbria, East Anglia and the eastern Midlands, western Mercia, and Wessex. Each area had its own elite and powerful patrons and protectors that it gathered around. Each area had its own distinctive regional form of government. Kings had to manage these groups as best as they could, and they found success to some degree in Northumbria, but in the Midlands this was difficult given the dominance of the family of Æthelstan Half-King, which dominated central England. Kings Eadwig and Edgar had tried to balance these families with other power brokers, but Æthelred had pushed the interests of the western Mercians at the expense of East Anglia. Æthelred's dynastic policies of championing the succession of his children by his second wife Emma at the expense of his elder sons created disgruntled princes around which disaffected provincial nobles could gather, and this resulted in the enormously complex manoeuvring of these powerful elites, each trying to serve their own interests while in the background a series of increasingly intense Danish raids inflicted considerable damage on the country. As a result of this situation, local feuds could easily translate themselves onto the stage of wider national politics.

The notion that the kingdom of England in the form that it appears in 1066 was a natural development of events in the late ninth century is simply wrong. In the 950s, the Mercian and Northumbrians broke away from the rule of King Eadwig and instead proclaimed his brother Edgar king. Although Eadwig's death allowed the kingdom to be re-united, the same division occurred in 1016 between Cnut and Edmund Ironside, with the latter taking Wessex and the former everything else. This may have been purely tactical and only lasted as long as Edmund was alive (he died soon afterwards from his wounds suffered at the battle of Assandun in 1016), but we cannot simply assume this was the case. With the death of Cnut in 1035, the kingdom was again divided between his sons, with Harthacnut controlling the south and Harold Harefoot the north. In this instance Harthacnut's failure to return from Denmark allowed Harold to become the *de facto* ruler. We must reject a simple teleological view of history that suggests that Northumbria would inevitably become part of England. In fact, it might easily have become part of Scotland, as the northern part of Bernicia (Lothian) had already done during the reign of King Malcolm III (1005–34). In the twelfth century, the Scots King David, exploiting the conflict in England between Matilda and her cousin King Stephen (1135–54), extended his southern border to the Tees, incorporating the whole of Bernicia, until his son was forced to return it to Stephen's successor, Henry II.

The territories to the north and east of Watling Street were subject to a complex series of evolving relationships with the south, whose control waxed and waned over the whole period. It is clear that Northumbria retained a degree of cultural separateness from the southern-based English 'state' that survived the ending of its political autonomy with the passing of the kingdom of York. English kings did not hold much property in these areas, nor did they have any reformed monasteries to channel royal influence. The king had no capacity to extend his itinerary circuits into the East Midlands and Northumbria, and if he did appear in these areas, it was at the head of an army.

It is unlikely that Northumbria was shired much before 1066 and the Domesday commissioners ended their survey on the Tees because the area beyond lacked the administrative infrastructure to provide information comprehensible to the southern bureaucracy.

The importance of the rhythms of regional identity persisted strongly into the eleventh century, as can be seen in the feud pursued by the descendants of Uhtred and Thorbrand, which continued beyond the Norman Conquest.[61] Royal English law codes had long recognized the social necessity of kin to revenge attacks and sought to restrain and regulate these, but local custom was too engrained. The kingdom was still a fragmented society that saw a constant re-articulation of local identities in terms of older traditions and was shaped by its interactions with the royal administration. A sense of nationhood was still nascent and superficial. The political stresses of the period could easily have seen its constituent parts broken up and re-constructed as something new.

Anderson and Gat can both find evidence to sustain their argument in the evidence we have. A concept of 'Englishness' did exist in the eleventh century. The kingdom of England was sufficiently coherent by this period to make it conquerable by an outside force. But there was nothing permanent about its constituency, nor was this identity exclusive but overlaid many other forms of regional identities, mediated through the key relationship of elites who were also both local and national. Most historians would now, therefore, admit that the Norman Conquest was less of a disjuncture in English history, which is best understood in terms of long-term structural changes that continued to develop over the next few centuries. It is perfectly feasible to argue that, should Harold have won at Hastings, in the same way that Scandinavia itself was gradually brought into the mainstream of Latin European civilization between the eleventh and thirteenth centuries, so England would have become more closely aligned to Europe, albeit at a more gradual rate of change.

'The Norman Conquest is the great turning-point in the history of the English nation,' wrote Edward Augustus Freeman in 1867.[62] Our tendency to present the Battle of Hastings as a turning point in English history ignores the reality that 'England' as a concept has been subject to a continual evolution ever since its creation in the tenth century. The great historians of the Victorian era who saw themselves in Harold and his army of Anglo-Saxons, developed the idea that would become commonplace in the twentieth century – the view of England (or Britain, depending on your point of view) standing against a hostile continent. The year 1066 became associated with

1588, 1804 and 1940: other turning points when 'our' island resisted foreign invasion, though the fact that 1066 had represented a failure was quickly overtaken by the Normanist view begun with Thomas Carlyle, who, in 1858, rather uncharitably described the English as:

> A gluttonous race of Jutes and Angles, capable of no great combinations; lumbering about in pot-bellied equanimity; not dreaming of heroic toil and silence and endurance, such as leads to the high places of this Universe, and the golden mountain-tops where dwell the Spirits of the Dawn. [63]

In other words, according to Carlyle, it was the Norman Conquest that laid the foundation for English greatness. Hastings, therefore, perfectly encapsulated the notion of a decisive battle because it seemed to mark such a watershed moment in the history of the nation.

Such views show that as the observers of the eleventh century wished to see Hastings in moral terms, as a conflict between the just and unjust, so later generations have followed in a similar vein and applied this battlefield dichotomy to Hastings, which has become representative of a notion of national identity that exists in conflict – of England against Europe. Such thinking reflects the way that our understanding of the battle has been continuously shaped by the changing concerns of different eras, and how our desire to know 'what happened' is never as straightforward as we may believe.

CHAPTER 3

An English Army?

THE POLITICS OF THE ENGLISH STATE

Having explored the complex background to the kingdom of England in the tenth and eleventh centuries, we can now focus on the key issue. When Harold faced William on the hill that was later named Battle, should we describe him as fighting for England or as the disputed leader of a fragmenting political entity? The portrait of Harold as a defender of English liberty that we find in the elaborately written account of Edward Augustus Freeman has long been recognized as a product of an over-stimulated Victorian imagination. Even so, we still tend to view Harold through a prism of national identity.[64] In one sense, this is fair: as the legitimate king of England, Harold was the sole unifying figure for a socially complex and ethnically diverse population. However, we can suggest another, more realistic, interpretation of these events by characterizing 1066 as a ruthless power-struggle between over-mighty warlords who exploited the dynastic instability in England in an attempt to seize control of the powerful administrative systems that the English monarchy had developed over the previous two centuries.

Eleventh-century English kings could exert considerable control over their most important subjects. Royal government was structured so that earls were appointed by the king, who had the power to summarily dismiss them or adjust their territorial jurisdictions, as he felt appropriate. This challenges the prevailing view of Edward the Confessor as a weak king controlled by the Godwin clan. Stephen Baxter has strongly criticized the use of the term 'over-mighty subject' for this period, and questioned the canard that Edward held fewer estates than his aristocrats.[65] Royal patronage was so important to an English earl that assemblies of the king's council were very well attended as one's future depended on the relationship with the man on the throne. The rapid turnover of aristocrats under Æthelred and Cnut would certainly bear this out to some extent. The high politics of the reigns of eleventh-century kings have been re-constructed through the names appended to surviving royal charters as witnesses to grants of land. Who was signing and in what order their names were recorded provides a much more effective insight into the dynamics of court politics than can be found within our intermittent chronicle evidence. As charters were produced by the king's administration, they, by their very existence, imply the paramount importance of royal government as an organizing principle in Anglo-Saxon England. They also suggest that the upper strata of society bought into a notion of Englishness strongly bound up with the monarchy. This can be contrasted with the more chaotic conditions in north-west France with which Duke William of Normandy had to grapple: rebellious vassals, secure in their castles, who could only be controlled by force of personality. It seems obvious why a Norman duke would covet the English crown.

It is possible to criticize this vision of an all-powerful 'Anglo-Saxon state' as it easily falls into the trap of English exceptionalism. Western Frankia (France) certainly witnessed a collapse of centralized royal authority in the tenth and eleventh centuries, which saw local aristocrats 'privatize' many of the powers previously exercised by the Carolingian monarchs and their immediate successors. This period is often described as a 'feudal revolution' distinguished by local aristocrats building castles to defend their territory against seizure in endemic private warfare with their neighbours. This strongly contrasts with an orderly and stable England. There was no English version of the 'Peace of God' movement that emerged in the late tenth century in south-west France, when local church leaders attempted to exert control over the violence in their localities owing to the absence of a strong central authority. However, one wonders how far these contrasting images are products of our surviving evidence rather than reflections of reality. We lack a Domesday Book for western Frankia and so rely on chronicle evidence, whose religious sentiments often reflect their authors' moralizing and pessimistic world view. A brief survey of the often bare narrative of the *Anglo-Saxon Chronicle* sees occasional mention of castles and the wasting of territory across England by both locals and outsiders. The ravaging of the whole of Worcestershire in 1041 ordered by Harthacnut in revenge for the killing of two housecarls who had been collecting taxes shows that royal government was not always benign.

Earls were vital intermediaries between the king and his subjects who ensured local compliance through the complex network of personal relationships on which Anglo-Saxon lordship was constructed. Royal institutions could replicate their local powers to some degree through the shire reeve (sheriff), but they often lacked the informal bonds of lordship where reciprocal loyalties were as important to effective government as the bureaucratic instruments of control that have struck modern commentators with such awe. Cnut's political legacy of three dominant earldoms in England – Wessex, Mercia and Northumbria – severely limited his successors' freedom of movement. Harold Harefoot, Harthacnut and Edward were only able to ascend to the throne with the acquiescence of these earldoms. The king's ability to mobilize military manpower was limited without the co-operation of their major subjects. The Godwins appear to have pursued their own separate foreign policy in the late 1040s when they allied with the Count of Flanders who was opposed to Edward's support for the Emperor Henry III. The outrageous behaviour of Godwin's son Earl Swein indicates that some of the Godwin family felt they could almost act with impunity. He was exiled after kidnapping the abbess of Leominster in 1046, a crime he committed probably for political motives, and immediately after making his peace with the king he murdered his cousin, Earl Beorn, which again led to his exile. One could argue that his exile shows royal power, but his actions indicate this was no real deterrence.

The main difference in political life between northern France and England was that in England the monarchy still acted as the principal conduit for advancement. This did not necessarily mean politics in England was more civilized. The return of Godwin and his sons in 1052 (after Edward exiled them in 1051) was, as Stenton has strongly argued, a result of military pressure rather than a neatly arranged diplomatic episode, though their return did culminate in a compromise agreement rather than a civil war owing to the pressure of the thegns to avoid such a conflict. Harold's attempt to force a landing at Porlock in Somerset in 1052 was opposed by local thegns and in the subsequent fighting, thirty thegns were killed as well as a large number of local levies. Godwin had toured his fleet up and down the coast ransacking local communities until they accepted his authority. The Northumbrian Revolt in 1065 began in violence with the attack on the hall of one of Godwin's sons, Tostig, in York and the murder of his thegns, and was followed by the encampment of a northern army around Northampton, which raided the local area while it awaited a decision from the royal court. According to the *Anglo-Saxon Chronicle*, its return north was accompanied by the cattle and other goods it had seized, and was thus almost a northern invasion of the south.[66] All of the characters were not nascent English gentlemen, as so memorably portrayed by Freeman, but players of power politics in which the stakes were so high that failure could easily result in death.

It is possible, therefore, to portray the kingdom of England in the decades before the Norman Conquest as being prone to violent political feuding, invasion by foreign rulers and destabilizing succession crises. The ability of the kingdom to survive these shocks is evidence of its inherent strength and resilience, but we could posit an alternative interpretation: that the kingdom was fragmenting. The paradox is that while the two centuries after the end of the First Viking Age witnessed periods of endemic political crisis, there was also considerable economic development in England with the creation of the countryside as we know it today. Nucleated settlements (villages) and a network of parish churches sprang up across the landscape, testimony to increased agricultural productivity. These were accompanied by the emergence of a rich thegnly class, who developed aristocratic residences with luxury goods and the conspicuous consumption of exotic foods and table manners that marked them out as being sophisticated elites. The funds that King Æthelred II was able to extract from his population between 991 and 1015 to pay off the sequence of Danish armies who rampaged through the kingdom are a remarkable testament to the wealth that was being produced.[67] This is another way that England in the eleventh century resembles contemporary Western Europe, as the political turmoil it experienced also stimulated similar economic trends.[68] It was the desire to control this wealth that made the country so attractive to foreign invaders and made the internal struggles between the different aristocratic factions so intense.

THE INFLUENCE OF THE GODWIN FAMILY

If we are to understand the Battle of Hastings in its domestic context, we need to understand Harold's perspective as he stood with his army facing the Norman forces. The gamble he took in confronting William immediately rather than waiting has been heavily criticized, but one needs to appreciate how precarious his political position was. The careers of Harold Godwinson's grandfather and father illustrate the vicissitudes of Late Anglo-Saxon political life. By 1007, Æthelred II had increasingly come to rely on the support of the Mercian ealdorman Eadric Streona and his kin-group to maintain control of his kingdom. They helped the king execute his policies in handling the persistent and existential Danish threat. Æthelred found managing the factional nature of Anglo-Saxon politics difficult, especially when trying to arrange the succession in favour of his sons, Edward (the Confessor) and Alfred Ætheling, from his second marriage to Emma of Normandy. He relied on murder and mutilation to remove opposition and Eadric served as the king's hatchet-man, assassinating the previously dominant ealdorman Ælfhelm and blinding his two sons in 1006.

Their political position secured, Æthelred and Eadric then developed a new strategy against the Danes, constructing a huge fleet in 1009 and assembling the leading men of England at Sandwich to serve in it. The politicking did not end there. Eadric, probably eyeing the opportunity to extend his control into the South East, turned on Harold's grandfather Wulfnoth, a leading thegn in Sussex, who was accused of disloyalty to the king by Eadric's brother Beorhtric. Wulfnoth detached twenty ships from the royal fleet and made a run for home, ravaging the south coast en route (presumably avoiding his own estates) while being pursued by Beorhtric with eighty ships. Mercia's landlocked nature was not ideal for gaining naval expertise and this inexperience probably contributed to subsequent events. As the king's men lost control of their ships, Wulfnoth was able to swing round and set fire to them. Wulfnoth then vanishes from the historical record, presumably fleeing into exile.

Despite his spectacular *volte-face* in 1016, when he deserted Æthelred's son Edmund Ironside, Eadric's pre-eminence under the previous regime meant that Cnut quickly disposed of him (amongst other leading figures) in the political manoeuvring that followed his accession to the throne. Godwin himself had nearly been buried by the exile of his father and so it is no surprise that he rallied to Cnut in a bid to restore his fortunes. After helping him secure the throne in England, Godwin campaigned for his new patron in Denmark, helping Cnut establish his North Sea dominion. Godwin received his reward by being given the earldom of Wessex, which was a significant promotion for someone whose family had no track record of elevated royal service. He consolidated this dominant position in the new regime with his complete loyalty to Cnut, whose kinswoman Gytha he married. The death of Cnut in 1035 led to an extended succession crisis that very nearly ruined Godwin's carefully constructed position. Godwin was closely allied to Cnut's wife Emma, who wished her son by Cnut, Harthacnut, to succeed his father. The other principal earls, Siward of Northumbria and Leofric of Mercia, rallied around Harold Harefoot, Cnut's son with his first wife Ælgifu. Harold Harefoot was in situ in England at the time whereas Harthacnut was in Denmark when his father died and he was not in a position to make a bid for power. The tardiness in arranging a fleet to support his candidacy undermined his credibility and left Harold Harefoot with the opportunity to establish his control bloodlessly, which he did by expelling Emma from the kingdom. His success left Godwin in a dangerously vulnerable position in relation to the new king's favour.

Godwin had to rapidly re-position himself and secure a rapprochement with the new king if he were to survive. It was probably to achieve such an accommodation that he arranged the interception and incarceration of Alfred Ætheling, Emma's son by Æthelred, who had made his own bid for the throne in 1036 supported by northern French mercenaries, largely from Boulogne. The massacre and enslavement of Alfred's supporters and the mutilation of the young *ætheling* demonstrates Godwin's ruthlessness, even if his precise role in the violence has been somewhat obscured by several sources, which sought to exculpate him and blame Harold Harefoot. While this helped secure Godwin's position, these events soured the relationship between Godwin and Harthacnut when the latter succeeded after his half-brother's premature death in 1040. Not only did Godwin's actions show his primary loyalty to self-interest, but Harthacnut had a social obligation to avenge his half-brother Alfred Ætheling. On Harthacnut's death in 1042, he was succeeded by his half-brother Edward the Confessor. The new king's weak political position meant that he was dependent on Godwin's support. This is clearly demonstrated by the Godwin ascendancy between 1042 and 1045, during which Godwin's sons Swein and Harold were promoted to earldoms and Edward the Confessor married Godwin's daughter Edith. Personal and political differences were always under the surface, however, and the fate of Alfred undoubtedly haunted their political and personal relationship. This spectacularly erupted with the crisis of 1051 when Edward moved against the Godwins and, after an armed stand-off at Gloucester, exiled them. Godwin and his sons had raised significant bodies of loyal men to defend themselves, but Edward secured the support of Leofric and Siward, and the Godwins' support quickly dissipated, leaving them with no option but to scurry overseas as quickly as they could, much to the astonishment of contemporaries.

Some historians have suggested that the trigger for the 1051 crisis was Edward's plans for Duke William of Normandy to succeed him against Godwin's wishes.[69] Edward seems to have promised the throne to a range of people: as Frank Barlow has argued, this is probably best understood as a tactical means of Edward enhancing his power through the creation of domestic and foreign alliances.[70] It is possible that Edward planned for a Norman succession as vengeance on the Godwins or even because of his 'French' sympathies (he was exiled in Normandy for many years, after all). However, either interpretation rests excessively on hindsight and arranges all the events in the decades before 1066 as mere precursors to Hastings. Presenting the Godwins as the defenders of English liberty against French acquisitiveness certainly persuaded Freeman as a cogent interpretation in the nineteenth century, but we cannot fall into such an anachronistic trap.

One of the main assertions made in the *Anglo-Saxon Chronicle* and the *Vita Ædwardi* ('Life of Edward') supporting Godwin's return was that the whole episode with Edward had been the result of evil advice and malevolence on the part of arrogant 'Frenchmen' in England. It is true that Edward had spent twenty-five years in Normandy and his outlook had been strongly shaped by his experiences. He was undoubtedly sympathetic to Frankish cultural developments as can be seen from his re-building of Westminster Abbey in the Romanesque style, which was being adopted on the continent. He brought a group of Normans with him across the Channel in the 1040s, including Robert of Jumièges, who was promoted to the archbishopric of Canterbury in 1051 and who was particularly unpopular with the Godwins. The *Vita Ædwardi*, written just after 1066 by the personal chaplain to Queen Edith, Godwin's daughter (and thus reflecting a very pro-Godwin family perspective), blames Robert's machinations entirely for the 1051 exile.

National readings are only of limited aid in understanding these matters properly. Edward came to England with a group of followers as he lacked any local connections in 1041. Not all of these men were politically ambitious: many of Edward's household servants, such as William the Falconer, had French names. All kings relied on people they could trust to carry out their orders. In a world where personal relationships were formalized through oaths and a culture of loyalty, a king needed a network of capable men to exert an influence on events. Cnut's power was based on the army of housecarls he maintained in England after demobilizing his fleet in 1017, but Edward lacked this independent power base. The 'Frenchmen' mentioned in the texts are defined by their geographical background, not their political and ethnic affiliations. Three senior Frenchmen at court – Robert fitzMarc and Ralph, who were both stallers (i.e. senior officials in the royal household), and Earl Ralph, the king's nephew – had strong English connections: kinsfolk through marriage, the commendation of small local landowners, and the patronage of religious houses. There was little to distinguish them from major English landowners. Although the Godwins fell out with senior clerical Normans like Robert in the 1051 crisis, they were not opposed to the Lothringian clerics that Edward introduced or the continental secular elites. Edward still retained a party of 'French' followers with him after the settlement of 1052. These were 'king's men' whose knowledge and military expertise were useful, as can be seen by their introduction of castles to defend the vulnerable Welsh Marches. Even King Macbeth of Scotland used Normans to fight for him against the invasion of Earl Siward in 1054. Many of the English nobility had family and other personal connections with Ireland, Wales, Norway, Denmark and mainland Europe, or had people from these areas amongst their entourages. Class, not nationality, counted in the eleventh century. The Godwin family's opposition to a Norman succession was not due to 'English' hostility to a 'foreign' ruler: it had served Cnut from his first arrival in England and was culturally connected to the Scandinavian world. What the Godwins did not want was a successor over whom they had no control, and who would need to re-allocate land to reward followers.

Swein's death while on a pilgrimage to Jerusalem in 1052 (presumably attempting to do penance for his sins) was followed by the death of his father, Godwin, at Winchester in 1053 while dining with the king. This meant that Harold became the dominant member of the family 'firm', but this did not mean that he simply inherited his father's influence. It could be inferred from some accounts of Edward the Confessor's reign that Godwin and his sons were the only dominant aristocratic grouping. Narratives of this period often telescope their rise and fall to the exclusion of all other matters. Harold's hold on Wessex was still not complete in 1053, however, and the English kingdom was influenced by other leading figures: Siward in Northumbria, Leofric in Mercia, as well as Edward's kinsmen Ralph and Odda in the south Midlands. The Godwin crisis of 1051–2 is the best example where we can see the formation of political consensus among this small elite. When Godwin and Edward had their standoff at Gloucester, both the 'D' and the 'E' recensions of the *Anglo-Saxon Chronicle* record that leading figures (John of Worcester identifies Leofric) argued against fighting as civil conflict would only leave the country weakened and exposed to foreign invasion. The same arguments were used in 1052 when Godwin staged a return from exile and confronted Edward with an army at Southwark. This has been presented as evidence of a precocious political culture that placed the national interest above sectarian concerns, but it can just as easily be argued that the leading figures were being driven first and foremost by calculating self-interest and were reluctant to risk losing their political assets in the uncertainty of combat.

Given the failure of Edward and Edith to produce children after a decade of marriage, it was very unlikely that their marriage would resolve the succession. Godwin's strategy of maintaining his family's influence by seeing his daughter's progeny on the throne was in vain. Our lack of information means that we can only speculate about how this changed political calculations, but, as we have reiterated, the principal concern of the main players was preserving, or even enhancing, their own internal position within the kingdom. There was probably a consensus that the succession needed to be managed to ensure the leading families remained in situ. It seems unlikely that Harold was aiming at securing the throne at this stage. A wide range of potential candidates had better claims, such as Cnut's nephew King Sweyn of Denmark, and Earl Ralph of Hereford, who was the son of Edward's sister. The diplomatic mission sent in 1054 to bring Edmund Ironside's son, Edward the Exile, back from Hungary has been seen as a challenge to Harold's ambition, but it is much more plausible that Harold supported this initiative. By bringing in an outside figure without any domestic power-base, like Edward the Confessor, they could provide a framework of rule acceptable to the powerful earls, preserving the *status quo*. An internal royal succession by an existing aristocratic family was an anathema as this would upset the balance of power by monopolizing royal patronage, which could then be used against their rivals.

A series of deaths in the mid-1050s left the Godwinsons and the Leofricsons as the main rivals for pre-eminence within England. Leofric's son Ælfgar had been made earl of East Anglia in 1051 after the expulsion of the Godwins, but with their return in 1052 this appointment was reversed: Ælfgar was deprived and the earldom returned to Harold. With the death of Godwin in 1053 and Harold's promotion to Wessex, Ælfgar was restored. This meant Leofric's family held a swathe of territory from Cheshire to Essex across the middle of the country and a major territorial bloc in a strategically vital area. The death of Earl Siward of Northumbria in 1055 swung the balance of power back towards Harold's family as his brother Tostig was appointed as his replacement to the earldom. This choice has been used to suggest that Edward's policy was now being shaped entirely by Harold, or that Edward was becoming increasingly indifferent to the government of his kingdom. This is probably unfair. Harold never appears as anything other than a loyal subject to Edward. There is evidence from the *Vita Ædwardi* that Tostig was personally popular with both Edward and Edith, and so it is perfectly possible that Edward was rewarding a loyal courtier whom he believed he could trust.

On the appointment of Tostig, Ælfgar was exiled. The three versions of the *Anglo-Saxon Chronicle* demonstrate their different political sympathies when describing this incident. Version C says that Ælfgar 'was outlawed without guilt'. The 'D' recension, which includes significant northern material, says he was 'outlawed having hardly committed any crime'. Recension 'E', which is more favourable to the Godwin family, says that:

> Earl Ælfgar was outlawed because he was charged with being a
> traitor to the king and all the people of the country. He admitted
> this before all the people who were assembled there, though the
> words escaped him against his will.

While we cannot make an objective assessment of these charges, the different chronicle versions allow us to see contemporary political arguments surrounding Ælfgar's treatment, and the differences reveal the continued divisive fault lines that the aristocratic factions continued to exacerbate. That the expulsion occurred at the same time as Tostig's elevation is probably no coincidence. Ælfgar may have felt this undermined his family's strategic position, and it was very likely that he had coveted the job for himself. There was a precedent as the Mercian Ælfhelm had served as an earl in Northumbria in the late tenth century. Harold and Tostig were able to use Ælfgar's intransigence as evidence of his disloyalty to the king, forcing Edward to act against him.

What is striking about Ælfgar's response is how he followed Godwin's tactics in 1052. Rather than merely accepting his exile, he travelled to Ireland and hired a Viking fleet. Returning to Wales, he made an alliance with one of the Mercians' major rivals, King Gruffudd ap Llywelyn of Wales, and this joint Mercian-Welsh force attacked the strategically important castle at Hereford, comprehensively defeating the defending forces under Earl Ralph, and then burning down the town. This embarrassing defeat is argued by the *Anglo-Saxon Chronicle* to have been due to Ralph making the English fight on horseback, who then fled. But the Welsh *Chronicle of the Princes* describes it as a 'bitter-keen struggle', which seems more likely given the persistent warfare that had flared up on the English-Welsh frontier since the late 1030s with the rise of the powerful Gruffudd. In the subsequent negotiations, Ælfgar was able to have his earldom returned to him. English earls were now quite prepared to bring in external forces to help resolve their own internal disputes, a policy that would eventually destroy them all when Tostig used it later. It clearly highlights the relative weaknesses of English royal government when dealing with its major subjects.

Harold managed to restore some order on the Welsh frontier by launching a limited invasion across the border and constructing a ditch around Hereford. In 1056, Harold's priest Leofgar was appointed as bishop of Hereford, who, the *Anglo-Saxon Chronicle* records, 'wore his moustaches' until his promotion. Shaving did not change his approach to his vocation and this martial priest then led a campaign into Wales, which ended fatefully, forcing Leofric and Harold to again return and re-structure the defences. The deaths of Earl Ralph and Earl Leofric in 1057 removed two senior figures from English politics, leaving Harold as the senior earl and the government's executive officer, as witnessed by his increasingly prominent role in the chronicles. The subsequent re-organization of the earldoms illustrates the increasing strength of his position. Ælfgar succeeded his father to the earldom of Mercia in around 1057, but East Anglia was passed onto Gyrth Godwinson, while the last Godwinson brother, Leofwine, was given an earldom in Kent and the south-east. Ælfgar's sons may have been old enough to be considered for promotion to the rank of earl at this time and, if so, they were passed over in favour of Godwin's sons just as Ælfgar himself had been in the 1040s. Ælfgar's marginalization was confirmed by another feud with the king that led to his second exile in 1058. Once again Ælfgar was able to restore his position using his alliance with Gruffudd ap Llywelyn and a Norse fleet under Harold Hardrada's son Magnus. This is dismissed by Version C of the *Anglo-Saxon Chronicle* after a couple of lines: 'It is tedious to relate how things went.' This is remarkable given that this represented another major Scandinavian intervention in English politics, which indicates how the English internal affairs were still a major focus of Norwegian and Danish royal ambitions.

The pre-eminence of Harold was clear by 1059: he can be seen witnessing royal charters as the premier earl. By now, Ælfgar had returned and been rehabilitated, as his appears as the second name in the two surviving examples. The next year, Tostig's name appears second, with Ælfgar third, which is how matters stayed until the earl of Mercia's death in *c.* 1062. It was probably after Ælfgar's death that, in 1063, Harold and Tostig launched a series of naval and land expeditions against Gruffudd that broke his power and culminated in August that year with one of his followers killing him. While this was a notable achievement in restoring peace on the frontiers given the longevity of Gruffudd's threat, it is possible to interpret the action as Harold and Tostig defending their own narrow sectional interests. Eliminating Gruffudd marginalized Ælfgar's sons Eadwine and Morcar, as they could no longer use the threat of Welsh intervention as a counter-balance to the influence of the Godwinsons. Harold and Tostig were certainly in an unchallenged position of dominance: the former was famously referred to by John of Worcester as *subregulus* ('deputy-king'), which seems an appropriate description for this period. Their minds must have been firmly focused on the succession, given Edward's advancing age. Whatever the details of Harold's journey to Normandy and his meeting with William (traditionally dated to 1064), the nature of Anglo-Saxon politics means that it was undoubtedly related to calculations about how Harold maintained his immense power.

TOSTIG'S RULE IN THE NORTH

What is not clear is at what point we can say that Harold decided to seize the crown for himself. Harold's hegemonic position created new problems. The marginalization of the Leofricsons may have had the consequence of accentuating the rivalry of Harold and Tostig. The *Vita Ædwardi* suggests that Edward and Edith were more favourably inclined towards Tostig than they were to Harold. The amount of time Tostig appears to have spent at court with the king may have been calculated to give him an edge on his brother when it came to the succession, or that may be what Harold feared. What undoubtedly acted as a catalyst for the political drama of 1066 was the Northumbrian Revolt in late 1065. On 3 October, several local thegns with 200 armed men broke into Tostig's base in York, captured his weapons and treasure, killed his housecarls ('both English and Danish') and then executed more than 200 of his followers outside the city walls the following day. The rebels' complaints against Tostig were that he was avaricious and unjust, but the resentment was principally caused by his failure to respect local traditions. He often spent time away from Northumbria, attending the royal court in the south (he was hunting with Edward when he learned of the revolt) or carrying out other political roles, such as invading Wales in 1063. He delegated the administration to a small group of loyal servants, such as Copsi, a local Anglo-Danish thegn. Copsi continued to serve Tostig after his expulsion from the earldom and his attempts to re-assert himself by force. After Tostig's death, Copsi got himself appointed earl of Northumbria by William in 1067 before being murdered in an ambush a few weeks into his role by Oswulf of Bamburgh. Tostig's use of such men showed that he was not interested in being popular: he was aiming to override traditional practices and assert himself.

The generally pro-Tostig *Vita Ædwardi* depicts the Northumbrians as a wild and lawless people in need of strict government and discipline. The rebellion was led by 'a party of nobles whom he [Tostig] had repressed with the heavy yoke of his rule because of their misdeeds'. When one takes into account the author's rhetorical exaggerations, the views of the *Vita* probably reflect the views of Edward's court, which never travelled north of Watling Street. As we have seen in Chapter 2, controlling the north had been a long-term objective for the southern-based monarchy. An outsider whom the king could trust was an optimal appointment if the north were to be brought into line with the rest of the kingdom after its relative freedom under Siward. Tostig was probably appointed to his earldom with a mandate to apply uniformity with southern administrative practices, but the conservative northerners were deeply angered by these assaults on their customary autonomy. Symeon of Durham's *Historia Regum*, a compilation of northern historical traditions written in the twelfth century, writes that the rebellion was 'on account of the huge tribute which he unjustly took from the whole of Northumbria.' It was, of course, the novelty of the monetary imposition, not its objective (un) fairness, that caused such anger.

Tostig's handling of the Northumbrians was not entirely maladroit and lacking respect for local sensibilities. He and his wife Judith were both generous benefactors to the influential shrine of St Cuthbert at Durham. However, his handling of opposition from the local elite was far more ruthless, employing strategies more commonly used in Southumbria (south of the Humber). Symeon of Durham records his murder of three eminent thegns: Gospatric was murdered while attending the king's court, a matter arranged by Queen Edith on behalf of her brother; Gamel and Ulf were killed while being hosted in Tostig's chamber at York, breaking traditions of hospitality. The resilience of feuds in Northumbria, such as the one pursued by the descendants of Uhtred and Thorbrand over decades, meant that Tostig was unleashing forces he could not control. Ultimately, it was Tostig's failure to fulfil his most basic role as a defender of the region that undermined his position. While Tostig was on pilgrimage in Rome in 1061, the king of Scots, Malcolm Canmore, launched a raid on Northumbria that inflicted considerable damage across the region, notably on Holy Island (Lindisfarne). Tostig's policy with the Scottish kingdom had been one of *détente*. In 1057, he had campaigned with Malcolm in Scotland against his rival Macbeth and brought the Scottish king to Edward's court at Gloucester in 1059 to give thanks for English help in re-claiming his throne. However, warfare and plunder was the most effective way Malcolm could consolidate his support amongst the autonomous Scottish aristocracy, and so the opportunity of exploiting Tostig's absence was simply too tempting. Tostig's military successes against Gruffudd in 1063 would have done nothing to reassure the inhabitants of Northumbria that he was prioritizing their interests.

The 'D' recension of the *Anglo-Saxon Chronicle*, compiled in Worcester, but using northern sources from its connections in York, preserves numerous details about the rebellion, and the likelihood is that it preserves the original demands articulated by the rebels through their leading clergy. The 'northern men', as the chronicler calls them, maintained a coherent sense of political identity. The plot was well organized and expertly carried out. Tostig was declared an outlaw and Morcar, the younger son of Ælfgar, was invited to become the new earl. The attack on Tostig's supporters was swift and ruthless. We have discussed the extensive separatist tradition that existed in Northumbria during the tenth century, but the rebellion does not appear to have been aimed at independence. What it aimed for was a re-calibration of its relationship with the English kingdom in line with the distinctive traditions of Northumbria. William Kapelle argued that this was a strong cultural movement based on memories of Northumbria's independence. The display of the preserved body of the seventh-century Northumbrian martyr, King Oswyn, in early 1065 by the sacristan of Durham stimulated local identity and focused resentment at Tostig's rule.[71] This view has been criticized, but saints were important symbols of local identity amongst northern British communities, as we can see in the important role that St Columba played in the emergence of the Scottish kingdom in the ninth and tenth centuries.[72] The choice of Morcar shows how well the Northumbrian elites understood national politics: their demands were entirely compatible with traditional royal policy in Northumbria. Previous kings had appointed earldormen and earls with northern interests, who were also active in southern politics and could acting as a bridge between the two regions. The northerners wanted a return to the *status quo ante* Tostig.

The rebellion demonstrates the sophistication and complexity of how national politics was conceived in mid-eleventh-century England and how far they were shaped by long-term regional traditions. Morcar showed considerable awareness of Northumbrian political dynamics as, on assuming the earldom, he split it into two and appointed as earl of the northern half Oswulf, Uhtred's grandson from the ancient house of Bamburgh. This is further evidence that the plot had been well planned and involved a large proportion of the Northumbrian elite. We do not know how old Morcar was, but he was not particularly experienced. The Northumbrians' choice of Morcar also exhibited an understanding of English court politics. By strengthening the House of Leofric, they could act as a counterweight to the influence of the Godwinsons, whose strength had been remorselessly growing since the mid-1050s. Having gained complete control of Northumbria, the rebels marched south and demonstrated their carefully considered strategy. They moved through areas with their own distinctive regional traditions that stood apart from Wessex – Nottinghamshire, Derbyshire and Lincolnshire – before arriving at Northampton, which town Tostig had held as earl to help underwrite his northern lordship. The Watling Street boundary also had deeper significance as an internal frontier with a long cultural memory of marking a north–south divide within the English kingdom, a divide that had been expressed most recently in Cnut's division of the kingdom with Edmund Ironside in 1016.

Northampton was where the northerners put their articulation of Tostig's outlawry into action: they proceeded to ravage the entire area. According to Version D of the *Anglo-Saxon Chronicle*:

> They killed people and burned houses and corn and took all the
> cattle they could get – which was many thousands – and captured
> many hundreds of people.

The chronicler's comment that the vicinity took years to recover is graphically supported by the poor state of the area in Domesday Book. There were a series of tense meetings at Northampton, Oxford and the royal court over how to respond. Harold acted as the intermediary between the king and the rebels. According to the *Vita Ædwardi*, Edward demanded that the rebels stand down three different times and accept his judgment, but they refused. In a tense meeting at Britford, Tostig was accused of corruption and incompetence as earl, but then made the stunning accusation that the whole rebellion was a plot by Harold. The author of the *Vita* artfully declares that he 'would not believe that such a prince was guilty of this detestable wickedness against his brother.' Yet, why mention it if he did not think it was true? Harold swore oaths declaring that he was innocent, though the *Vita* author comments acidly that Harold was 'rather too generous with oaths, alas!' This clearly suggests that Harold emerged from the crisis stronger. He conveyed a settlement to the rebels in which the king approved their choice of

Morcar as earl, and granted them 'The Laws of King Cnut', which meant, in effect, recognizing Northumbria's traditional autonomy. They accepted this and returned home with their plunder. The *Vita* claims that Edward wanted to mobilize an army to crush the rebels, but he was frustrated by his leading subjects (i.e. Harold), who first argued that it was too late in the year, but which suited them as 'in that people [the English], horror was felt at what seemed civil war.' After many 'senior figures' argued against the strategy, they then simply refused to obey Edward. The king, according to the *Vita*, was devastated to lose Tostig, who was sent abroad with gifts and apologies for the king's lack of power (*impotentia*). The author says this humiliation led to Edward's fatal illness: he had become superfluous.

HAROLD'S POSITION IS AUGMENTED

The sons of Ælfgar had re-built their grandfather's dominant political position in the kingdom. This must have been their aim when they seized the opportunity to exploit Tostig's vulnerability in the autumn of 1065. Morcar's brother Eadwine brought an army from Mercia to Northampton to provide support for his brother in the negotiations with the government. This army included Welsh auxiliaries, which implies that Eadwine had reconstituted his father's cross-border alliance that had proved so important in his political difficulties of the 1050s. Despite this, it was Harold who emerged from the Northumbrian crisis in the strongest position: his main rival was banished and he now had an alliance with Edwin and Morcar sealed with his marriage to their sister Ældgyth, a marriage that had been arranged at some point in the rebellion's aftermath. This laid the foundation for Harold to be crowned the afternoon after Edward's burial on 6 January 1066.

Some historians have tended to see Harold as an opportunist, while others portray him as a Machiavellian figure, manipulating events over time to suit his own ends. It seems more credible to suggest that there was nothing inevitable about Harold's succession to the throne: it was the product of a complex series of accidents and fateful events that ultimately made his own candidacy the best option to preserve his position. Tostig's fall presented Harold with a stark choice: an uncertain future defending his brother's honour against the combined power of Mercia and Northumbria, which would expose England to foreign invasion, or to make an alliance with Ælfgar's sons, which would mean that he had the support of all the main regions in the kingdom. As we have illustrated already, the precedents for leading families managing the succession without losing status, land and wealth accumulated over decades, were not good. It could be argued that as soon as events moved against Tostig, Harold quickly made his calculations and made contact with the rebels – something Tostig was clearly aware of. The marriage to Eadwine's widowed sister, whose first husband, Gruffudd, Harold was responsible for killing, must have been arranged swiftly. The intense rivalries the Godwinson ascent had created meant that there could be no trust. It is fashionable to see Harold's claiming of the throne as a hubristic mistake, but by 1065 it was the best way he could guarantee his status: one could either go forwards or backwards, there was no standing still. Like all the main warlords in the eleventh century across the whole Northern European coastal zone, from Scandinavia to Normandy, he saw England not through national eyes, but through the perspective of his own dynastic interests. This approach was inherently unstable, but there was no other choice. When the *Anglo-Saxon Chronicle* says that 'Earl Harold was now consecrated king and he met little quiet in it as long as he ruled the realm', this would have probably been the case even if Duke William of Normandy had not claimed his throne.

Some contemporary sources convey disquiet at what transpired, though all are difficult to use as reliable guides to opinion in January 1066, given that they all wrote with hindsight. Baldwin, Edward the Confessor's physician, became abbot of Bury St Edmunds *c.* 1065. He attended the king's deathbed and his experiences were probably recorded by a continental author, Herman, who had been commissioned by Baldwin to write about the abbey's patron saint and who was possibly writing as early as 1070.[73] Herman writes:

> Harold, son of Godwin, who had seized the kingdom in a cunning way promptly at the start of mass sat himself on the royal throne and so triggered off his own demise.

Crucially, Harold's temporary alliance of convenience with Eadwine and Morcar did not overcome the traditional aversion of northerners to southern rule, which appears to have become more assertive in the aftermath of the Northumbrian Revolt. William of Malmesbury, writing in early twelfth century, provides an account of King Harold travelling north accompanied by Bishop Wulfstan of Worcester in his *Life of St Wulfstan*. This makes a clear statement of Harold's unpopularity in the region:

> For the moment, Harold won the crown by favour, or extorted it by
> force, and took over almost the whole realm. The only people to put
> off taking allegiance were the Northumbrians, 'with all the pride
> of their race', as they frequently put it, they did not care to see their
> northern granite subject to those [softies] in the south.[74]

This account is not simply a reflection of the character assassination
Harold received after the Conquest. William of Malmesbury's *Life
of St Wulfstan* was based on an earlier Old English life of Wulfstan
written by Coleman, an English monk of Worcester who knew
Wulfstan personally, between 1096 and 1113. While one need not
accept the story that Wulfstan was able to appease northern hostility
to Harold through his personal appearance – a cliché typical of the
genre – the general view of the Northumbrian attitude to Harold in
the work is credible.

The tradition of factional struggle amongst the senior nobility
in England meant that Harold's settlement in 1065 would only be
temporary. Tostig followed what was by now the standard tactic for
exiled earls, which was to find an external ally and force his political
rehabilitation. There is some indication that he had support from
disgruntled elements in the kingdom. Version C of the *Anglo-Saxon
Chronicle* refers to his move on the strategic position of Sandwich
and when Harold responded, Tostig 'went from Sandwich and took
some of the sailors with him, some willingly, some unwillingly.' The
northern Version D is more dismissive of Tostig, his poor record
as earl prompting little or no sympathy for him. Versions D and E
omit the earlier events in the south, and focus on the north, where
Tostig's attack on York was pre-empted by Earl Edwin. After Tostig's
rebuff, his 'sailors deserted him.' This forced Tostig to try his luck
with Malcolm Canmore before he intercepted the Norwegian fleet of
Harald Hardrada. Tostig could now try to replicate Ælfgar's tactic in
1058 of using Scandinavian intervention to gain back his earldom, or
to go one better and replace his brother.

Assessing the loyalty of Edwin and Morcar to their new brother-in-
law is difficult in the absence of any clear evidence. If we place them into
a wider context, the great aristocratic houses experienced sufficient
vicissitudes in the late tenth and eleventh century for them to understand
that alliances were temporary and their survival depended on their
own strength. Some have suggested that Edwin and Morcar were very
loyal to Harold.[75] Domesday Book shows that Harold and Edwin
held significant amounts of land in Morcar's earldom, presumably
when they carved up Tostig's estates in 1065. This was quite common

practice: Tostig and Harold both held land in areas where their brothers Gyrth and Leofwine were earls. From Orderic Vitalis' perspective in the early twelfth century:

> The Earls Edwin and Morcar, sons of the great Earl Ælfgar, were close friends and adherents of Harold and gave him every help in their power; for he had taken to wife their sister Edith.

This is a view shared by Frank Stenton and, more recently, Nicholas Higham, who argues that their actions in the summer of 1066 – chasing off Tostig in Lincolnshire and raising an army to fight Harald Hardrada at Fulford Gate in September that year – show their willingness to fight for Harold.[76] However, this interpretation is not without its problems.

Version C of the *Anglo-Saxon Chronicle* gives the most detail on the northern invasion of 1066 and the negotiations that followed the defeat at Fulford Gate:

> After the fight, Harold, king of Norway, and Earl Tosti[g] went
> into York with as large a force as suited them, and they were given
> hostages from the city and also helped with provisions, and so went
> from there onboard ship and settled a complete peace, arranging
> that they should all go with him southwards and subdue the
> country.

One has to be very cautious in placing too much emphasis on such allusive material, but there is no indication in the sources that Eadwine and Morcar anticipated Harold's sudden arrival: he was busy with the defence of the south coast. Their defence of the north was probably driven by local considerations as much as it represented a national strategic response to the Viking threat. Ælfgar's sons were undoubtedly more concerned with preserving their own position than defending Harold's interests. As we have pointed out, a division of England into a northern and southern entity was not inconceivable, having already been achieved in living memory. This is not to say that the north was giving up on its union with the south: a decision for a mutual southern invasion, if it ever happened, may well have been a tactical one by Eadwine and Morcar in an attempt to play for time. Then again, their marriage alliance and sharing the spoils of Tostig's fall did not make their alliance anything but expedient. Harold had turned against his own brother: his brothers-in-law would have no guarantees.

THE BATTLE OF STAMFORD BRIDGE
AND ITS AFTERMATH

Harold's prompt response to Harald Hardrada and Tostig's invasion is one of his most highly praised actions, given that it led to the spectacular victory at Stamford Bridge. Ultimately, though, Tostig's invasion was catastrophic as it gave Duke William the opportunity he needed to cross the Channel. In the context of the continued fragility of the southern control over Northumbria, so recently demonstrated by the events of 1065, Harold's rapid response may have been due to his fears of a resurgent, independent north and insufficient faith that the northern earls would defend the integrity of his English kingdom against the invader and would instead be more inclined to make arrangements that would safeguard their own interests. Frank Stenton wavered in his view of Edwin and Morcar's loyalty to Harold. Generally, he is convinced of their loyalty, but in this instance he suggests that they:

> Made peace for themselves on terms which show that the recent northern progress of Harold Godwinson had failed to conciliate them.[77]

The victory over the forces of Harald Hardrada and Tostig at Stamford Bridge were the apogee of Harold's nine-month reign. The 'C' recension of the *Anglo-Saxon Chronicle* ends with the battle. Versions D and E both display pride at Harold's victory. Version D notes that '... Harold, our king, came upon the Norwegians by surprise', while Version E proudly notes how Harold 'valiantly overcame all the invaders'. However, in the intervening period between this glorious moment in Harold's career and the subsequent catastrophe at Hastings, something went wrong. It is clear that, from the chroniclers' perspective, Harold's quashing of the threat from the north was not translated into unanimous political support. The hints are clear in the two surviving chronicle accounts of the battle. Version D reports that on William's invasion, Harold responded, but that his attempt to stop William was undermined:

> The king nevertheless fought hard against him [Harold], *with the men who were willing to support him* [my italics] and there were heavy casualties on both sides.

Version E gives a slightly less sinister account of what happened:

> Harold came from the north and fought with him [William] before
> all the army had come, and there he fell and his two brothers Gyrth
> and Leofwine.

This account is a contrast to the 'great force of Englishmen' that were
said to have accompanied Harold in his fight at Stamford Bridge. The
sources clearly suggest that Harold's army was not as large as it could
have been. We do not know how many men Harold took to Stamford
Bridge. The usual reading has been to see Watling Street crowded with
southern soldiers marching north, but this is supposition. The *Anglo-
Saxon Chronicle* mentions Harold's fleet returning to London in early
September and experiencing damage. Perhaps a better interpretation
would be that Harold and his household troops travelled by ship, and
he assembled the fyrd en route. The only evidence for the English who
fought at Stamford Bridge comes from Domesday Book: it mentions
two thegns, one from Worcestershire and one from Essex. Abbot
Æthelweg's uncle from Kent also died. It could easily have been a
mainly northern army that fought at Stamford Bridge.

Many historians' answer to this apparent numerical shortfall in
Harold's force at Hastings is that he raced from York to the south
coast with undue haste and did not wait to assemble enough men.
Harold was perhaps attempting to repeat the tactics of Stamford
Bridge by surprising the Normans before they were prepared for his
attack. The lack of preparation of the Viking army is made clear in
the evidence of the battle preserved in the later *Helmkringa* saga,
which emphasizes that the Norwegians were unarmoured. Harold's
decision to repeat these tactics on William would have been a sensible
realization that any advantage in a battlefield situation was critical
given the uncertainty of conflict. John of Worcester reports that
Harold fought:

> Though he well knew that that some of the bravest Englishmen
> had fallen in his two [former] battles and that one half of his army
> had not yet arrived ... before a third of his army was in order
> for fighting, he [Harold] joined battle with them nine miles from
> Hastings.

John goes even further than Versions D and E of the *Anglo-Saxon
Chronicle* in suggesting a strong vein of disloyalty amongst Harold's
forces as 'many retired from the ranks, and very few remained true
to him'. This, of course, highlights Harold's heroism in resisting the
Normans, which is clearly John's intention, as he held Harold in

high regard. Still, Edwin and Morcar are explicitly acknowledged as having played an ambivalent role in the encounter. John says that they had 'Withdrawn themselves and their men from the conflict'.

William of Malmesbury gives some context to this by recording that Harold had alienated many by his refusal to share the triumph of Stamford Bridge as he:

> Would not share any part of the loot with his comrades in arms, wherefore many, when they got the chance to slip away, deserted him on his march to Hastings.

This tradition is contradicted by the Anglo-Norman Geoffrey Gaimar, who says that the loot was handed over to Bishop Ealdred without any controversy

> He [Harold] handed over to Bishop Ealdred all the booty and equipment he had seized from the Norsemen.

Gaimar's later account in Old French emphasizes the huge losses at Stamford Bridge when he reports that it:

> took him [Harold] five days to gather his troops, but he had great difficulty in bringing together a sufficient quantity because of the large number of losses he had sustained in the victory which God had granted him over the Norsemen. Taking with him as many troops as he could muster, Harold came as far as Sussex, and his two brothers Gyrth and Leofwine, who had themselves been gathering troops, joined forces with him to do battle against the army from across the Channel.

The issue, therefore, lies with the question of the significant losses suffered by the English at Fulford Gate and Stamford Bridge and whether these losses ensured that Harold could get no help from the North, or if, as we have discussed, the imperfect relationship amongst the leading earls of England, riven by regional tensions caused by Harold's succession, meant that Harold was left to fight alone. It seems certain that Edwin and Morcar would have been deeply impeded by the losses they suffered and in the context of the difficult events of the previous eighteen months the north's manpower would have been severely impacted. But then again, they probably calculated that whoever won at Hastings, they would stand a better chance negotiating a better deal for themselves if they kept their armies intact. As we have seen on so many occasions in Edward's reign, the aristocratic mantra was to avoid combat whenever possible, as the political risks were so great. The view of the excessive casualties at Stamford Bridge bringing Harold down, almost a victim of his success, sounds like an attempt to rehabilitate his memory, in the same way that William of Malmesbury's moralizing account places the blame on Harold's avarice. Such accounts are more to do with later debates over the reasons for Norman success rather than accurate representations of the complex reality in 1066.

HAROLD'S ARMY

The major obstacle to understanding the nature of Harold's army at Hastings is the lack of information about its composition and the fact that many collections of combatant names in secondary works are incomplete. Domesday Book and chronicle evidence preserve varying degrees of information about thirteen individuals, excluding Harold, who fought at Hastings. Harold's family was a significant part of his support, with Gyrth and Leofwine, as well as his uncle Abbot Ælfwig of Winchester, who, according to the *Warenne Chronicle*, was fatefully accompanied into battle with twelve of his monks clad in chain-mail. It has been suggested that Hakon, Harold's nephew, who had been brought back from being held hostage in Normandy at some point, also fought, but this can only be supposition as we have such little information about him. The Anglo-Saxon 'E' recension records that Abbot Leofric of Peterborough, the nephew of Earl Leofric (and thus the cousin of Edwin and Morcar), fell ill during the campaign and returned home to die. As major landowners, both clergymen would have presumably brought significant armed contingents with them to the battlefield. We know of two sheriffs who would have also presumably led detachments of men from their shire to fight for Harold. Esegar the Staller, who was sheriff of Middlesex, is believed to be at the battle from a reference in the *Carmen*, while the other was Godric, sheriff of Berkshire, who, according to the *Abingdon Monastic Chronicle* held land from the abbey. Thurkill, another wealthy thegn of Berkshire who held land in Abingdon perished. Ælfric from Cambridgeshire, who held land from St Benedict's monastery of Ramsay, caused problems for his former landlords, who had their land disseized by Aubrey de Vere after the abbot had taken them back. The Domesday Book mentions two men who held land in Tetherley in West Hampshire to have fallen at Hastings. Another lesser tenant killed at Hastings was Breme, who held 1½ carucates of land. Eadric the Deacon, who held land in Cavendish in Suffolk as a 'free man' from Harold, and a nameless tenant from Bury St Edmunds who held 12 acres worth 16 pennies, complete the picture.

It would be foolish to place too much weight on any generalization drawn from such a narrow sample, but it does suggest that those who fought at Hastings were generally from the south and east of the country, confirming the reasoned suspicion that the northerners did not appear. Some have noticed the absence of leading figures outside of those close to the Godwin family, and this is possibly due to the speed with which Harold assembled his forces. However, as we have argued, one of the reasons for Harold's precipitate march south was the political imperative to establish his authority over the whole kingdom and overawe Edwin and Morcar's clients. The strong ambiguity of the northern approach to Harold both before and after his accession emphasizes how the mutual suspicions of the great houses of Anglo-Saxon England undermined any united response to the Norman threat. Therefore, we can suggest that the army that Harold led to Battle in October 1066 was not an 'English' army in the sense that it was fighting to defend England. In many ways it was fighting to allow Harold to control England, as much as it was fighting to prevent a Norman Conquest.

CHAPTER 4

Deconstructing the Armies

The paradox of Hastings is that we have more written accounts than any other eleventh-century battle, yet, like so many other historical battles, these accounts give us very little concrete information about the two armies, which faced each other on 14 October 1066, that can be accepted without qualification. Any attempt to reconstruct the weapons, armour and nature of the Norman and English forces extensively relies on the broader contextual evidence of military service, archaeology and an understanding of how the two societies functioned. Even this information is often controversial and subject to interpretations weighed down by anachronistic assumptions! Crucially, though, we can suggest that Anglo-Saxon society possessed a militarized elite that functioned in a very similar way to the elite of Norman society.

SCHOLARLY TRENDS

Although it appears to be first and foremost a technical question, the issue of how the two armies were organized at Hastings has deeper implications for historians than simply providing a catalogue of weapons, armour and tactics. The battle has become a mirror that reflects the perceived merits and demerits of the participants' social and political structures. This evaluation began almost as soon as the fighting ended. The contemporary sources present the result as evidence of Norman moral superiority. From the English perspective, it was divine punishment. The *Anglo-Saxon Chronicle* 'D' recension states that 'God granted victory to them [the Normans] because of the sins of the [English] people.' For the Normans, the justice of William's cause and his heroic qualities proved decisive. By the early twelfth century, these traditions had evolved into contrasting ethnic stereotypes. When writing about the opposing armies on the eve of the battle, William of Malmesbury contrasted the ribald drunkenness of the Anglo-Saxons, which became a common negative stereotype of the English in the twelfth century, to Norman piety, their soldiers quietly wishing to confess their sins. It was clear to contemporaries that both sides thus got what they deserved, but such moralizing tended to conform to pre-existing opinions rather than provide any useful insight for modern readers interested in what actually happened.

These views of the ethnic attributes of English and Norman warriors, when stripped of their religiosity, shaped the debates that emerged with the professionalization of historical study in the mid-nineteenth century. The battle was replayed in the late Victorian scholarly jousting of Edward Augustus Freeman and J.H. Round, aided by their respective followers, over the relative quality of English and Norman societies in the eleventh century. Round's belief that the Norman Conquest enhanced the subsequent development of English history by reinvigorating its institutional strength ultimately trumped Freeman's romantic nationalist views of the Anglo-Saxons and his belief that they were the prototype of a democratic society, subverted by continental tyranny. For Round, the strength of Norman feudal society, with its cavalry and castles, was simply too formidable for the Anglo-Saxons to resist, while Freeman bemoaned the tragedy that befell brave Harold and his men in fighting such a perfidious foe. These debates also shaped the views of another contemporary, the influential military historian Charles Oman, for whom cavalry was the decisive arm of medieval armies. Oman had little good to say about the English army in 1066, claiming that it had the barest knowledge of military technology. Anglo-Saxon military science ran to no higher concept than 'the stationary tactics of a phalanx of axemen'.[78] This explanation ultimately derives from William of Poitiers' description of the English lack of discipline and the Bayeux Tapestry's portrayal of English warriors with no armour, both of which supported the view that much of Harold's army was an untrained rabble. The superiority of Norman tactical formations and technology, alongside William's qualities as a general, became the conventional interpretation in explaining the outcome of the battle in most of the accounts written during the twentieth century. Major Fuller's influential popular account of Hastings in his *Military History of the Western World* recognized the bravery of the English warriors, but suggested that their lack of discipline proved decisive.[79] According to Allen Brown's article on the battle, delivered as a lecture for the inauguration of the annual Battle conference in 1978, the triumph was due to Norman cavalry.[80]

While individuals, the 'great men' of history, have retreated from scholarly focus in recent decades, the comparative study of English and Norman social structures is still seen as the best means of

Anglo-Saxon soldiers: peasant militia or light infantry? (From Bayeux Tapestry illustrated by Anne Crofts.)

understanding the outcome of Hastings. Published in the early 1990s, Robert Bartlett's influential work, *The Making of Europe: Conquest, Colonization and Cultural Change, 950–1350*, developed from the study of medieval frontier societies, where different cultures met in conflict and co-operation. Bartlett looked to the dynamic militancy of the northern French aristocracy to explain the emergence of homogenous social and cultural patterns that we recognize as being characteristics of 'Medieval Europe'.[81] The development of missile technology (especially crossbows), castles and heavy cavalry in the aftermath of the collapse of the Carolingian Empire during the early tenth century, gave these elites a qualitative superiority over the more traditional societies that neighboured them. This permitted several centuries of territorial expansion, accompanied by the colonial introduction of these superior military practices as well as a range of new customs (such as land-holding patterns based on patrilineal primogeniture). The Norman victory at Hastings could, therefore, be understood as a wider phenomenon, alongside parallel expansionist enterprises such as the establishment of Norman lordships in southern Italy, the First Crusade and its creation of Frankish domains in the Levant, as well as the *Reconquista* of Spain, and German expansion into the Baltic region.

Since Lynn White's controversial attempt to link the development of medieval society with the invention of the cavalry stirrup under the Frankish Charles Martel in the early eighth century, technological determinism has been treated with considerable suspicion by historians as an explanation of historical change.[82] The importance of castles in facilitating the Norman conquest of England has long been recognized, an observation first recorded in the writings of Orderic Vitalis, who said castles were almost unknown in England before the arrival of the Normans. To argue that they were fundamental to the relative lack of English resistance to William the Conqueror places too much weight on a single factor, however. The implication that north-west Frankia was superior in military terms (at least to England) can also be challenged. Bartlett's theory implies that the technology of castles was unknown in England in 1066. This is not true. There is evidence for three motte and bailey castles in Herefordshire and one in Essex built by the Frankish followers of Edward the Confessor in the 1040s and 1050s. The archaeological excavation of what appears to be fortified aristocratic residences at Goltho (Lincolnshire) and Sulgrave (Northamptonshire), which date to the early eleventh century, have also supported those who argue that 'castles' were, in fact, part of a broader social process that had already begun in pre-Conquest England.[83] Ann Williams has argued that many burhs should be considered as thegnly residences rather than communal or urban structures, and so fortified aristocratic residences should be considered as a significant feature of the first half of the eleventh century.[84]

This idea has been bitterly opposed by scholars such as R. Allen Brown and the evidence is certainly not unproblematic.[85] Ann Williams has pointed out, for example, that these residences did not appear to have been bases for rebellion or other military actions. However, the more traditional definition of a 'castle' as a defensive site reflecting lordly and military power is a reductive and excessively narrow definition and understates their role as a status symbol and lordly residence. Knowledge of castles in Normandy before 1066 is fragmentary, as known examples date from the late eleventh and twelfth centuries. The 'motte and bailey' types, with their towers representing an explicit military purpose, were probably in the minority in pre-1066 Normandy, and predominantly controlled by the duke and his relatives. Despite William of Malmesbury's claim that Anglo-Saxon dwellings were more modest than the Normans, with their taste for stone buildings, there is little evidence that this was the case in this period. Most lords used ringwork-style castles without towers, or lived in hall complexes with banks and ditches. Bartlett acknowledges the ambivalence in definitions between the fortified *burhs* used by the Anglo-Saxons and later castles that were used after

1066. Whether one explains the lack of castles in England because of the strength of English kingship before 1066 or the pre-existence of *burhs*, the key point is that the lack of castles was due to a social and political choice on the part of Anglo-Saxon elite and not due to an inherent incapacity or ignorance. We cannot simply use Norman technological or social superiority as an explanation for the result of Hastings.

While Bartlett's thesis on northern French military superiority does not necessarily work for their conquest of Anglo-Saxon England, it certainly explains later Norman expansion across the British Isles into the politically fragmented territories of Wales, Ireland and the Scottish kingdom. However, this focus on the successes after 1066 marginalizes the old English kingdom's military hegemony. The English kingdom possessed an effective military capacity. The sustained Viking threat to English rule was fought to a standstill by Alfred the Great in the late ninth century and the expansion of Wessex in the tenth century shows considerable capability. Edward's earls led major expeditions into neighbouring territories, emulating the successes of Æthelstan at Brunanburh in 937. In 1054, Siward's expedition into Scotland, which was accompanied by a fleet as well as a land force, defeated King Macbeth and his Norman mercenaries. Harold and Tostig's naval and land expedition into Wales in 1063 to crush the formidable Welsh king Gruffydd ap Llewellyn was another major success. As has been argued in Chapter 3, the ability to mobilize three armies in the period from 20 September to 14 October to fight at Fulford Gate, Stamford Bridge and Hastings is evidence of a formidable military machine.

Large numbers of men yomping or riding along Ermine Street to and from the north in the early autumn seems unlikely. While arguments from silence should not be encouraged, it seems just as plausible to argue that Harold transported the core of his army up the coast, using the fleet he had brought back to London in early September, despite the problems and damage caused by storms referred to in Version C of the *Anglo-Saxon Chronicle*. The tradition of investment in ships for defence first appears under Alfred the Great, but the late Anglo-Saxon state had considerable naval resources at its disposal. The *lithesmen* were a permanent fleet maintained by Cnut and his successors in London before Edward the Confessor abolished them, and the tax (*heregeld*) that had maintained them, in 1050. The *scipfyrd* (navy) obligations on the population are demonstrated by the great fleet constructed in 1009 from all the kingdom's shires, both coastal and inland: each 310 hides had to provide one ship – over 200 in total, if one assumes the sum of 70,000 hides recorded in Domesday Book applies earlier. Coastal communities provided manpower by serving as the *butsecarlas* ('seamen'), who are mistakenly identified as a standing army by some modern authors. It is possible to argue that the number of successful naval invasions in the eleventh century by Cnut and William, and the inability of royal naval forces to prevent Harthacnut, Godwin and Ælfgar imposing their political demands using sea-power, hardly reflects unmitigated success. However, both King Magnus of Denmark and Emperor Henry III sought an English alliance in the late 1040s because the kingdom's naval might would swing the balance of power in their struggle, which indicates that the English navy was far from negligible in its potential impact. Medieval sea-power was more effective as an offensive rather than a defensive weapon, which ultimately gave William an advantage. His reluctance to risk an early departure from Normandy in August and September 1066 was probably due to fear of Harold's naval power.

We can, therefore, challenge many of the assumptions that have underpinned understanding of the broader social context in which Norman and English armies were raised and maintained. The notion of medieval military primitivism has been broadly rejected by scholars in the previous decades and the notion of the qualitative difference between the Norman and Anglo-Saxon military traditions, both in terms of organization and effectiveness, vulnerable to correction. We will now look at how the armies were raised and equipped before summarizing what this, in turn, informs us about our wider understanding of the two protagonists.

THE NORMAN ARMY

Identifying who served in William's army is not straightforward. William of Poitiers listed a few names in his account; Orderic Vitalis added some more; and Wace extended this even further. A list of all those who fought with William hung in Bayeux in the nineteenth century and a bronze tablet listing 315 names survives today at Falaise in Normandy. However, it is easy to be sceptical about this information given the social cachet in the twelfth century of being able to claim descent from a 'companion of the Conqueror' and D.C. Douglas argued that most of these names are difficult to confirm as genuine.[86] William's mobilization of an army capable of successfully invading England, which as we have already argued was a formidable military power, and assembling the necessary naval resources to cross the Channel, is testament to the administrative power of the duchy. What makes this doubly impressive was the management of

94

the military logistics that maintained the integrity of the army at the two ports where it was based, Dives-sur-Mer and St-Valery-en-Ponthieu, in the months before the invasion was finally launched in late September. Bernard Bachrach's discussion of the logistical statistics that ensured William's army was fed and healthy makes for startling reading. To isolate a few select facts: 2,340 tons of grain and 1,500 tons of hay would be required for one month in camp, as well as the more mundane matter of disposing an estimated 5,000,000 pounds of horse faeces and 700,000 gallons of urine.[87]

Bachrach's figures, which appear scientific, are speculative and can be criticized. His assumption that William used a fort on the Roman model, preserved into the medieval era through the late Roman military author Vegetius, ignores the existence of Danish forts from the late tenth century and Carolingian precedents.[88] Their deeper validity cannot be denied and are generally supported by the details we have of William's campaigns before 1066. These show his mastery of both offensive and defensive strategies that typically relied on avoiding pitched battles and instead emphasized movement and the organization of supplies, as can be seen in his gradual conquest of Maine, which culminated in 1063, and the repulse of the French king's invasion in 1054.[89]

How William recruited his forces is less clear. The traditional view followed the work of the early twentieth-century American scholar C.H. Haskins (who served as one of Woodrow Wilson's principal advisers at the Paris Peace Conference in 1919). This work developed the theories of 'feudalism' of J.H. Round when looking at the Norman evidence and considered the army to be the archetype of a feudal force, composed of those who held land from the duke in return for military service for a fixed time period.[90] Their personal service was supplemented by contingents of knights, set by established quotas, to whom the Norman magnates had in turn granted land (subinfeudation). As Marjorie Chibnall argued in 1982, such a schematic picture is no longer tenable, as the evidence that supported such arrangements, such as the notion of vassals providing forty days' service, all derived from the twelfth century and could no longer be simply applied retrospectively to understand arrangements in the previous century.[91] 'Fiefs' – clearly defined estates granted for military service, and the building blocks of the 'feudal system', as it appears in most textbooks – did not exist in Normandy before 1066. Their emergence was due to the consequences of the Conquest in the development of land-holding patterns in England, which were then imported back over the Channel.

But even if there were no 'feudal system' in Normandy, contemporary documents show a duchy full of knights and soldiers. The best reconstruction of how William raised his army was a complex web of individual arrangements between the duke and his followers, where land was granted for life as a reward for military service (*beneficium*) while other families held hereditary lands of strategic value (*allodium*) granted in previous reigns. The capacity to turn these general obligations into military resources depended on the effectiveness of the duke's personality and his administration. This was a range of *ad hoc* arrangements rather than a system, and its effectiveness would be affected exponentially by the military success or failures of the duke. Guy, count of Ponthieu, was released after his defeat and captivity in 1054 with an obligation to provide annual military service of 100 knights. A reputation for success would mean more supporters, who would come to serve the duke, confident of reward.

William, like previous dukes, relied on significant household military contingents made up of soldiers with personal ties or obligations to his family as well as those who served for salaries. These military resources were particularly important in maintaining control of strategically important castles across the duchy, which underpinned the duke's power. He also relied on personal connections with subordinate figures who possessed similar military contingents. Men like his half-brothers Bishop Odo of Bayeux and Robert of Mortain, and the son of his former steward, William FitzOsbern, provided reservoirs of warriors and political loyalty. The situation in Western Frankia during the tenth and eleventh centuries meant that the accumulation and assertion of military power was fundamental to any projection of authority. Many abbeys possessed knights to protect their property and their senior figures as they travelled around the continent conducting business. The support of ecclesiastical institutions in terms of ships and men was particularly important in 1066. The development of trained cavalry who could fight co-operatively was also essential to the social and cultural foundations of Normandy, as can be seen in the system of the *conroi*, which organized horsemen into multiples of five and ten. The nascent threads of chivalry can be seen in the rules of war that regulated sieges and the treatment of captured combatants. These appear to have applied in Normandy more consistently that they did in England, where the treatment of social equals was arguably more brutal when political disputes arose.[92]

William mobilized these diverse pools of manpower and was assisted by contingents from across Frankia and potentially further afield. The Bayeux Tapestry refers to William's troops as 'Franci' rather than

'Normanni', implying they were seen as coming from across north-west Europe and not just Normandy. The most famous participant was Count Eustace of Boulogne, presumably accompanied by a considerable contingent of followers. William of Poitiers mentions men of Maine, France, Brittany and Aquitaine serving. The extent of broader support William received is controversial. The number of locations that provided troops recorded in the written sources increases with the passage of time, ultimately including Normans from the south of Italy. John of Worcester claims that William brought auxiliaries from across the 'whole of Gaul', which, as an English source, could be argued to be reliable, save that its compilation in the early twelfth century meant that it is very likely Norman sources were used, thus weakening the likelihood that it was an independent tradition. The idea that papal support for William's expedition was a crucial factor appears to be a retrospective projection of the response to the First Crusade (1096–99) onto 1066. Papally summoned expeditions in the intervening years, such as Pope Gregory VII's call in 1074 to aid Byzantium, did not achieve much traction, showing that other factors than purely spiritual ones were important.

Sten Körner is very sceptical about the validity of such claims to broad regional support, given the difficult relationship that the Normans had with their neighbours.[93] This does not preclude William's ability to attract large numbers of participants, given the loose control many lords had over their vassals in this period. Maine was subordinate to William and so troops were probably demanded on that basis, while Brittany had been defeated in 1065 in a campaign that is depicted in the Bayeux Tapestry; the peace treaty that resulted may have demanded military service. William of Poitiers and others claim the Bretons made up the entire left flank. The presence of Frankish and Norman mercenaries across Italy, Byzantium and Spain during the eleventh century indicates how the political instability in Frankia produced large numbers of men who relied on their military skills to sustain themselves and eventually secure estates and lordships for themselves. The penitential ordinance imposed on William's army by the Church gave stricter penances to those who had served for material gain than those who had served through lordly obligation, which implies that this was a significant group. Northern Frenchmen had already made their military presence felt in England (and Scotland) before 1066, with the Flemings that accompanied Alfred Ætheling in 1036 and the Normans and other French followers of Edward the Confessor. Even if William did not have official support from his neighbours, the same lack of fixed control over his vassals also applied to them and probably ensured there was a large reservoir of potential manpower quite happy to serve for land and plunder.

THE ENGLISH ARMY

As with William's forces, the details of Harold's army are elusive. We have already argued in Chapter 3 that it was probably drawn from the southern shires and relied on several key family figures: his brothers Leofwine and Gyrth, as well as Ælfurg, abbot of Winchester. Alongside the great, our information includes a few smaller landowners such as the nameless tenant of St Edmunds in Norfolk, who only held 12 acres. William of Poitiers claims that Harold had a significant contingent of Danes in his army, while William of Malmesbury says that Harold's army consisted mainly of mercenaries. Both accounts wish to minimize Harold's support so can be dismissed. We, therefore, need to reconstruct the nature of the army from the wider information about Anglo-Saxon military institutions. Despite the relatively abundant evidence for royal administration, it is complex and controversial.

The English military system was shaped by the response to the Viking threat under Alfred, which replaced the royal war bands made up of a king's retainers and their followers with a standing army, the *fyrd*. References in the *Anglo-Saxon Chronicle* and documents such as the Burghal Hidage, which probably dates from Alfred the Great's son Edward the Elder (899–924), suggests that all freemen were subject to a trinity of defence obligations: bridge building, fortress construction and military service (the *trinoda necessitas*). The principle appears to have been that all able-bodied men were eligible to serve in response to a military threat, and this idea of a national army constructed on the participation of all free men (especially the humbler sort of landowner, the *ceorl*) was persistently championed by Anglo-Saxon scholars in the late nineteenth and early twentieth centuries. This was a reasonable assumption given the *Anglo-Saxon Chronicle* entry for 1016, when Edmund Ironside summoned the *fyrd* so that 'every man living should come forth'. This sustained the long-held view (still beloved by school-children) that the *fyrd* was made up of poorly armed rustics of the sort often interpreted as appearing in the margins of the Bayeux Tapestry.

The lack of concrete information on administration means that the precise workings of this military system are obscure. The idea of a 'nation-at-arms' was persistent: the great Anglo-Saxon scholar of the first half of the twentieth century, Frank Stenton, recognized the importance of aristocratic participation in armies, but saw this as consequence of their rank, not as an obligation for land they held. He believed that the system existed to protect the interests of a class of relatively humble and free landowners. However, Stenton's views were challenged by an increasing recognition during the 1950s and 1960s that the Anglo-Saxon military system was based more on land-holding and lordship obligations than had been previously acknowledged. We get occasional glimpses of the Anglo-Saxon system in the Domesday Book survey. For example, the entry for Berkshire states:

> If the king sent out an army somewhere from five hides only one *miles* went out. And for his supplies [*victus*] or pay [*stipendium*] he was given 4s for two months from each hide. This money was not sent to the king but was given to the *milites*.

Five hides is a crucial definition as it is the standard threshold for thegnhood in other Anglo-Saxon texts. Thegns had evolved from the seventh century as a land-owning class that maintained a variety of rights and obligations based on personal service to a higher lord ('thegn' literally means 'one who serves'). The Domesday entry for Berkshire implies that a soldier was supposed to be of thegnly status, though the idea that every five hides was to produce a soldier could also be interpreted as being representative service of one individual on behalf of a collective that held lands equivalent to five hides, which Stenton and others argued showed the persistence of the military role of the *ceorl*. On the other hand, it could also be interpreted as a system that ensured a smaller, better equipped force made up of higher status men. As Richard Abels has strongly argued, *contra* Stenton, the allocation of land and the assessment of its economic value was accompanied by clear military obligations that transcended personal obligations of lordship.[94]

The 'five-hide' reference has other parallels in Domesday, such as the entry for Malmesbury in Wiltshire, but overall the 'system' appears complex as it is subject to regional traditions, especially in the 'Danelaw' region. Each shire seems to have had its own military identity given that its men served as a distinctive group, and this could explain the references to 'all men' being mobilized that were written in the different regional versions of the *Anglo-Saxon Chronicle*. All shires were called rather than just one. C. Warren Hollister introduced the concept of the 'general *fyrd*' and the 'select *fyrd*' to distinguish between these two apparently distinctive traditions.[95] The former was defined as a less well equipped *levée en masse* that would respond to a national emergency, such as the Viking invasions or 1066, while the latter was a smaller, more professional force of better equipped warriors. These terms commonly appear as standard descriptions in writing on Anglo-Saxon warfare, even though they were convenient labels created by Hollister and would not have made much sense to anyone in the eleventh century.

The crucial aspect in the Domesday entry for Berkshire is the issue of pay and supplies given directly to the soldier to sustain him. This implies that the military obligations on the lower orders were becoming increasingly fiscal. We can see this in the early eleventh century under Æthelred when the military system was again re-organized in terms of the nature of obligations. In 1008, the English shires were expected to provide a ship for every 310 hides and a helmet and suit of armour for every 8 hides. Domesday Book has 70,000 hides, which would suggest that the demand was to provide equipment for an army of just under 9,000 men, a smaller force than the 20,000–30,000 that formed the basis of earlier estimates of the armed manpower at the disposal of the English kings. Æthelred's reforms were probably a response to Danish military superiority by upgrading the armour of his troops and creating a smaller, more elite force. The employment of mercenaries, such as Thorkell the Tall's fleet from 1012 onwards, also shaped the patterns of military obligations as they were funded by a new tax, the *heregeld*, which survived until Edward the Confessor's reign. Thus, the principle of military service was being modified by the idea of fulfilling this obligation by paying for professionals to carry it out – a principle that would be developed vigorously by Norman and Angevin monarchs from 1066 to 1215, until it was opposed in *Magna Carta*.

The other crucial tradition was the requirement of military service as a key component of lordship. This was based on a personal relationship between a man and his lord, established through the practice of commendation, which was legally enforceable. Anglo-Saxon society was not entirely militarized and other obligations existed, such as maintenance of a lord's estate, defending his body and attending him on the hunt. It was not all one way: there was a reciprocal arrangement whereby the lord provided his bondsmen with protection and gifts. The importance of the lord providing weapons can be clearly seen in the custom of *heriot*, a form of death duty that appears in wills of the late Anglo-Saxon period and in the Domesday entry for Berkshire, where the gifts given in life were to be returned:

When a thegn [*tainus*] or a *miles* of the king's demesne [estates] was
dying, as a relief [*releua* = *heriot*] he left all his weapons to the king,
and a horse with a saddle and another without a saddle.

The elision of thegn and *miles* in this text strongly indicates how
military service in Late Anglo-Saxon England was becoming an elite
enterprise, underlined by the way the responsibility for raising *fyrd*
contingents increasingly fell to earls, shire reeves and religious lords
such as abbots and bishops.

While the king would naturally have the largest household, each
of his leading earls, abbots and bishops would have had their own
household followers, who formed the basis of their own military
retinue. The increasing wealth of Anglo-Saxon England in the tenth
and eleventh centuries meant that society was becoming more stratified
and consequently more men of this status could be supported. Harold's
retinue of *milites* that appear on the first scene of the Bayeux Tapestry
shows such a group in action. As John Gillingham has argued, the
survival of the old English word *cniht* as 'knight', rather than the
French word *chevalier*, clearly demonstrates that the knightly class
that existed in England after the Conquest was very similar to that
which existed before 1066.[96]

Alongside the *fyrd*, a distinctive feature of the late Anglo-Saxon
military system was the *huscarls* (housecarls). David Howarth
describes them as 'professional regular soldiers'.[97] Peter Poyntz Wright
uses the term 'the standing regular army', estimating their number to
be approximately 3,000.[98] Edwin Tetlow describes them as being 'men
who were trained to fight and had little other purpose in life except
to do so'.[99] John Grehan and Martin Mace describe them as being
'A body of paid, armed retainers ... men of high standing ... who
formed a disciplined military brotherhood'.[100] These views are largely
inherited from C. Warren Hollister, who emphasized the housecarls'
elite character and coherent identity as a body of warriors.[101] This
confident characterization of the housecarls as professional soldiers
and the bedrock of Harold's army obscures the lack of clear evidence
that explains the precise function of the housecarls.

Surviving detail about the corporate nature of the housecarls comes
from the *Lex Castrensis* ('Military Camp Law'), a late-twelfth-century
text that deals with the punishment of soldiers in the royal Danish
army. This relates how Cnut bought off most of the army that had
conquered England for him in 1018, retaining a force of forty ships
whose men became a royal guard, distinguished by their high-value
weaponry and aristocratic status. The soldiers were organized into a

military guild with a series of regulations that arranged matters such as the resolution of disputes. This resembled other semi-professional military associations common in medieval Scandinavian sagas such as the Jomsvikings, a brotherhood of pirate warriors who adhered to a common set of rules. Even if one is sceptical about the historical value of saga evidence, there is strong archaeological evidence to support the general point that disciplined and organized bodies of men were fairly typical in this period. Denmark had developed into a militarized society in the late tenth century, as can be seen from the excavation of five great late tenth-century 'ring fortresses' with circular ramparts and regular shape such as that at Trelleborg, demonstrating the increased regimentation of Danish society during the reign of Harold Bluetooth.

Most scholars now accept that the *Lex Castrensis* reflects late-twelfth-century Danish society and is, therefore, less useful as evidence for earlier periods. An example that supports the housecarls being a warrior guild intimately connected with the organization of the royal court is the murder of Earl Beorn by Earl Swein in 1049 recorded in the *Anglo-Saxon Chronicle* 'C' recension: 'The king and all his host [*here*] declared Swein a scoundrel [*niðing*].' The *Lex Castrensis* uses *niðing* as the term applied to housecarls who murdered their fellow members, which led Larson to argue that the Old English term *here* in this context was explicitly referring to the housecarls.[102] Such a narrow interpretation is not actually necessary as the term *niðing* was used in eleventh- and twelfth-century English law to refer to someone who had lost their legal status and protection of the law for crimes such as despoiling the dead. Although the word *here* in the *Anglo-Saxon Chronicle* refers to Danish armies during the ninth and tenth centuries and *fyrd* refers to their English equivalent, these were synonymous terms by the eleventh century.

Housecarls appear in a variety of eleventh-century English sources. Osbern, who was writing around 1080, describes 'Soldiers of his household who are called "housecarls" in the language of the Danes', accompanying Cnut during the translation of the relics of St Ælfheah, the martyred archbishop of Canterbury, to London in 1023.[103] In an account of Earl Siward's move into Scotland to overthrow Macbeth in 1054 found within the 'D' recension of the *Anglo-Saxon Chronicle*, there is a direct reference to the 'housecarls' of the earl and the king being part of the invading force. However, the 'C' recension is less explicit, and merely refers to 'Danes and English', without any mention of housecarls. The attack by local thegns on Tostig's household in 1065 during the Northumbrian Revolt, as mentioned in the *Anglo-Saxon*

Chronicle's 'C' recension, talks of the earl's housecarls being attacked and killed. On the other hand, the 'D' version of the Chronicle merely mentions Tostig's followers as *hiredmenn*, which Whitelock translates as 'bodyguard'.[104] Such inconsistent terminology cannot be simply attributed to stylistic freedom, but probably reflects that housecarls played a broader role than a purely military one.

In 1041, Harthacnut used his housecarls in Worcestershire to collect taxes, and they treated the local people so harshly that the local people rioted and two housecarls were killed. According to John of Worcester, who was in a good position to know, the kingdom's earls and the king's housecarls then ravaged the shire for four days as punishment. Housecarls also appear to have been an important method of royal control in the shires. The Domesday Book entry for Wallingford says that 'King Edward had fifteen acres where housecarls used to dwell', but it is unclear whether this was a garrison, as some have suggested, or merely reflects their role as landowners. In the Dorset entries of Domesday Book, the four main *burhs* of Dorchester, Bridport, Wareham and Shaftesbury are all recorded as making geld payments of silver for the use of the housecarls. Three of them (Urk, Bovi and Agemund) regularly appear as witnesses in Cnut's Dorset charters. There are significant numbers of wealthy landowners with Danish names in Wessex recorded in Domesday Book as a result of settlements under Cnut and his successors.[105] This would suggest that one could argue that the term 'housecarl' was synonymous with 'Dane'. However, in Worcestershire, Sigmund the Dane, who was criticized by the cathedral clergy for his acquisitiveness, is described as a *'miles* of Earl Leofric', and not as a housecarl, despite apparently being qualified to be one. Richard FitzScrob, on the other hand, who accompanied Edward abroad in 1016 and would appear to have been of Norman descent, was addressed as a king's housecarl in a writ of the early 1060s.

This strongly suggests that housecarls overlapped with pre-existing roles in Anglo-Saxon society. References in Domesday Book are inconsistent and often imprecise. Service to the king was paramount for him to maintain control over his kingdom. A charter of 1033 refers to an individual as a *fidelis minister* ('faithful thegn'), but who was then copied into the cartulary in Old English as King Cnut's *huskarle*. Urk, attested in charters between 1033 and 1045 as a thegn (*minister*), is addressed in a writ as the king's housecarl. It is, of course, perfectly possible that the Domesday commissioners were not that bothered about the precise nature of such titles by the time they collected their information in 1085–6 and English juries, too, were very vague about the term. Although housecarls had to be ready for service at any time, it is difficult to interpret them as being substantially different from the king's thegns who had a similar military obligation to their lord. Their status was derived from their relationship with the king's household, on behalf of whom the thegn also often acted as a local agent.

Stenton argued strongly that the fact housecarls became landowners did not mean that they were not still a full-time professional force, suggesting that:

> The force as a whole was set apart from other men by the severity of its discipline, its elaborate constitution and its intimacy with the king.[106]

While not necessarily condoning the characterization of their regulatory structure, James Campbell argued along similar lines by challenging Hooper's attempts to play down the significance of the housecarls.

> To call such a body, never to be numbered in more than hundreds, a 'standing army' may well be to strain a point. To deny it some of the functions of a standing army may be to miss a point.[107]

This examination suggests that they were very similar to the other retinues that made up the core of royal armies in the medieval period and are actually entirely consistent with the traditions that existed in the Anglo-Saxon period, also. Alfred the Great had employed a core of household warriors, some of whom came from outside of Wessex.[108]

Ultimately, the Norman and English armies were both drawn from a pool of semi-professional warriors who were drawn into service for their lords, both royal and otherwise, according to a complex series of obligations, both personal and tenurial. Although both areas had different traditions, in practice the differences are far less apparent than earlier historians have suggested. This largely remained the case after 1066 when the Norman kings relied on their military household of knights who served for pay, but were often of high social status, which made up what contemporaries called the *familia regis*. This served as the core of royal armies and provided a body of trustworthy servants who could be relied on to carry out important missions.

ARMS AND ARMOUR

The Bayeux Tapestry is the best visual evidence we have for the arms and armour used at the battle, and close study suggests that the basic equipment used by both sides was essentially the same. Does this reflect reality or medieval artistic conventions of representation? The tapestry generally illustrates cultural differences between Normans and Anglo-Saxons (for example, in hairstyle), which does lend weight to the tapestry reflecting reality. All warriors wore chain-mail coats made up of hundreds of individually formed and interlinked, riveted, iron rings that were worn over a tunic known as a *byrnie*, if you were Anglo-Saxon, or a *hauberk*, if you were Norman-French. On the chests of some Norman horsemen appear square sections, the purpose of which is uncertain, though it has been suggested that these form a *ventail* to give an added layer of protection for the throat or to reflect status. To provide extra protection, often these tunics were padded; in this way, any blows suffered in combat could be absorbed without creating injury and could even be supplemented with quilted or leather hoods. According to the tapestry, such tunics were often knee length. This has been questioned, given the impracticality of such an arrangement for Norman horsemen, but Ian Pierce has shown how these tunics were split at the front and back to allow horsemen to ride effectively, and experiments carried out at Battle itself in the 1980s demonstrated that once a rider was on the horse, it would appear as if the rider were wearing leggings similar to the infantry.[109] Flexibility was also a priority for the English when wielding their battleaxes so their mail was split under the arms to provide the necessary mobility. Head protection was provided by conical helmets with a nose-guard. Only a few high-status examples have survived.

Both sides seem to have used the same basic array of weapons: double-edged swords and spears. The English were also distinguished by their use of axes: the *æces*, a small weapon, with an edge of 4 inches, that could be wielded in one hand, along with the more famous large, two-handed axe traditionally associated with the housecarls (although there is no conclusive evidence that this weapon was not simply used by any high-status warrior with the means to wield them). Round and kite-shaped shields were used by both sides, though the Norman cavalry are exclusively portrayed with the latter. Both were constructed with wood and covered with leather. There has been a tendency to see the English warriors as being not as well-equipped as the Normans; hence Wace's late-twelfth-century description of English peasants carrying 'cudgels and great pikes, iron forks and clubs', as well as a warrior with a helmet made of wood. This is apparently consistent with the appearance of several individuals portrayed on the tapestry fighting Norman cavalry on a hillock without armour.

(*see* the image earlier in the chapter). The men shown in this scene are apparently of high status, given their moustaches, which would suggest that they were a detachment of specialist light infantry. The Anglo-Saxon custom of *heriot*, where a commended man returned weapons to his lord on his death, shows how important weapon-bearing was as a symbol of the individual's social status and indicates the considerable investment placed in the manufacture of weapons.

A major imbalance often cited by authors on the two sides at Hastings was in archery.[110] The Bayeux Tapestry shows large numbers of archers on the Norman side: four are seen supporting the first cavalry charge on the shield-wall, and twenty-one are embroidered into the lower border. Although one archer is shown in a full hauberk, the majority are shown with no armour, implying that, as in later periods, archers were drawn from those of lower social status. There is only one archer who appears on the Anglo-Saxon side. The significance of missiles is apparent in the Norman written sources and William of Poitiers explicitly mentions the Norman use of *ballistae*, which is often interpreted as indicating the use of crossbows. One has to be careful again not to draw excessively strong conclusions from this. The idea that the English simply did not have a tradition of archery is derived from older ideas of Anglo-Saxon military inferiority, which we have already refuted. *The Song of Maldon*, written in the early eleventh century, says that 'bows were busy', though the poem is not clear which side is being referred to, or whether it means a throwing spear, which is the same Old English word as arrow. It is worth noting that the solitary English archer in the Bayeux Tapestry does not differ in his equipment from the three on the Norman side. One explanation for a lack of archers was that they had marched north to Stamford Bridge and could not return south quickly enough. This assumes that Harold used the same army rather than summoning a different one. On current information, this is ultimately unresolvable.

ARMY SIZE

The question of how many men faced each other on the morning of 14 October 1066 is another that has confounded those seeking to unravel the battle's mysteries. A range of possibilities suggested by a survey of authors is included in Table 1. The literary sources are not especially enlightening. William of Jumièges claims that Harold had 'an immense army of English', but says little specific about the Norman force. William of Poitiers claims that Harold's force was large and records the Norman strength at 50,000 *milites*. Medieval chroniclers are notoriously unreliable when estimating the size of armies. They deployed them as part of their commentary on the importance the battle, not from any sense of realism. The incentive to magnify their patron's achievement by exaggerating the size of the English forces also makes contemporary Norman sources unreliable. The *Anglo-Saxon Chronicle* versions are not particularly helpful, either. Only John of Worcester gives any information on the Norman force, describing it as large. Interestingly, the 'D' recension says that Harold had managed to assemble a large army, but William's rapid movement meant Harold was not able to deploy it fully, which would make more sense if the army were, indeed, considerable in number. Both Version 'E' and John of Worcester say that Harold's force was incomplete and, therefore, smaller than it should have been. What these subjective terms mean in reality is much harder to ascertain.

One document that would appear to give a more realistic assessment of the size of the Norman army is the manuscript known as the 'Ship List of William the Conqueror'. This survives in a copy dating from 1130–60, which talks of fourteen vassals giving the duke 776 vessels. The text also discusses William's expectation that he would have 1,000 ships in total. Although some are sceptical about the authenticity of the document, those experts that have studied it closely champion its reliability.[111] This figure is partly supported by Wace, who claimed his father as an eyewitness to the departure of William's fleet from St-Valery: 'There were seven hundred ships less four'. These figures are usually seen as being more realistic than the claims made by William of Poitiers (1,000 ships), William of Jumièges (3,000) or Gaimar (11,000). Using these basic figures, Charles Oman (1907) and Major-General James (1923) calculated the Norman army that crossed the English Channel to have been made up of 11,000–12,000 and 11,000 men, respectively. James's methodology was to use the Bayeux Tapestry's images and the information recorded about ship capacity from English naval expeditions in 1254, 1346 and 1360 to suggest that nine men with horses or twenty-five men without horses would be conveyed in each ship, though he suggested that once camp followers and the sick were removed from the calculations, this would leave a force of around 8,000 men. This has been subsequently followed by most authorities as a general guide to the force's size.

The size of the English army is estimated on a similar basis, based on a general consensus that it was roughly the same size as the Normans, typically around 7,000–8,000 men. Much of the speculation about the English force is based on the length of the ridge where the battle is believed to have occurred, but as this cannot be established as the battlefield with any certainty, and the depth of the Anglo-Saxon shield wall is unknown, we simply do not know how big the army was. As in so many cases, estimates are ultimately shaped by the prior assumptions of the estimator, and so a scholar who has a more pessimistic view of the military capacity of the eleventh century will always be less open to larger numbers than one with a more positive view. M.K. Lawson, for instance, while acknowledging that the numbers are 'a range of possibilities', argues for a higher rather than a lower estimate.

Table 1 A summary of scholarly estimates of the size of the armies at Hastings

Authors	Norman Army (non-combatants)	Anglo-Saxon Army
W. Spatz	7,000	7,000
J.F.C. Fuller	8,000–10,000	6,300–7,500
C.H. Lemmon	8,000	8,800
A.H. Burne	10,000	9,000
C. Gravett	7,500	8,000
P. Poyntz Wright	5,000 (2,500)	8,000
R. Allen Brown	7,000	7,000
M.K. Lawson	12,000	12,000–13,000
J. Grehan & M. Mace	7,500–8,000	7,500–8,000

TACTICS

As we have already outlined, the arguments over the relative superiority of the Norman 'feudal' system and the Anglo-Saxon 'nation at arms' model can be viewed with some scepticism. This has implications for the issue of how both sides fought. As we have already seen, the stereotype of the stationary Anglo-Saxon infantry wall confronting Norman cavalry charges has been used to suggest the superiority of Frankish military techniques. Quite how the Normans used their cavalry is less clear. Typically, medieval cavalry is seen to have secured its power from the couched-lance technique, where the end of the lance was held under the arm with the point held to the front while the horseman charged at his opponent. The combined mass of horse, horseman and lance was factored into the charge, which greatly increased its power. Anna Comnena, the daughter of the Byzantine Emperor Alexius Comnenus, saw the impact of this technique at first hand during the First Crusade and famously said that a charge of a 'mounted knight is irresistible; he would break his way through the walls of Babylon'. However, it is doubtful that the Normans used this technique at Hastings as it is believed to have evolved at the end of the eleventh century, probably during the Crusade itself when large numbers of cavalry were brought together for a considerable period of time.[112] The Bayeux Tapestry implies that the Normans threw spears from horseback, but the key to the Norman strategy was the use of cavalry in conjunction with the infantry and archers. The idea of the dominant cavalryman can be exaggerated.

The Anglo-Saxon shield-wall was the infantry tactic used at Hastings, and we have some detail from the poem concerning the Battle of Maldon in 991. This is often seen as a crude defensive formation that required little co-ordination and training, but judgements should be reserved given the lack of detailed information we have. The tactic was apparently used offensively during the battles of Ashdown (871) and Sherston (1016). As we have already discussed, the military forces available to the English king in the eleventh century had men with equipment of considerable quality who undoubtedly possessed some training. They would have been used to co-ordinated action and the use of weapons through social activities such as hunting. It is unfair to characterize professional training in the medieval period as exclusive to cavalry. Similarly, as we have argued already, there is evidence that the Anglo-Saxons used specialist soldiers: the unarmoured infantrymen fighting the cavalry can be characterized as light infantry rather than amateur ceorls. The decision to fight on foot at Maldon and Hastings can be portrayed as a tactical decision rather than one reflecting cultural determinism. The Earldorman Brythnoth at Maldon wanted to send a clear message that he and his men were not going to flee, while at Hastings Harold was on a slope and facing an enemy whose tactics he well understood according to the details of his visit to Normandy preserved in the Bayeux Tapestry.

Most historians are still quite explicit that the main weakness of the English army at Hastings was its lack of cavalry, which gave the Normans a crucial competitive advantage. This does not mean that the English were alien to the use of horses in warfare. Harold's journey north to Stamford Bridge in September 1066 is usually seen as being by horse given the speed he travelled (even if he travelled via ship for part of the journey, he would still have probably travelled to Stamford Bridge on horse). While scholars accept that Anglo-Saxons rode to battle, the general view is that there was no role for horses to play in the actual fighting. Richard Glover was the first to challenge this view in the early 1950s by suggesting that the rejection of Anglo-Saxon cavalry capability was 'dogma' and emphasizing the testimony of Snorri Sturluson's *Helmskringla*, the epic that gives a detailed account of the Battle of Stamford Bridge.[113] This shows that the Anglo-Saxons did not just ride to the battle, but used their horses to attack the Norse lines:

> When they had broken the shield line, the English rode upon them from all sides and threw spears and shot at them.

The use of Snorri's evidence for eleventh-century details has been heavily criticized given that he was recording oral traditions in the early thirteenth century that were heavily shaped by contemporary assumptions. Glover argued that where the details could be cross-referenced, Snorri tended to get things right, and that the oral traditions were capable of preserving details for a considerable period of time. Nevertheless, this argument was dismissed peremptorily by R. Allen Brown as being entirely without merit, given that it failed to appreciate the social implications of what he was saying.[114]

As we have already argued, the social implications that Brown refers to – that cavalry were a product of a 'feudal' society – are no longer uncontroversial. Guy Halsall has argued more recently that the study of cavalry warfare has been shaped by developments in early modern warfare, which saw the evolution of discrete infantry and cavalry regiments with specialized tactical doctrines. The emergence of concepts of 'dragoons' and 'cavalry' created a distinction between mounted infantry and those who fought on horseback, which continued to reflect the evolution of cavalry during the nineteenth and early twentieth centuries. Such a distinction is artificial when applied to medieval warfare. Halsall argued that, unlike the Normans who fought on horseback, the view that the English merely rode to battle has been imposed as a crude template on the limited evidence we have for warfare in the tenth and eleventh centuries, developing the ethnic stereotypes of warfare that also developed in the twelfth century when lower status Englishmen did fight as infantry while the upper class 'Normans' provided the cavalry.[115] There was no clear distinction between the two methods: they were adopted when appropriate.

One of the most debated examples took place in 1055 at Hereford when Earl Ralph, the Norman nephew of Edward the Confessor, attempted to fight off a combined Irish-Welsh assault led by Earl Ælfgar. The 'C' recension of the *Anglo-Saxon Chronicle*, which was probably compiled with material from Worcester and so had access to local knowledge, states that 'the English army fled because they were on horseback and many were killed there'. John of Worcester later glosses this entry with a note saying that the English fled because such fighting went against their custom. For many historians, this is the crucial evidence showing that the English fought exclusively on foot.[116] While it may be true that the tactics Ralph was using from his northern Frankish experience were unsuited to the style of warfare more commonly used on the Welsh frontier, we are not given enough detail to be certain that horses afforded the English forces a better opportunity to escape rather than the English were not used to fighting on horseback. Again, John could simply be reflecting on the events of the eleventh century through the perspective of a twelfth-century context.

The mobility implied in our information about insular military encounters during the early medieval period suggests a long tradition of cavalry warfare. Anglo-Saxon stone sculpture from earlier centuries portrays mounted warriors, and the Northumbrians portrayed on the Aberlemno Pictish stone, which appears to show the Battle of Dunnichen in 685, are mounted. There is plenty of evidence to suggest that Anglo-Saxon aristocratic values were intimately connected with horses, as is clear in the Bayeux Tapestry, where Harold is shown on horseback in the first scene riding with his retinue to Bosham. How this applies to the eleventh century is more complex. R.H.C. Davis acknowledged in 1987 that horses were important in the period 946–1020, but:

> After that the balance began to change and by 1045 had been reversed completely; Duke William's Normandy was far more horse-minded than Edward the Confessor's England.[117]

For Davis, the military and political crises of the reign of Æthelred II would have destroyed the studs that produced the horses, and the emphasis on ships during the reign of Cnut explains why they do not revive. The documentary evidence also presented important contrasts between the Normans and the English. The eighteen documents that discuss horse ownership in the Anglo-Saxon documentary record appear over a century (the latest document dating to 1045), whereas the ten Norman records date from 1020 to 1066, implying that attitudes to horses were travelling in different directions within these two societies. The fact that Anglo-Saxon records did not concern themselves with the relative wealth of their horses, while the Normans did, was also telling for Davis.

James Graham-Campbell argued in 1991 that the accumulation of archaeological evidence actually suggests the opposite: that the Scandinavian impetus after Cnut was increasing the use of horses.[118] The earlier debate over the absence of stirrups in eleventh-century England was resolved when leather straps were discovered, but the most significant finds are the large numbers of horse-trappings of inferior quality, which have been discovered since the late 1980s and which, in turn, implies that they were being used across a range of social classes, and were not just the privilege of a tiny elite.[119] Davis' views had changed by 1989 when he argued that, under Edward the Confessor, horses became not only status symbols, but representative of the social order.

> Another fact that suggests the English army was becoming
> increasingly cavalry-minded is the introduction of the office of the
> staller ... by King Edward the Confessor at the beginning of his
> reign [1042].

A staller was the name for an important member of the king's household, and there has been some debate over whether it was of Norse or French origin. If we consider the stallers together with the evidence of the *heriots* or war-gear demanded by the king on the death of a thegn, which, under Cnut was four horses (two saddled, two unsaddled), it becomes extremely difficult to argue that the use of warhorses in pre-Conquest England was either unknown or totally different from that of northern France or Normandy. In 1962, Warren Hollister had already argued that cavalry was present on both sides, but only 'constituted a larger percentage of the total Norman force'.[120]

Our information informs us that the English chose to fight on foot at Hastings, but it can be strongly argued that this was not because they had no choice, but because Harold and his leading men decided that the army needed to know that they were standing and fighting. This was common in subsequent periods, too, famously at the Battle of the Standard in 1138, when Norman knights dismounted to fight with the infantry. What is important is that both armies were unused to set-piece battles that lasted all day. The unusual circumstances at the battle must be acknowledged. Norman and Anglo-Saxon leaders usually achieved their political objectives through violence focused on burning crops and ravaging the landscape, thus denying their opponents crucial economic resources. William of Poitiers' accounts of Duke William's campaigns before 1066 show this to be a regular

Stone marking the traditional site of King Harold II's tomb at Waltham Abbey.

Rear view of Harold's tomb (foreground) at Waltham Abbey in the shadow of the east end of the church.

Inscribed memorial stone marking the traditional location of Harold II's death in the abbey church of Battle Abbey, which was moved in 2016. The outline of the now-demolished church can be seen marked on the grass in concrete and gravel.

Nick Austin's proposed location of the battlefield at Crowhurst, East Sussex.

View of Caldbec Hill looking north from the Battle Abbey gatehouse

The south-facing slope of the traditional battlefield with the abbey at the summit
of the hill, looking northwest to the English right flank.

The hill on the west side of the battlefield suggested as the site where the English victims of the 'feigned retreat' sought refuge.

Looking north to the slope towards Battle Abbey across the nineteenth-century fishponds.

part of his tactics and, as we have seen in Chapter 3, it was how the Anglo-Saxons fought, too.

CONCLUSION

With the breakdown of the 'feudal' consensus that was the dominant intellectual paradigm of the twentieth century, the main framework for stressing the difference between Norman and Anglo-Saxon society disappeared. While denying all differences is itself a dogmatic position, as both sides had distinctive traditions that emerged from different historical circumstances, the extrapolation that the ultimate result of Hastings was due to the superiority of Norman military culture and structures is less tenable. As we have already discussed in Chapters Two, Three and Four, in the society that emerged in Western Europe during the 'feudal revolution' of the late tenth and early eleventh century, where warfare was being increasingly restricted to a social elite whose demand for expensive military equipment drove economic growth, such increased inequality looks increasingly less distinctive from what was happening in England at the same time. The idea of English infantry against Norman cavalry that appears in many of our later sources, which fill out the details of the battle, are probably reflections of the contemporary circumstances created by the Conquest, which were then transposed onto the past where, it was assumed, they also applied.

CHAPTER 5

Reconstructing the Battle

BACKGROUND

Only the most fundamentalist of military historians could argue that a battle can be understood without a framework of events that immediately preceded the engagement. According to Version D (and supported by Version C) of the *Anglo-Saxon Chronicle*, Harold had mobilized an army and fleet 'larger than any king had assembled before in this country' through the summer months of 1066 on the south coast to oppose any attempt by William to land. Version E hints at a possible skirmish between the English and Norman fleets off the south coast when it says 'he [Harold] went out with a naval force against William' (though, this could just as easily be referring to the English fleet maintaining a patrol of the south coast rather than implying a conflict). None of the Norman sources refer to such an action, but then their accounts are not likely to be complete given their eulogistic presentation of William. The *Anglo-Saxon Chronicle* narratives of 1066 are allusive and elusive in an almost obscurantist way, probably partly due to the shock and grief at the events of the Conquest. One does wonder what we are not being told. A typical example is Version C, which describes the effort Harold put into the defence of his throne, but which admits that 'in the end it was no use'. By early September, the duke of Normandy's lack of movement from the port of Dives-sur-Mer meant that Harold's army, running low on supplies, was demobilized. On 12 September 1066, William moved up the coast to St-Valery-en-Ponthieu, but still made no attempt to cross the Channel.

Earlier that summer, Tostig had fled to the court of his sworn brother King Malcolm Canmore after his failed attempts at raiding the English coast, and then made contact with the formidable Norwegian King Harald Hardrada, who had decided to emulate his predecessor Cnut by conquering England. It does appear odd that Harold does not appear to have anticipated Hardrada's invasion. Then again, he may have simply calculated that the southern threat was more serious and that the north could look after itself. Ultimately, our sources simply do not give us enough information to make any conclusive judgements on the matter. Once allied with Tostig, Hardrada's fleet set out and, by mid-September, was sailing up the Ouse to land at Riccal. Their force disembarked and then headed north for York, where, on 20 September, they met a northern *fyrd* assembled by the earls, Morcar of Northumbria and Edwin of Mercia at Fulford Gate, a couple of miles south of the city. The Northumbrian and Mercian armies were defeated, hostages were promised, and Hardrada and Tostig moved on to Stamford Bridge, to the north-east of York.

Harold responded immediately by travelling north, summoning men to assemble en route, and, riding from Tadcaster through York on the 24 September, he arrived at Stamford Bridge the following day, apparently taking Hardrada's army by complete surprise. Harold's victory was a notable triumph, celebrated by the English sources in some detail, but its legacy was problematic. Just two days later, on 27 September, William set sail from St-Valery-en-Ponthieu and landed at Pevensey Bay, where he established a base, before moving eastwards to Hastings. There he had a motte and bailey built and began to ravage the countryside for supplies: the quintessential method of warfare in this period. Many have speculated that William's intention was to force Harold into a confrontation by attacking the estates that was his patrimony, East Sussex probably having been his ancestral home.[121] This was a direct challenge to Harold's honour, his capacity as a lord and, ultimately, his ability as king to maintain the peace. Domesday Book reveals the extensive devastation that William's army inflicted on the area. It had still not recovered twenty years later. The stress placed on a lord's capacity to protect those bound to them in Anglo-Saxon society can be seen in 1051, when the crisis between Godwin and Edward broke out over the king's demand that the earl punish his own people in Dover over a violent incident that had occurred with the arrival of Eustace of Boulogne and his entourage. Both sides had been blamed for this incident, which had left several Franks and English dead. It is highly significant that the earl risked everything on an armed confrontation with Edward rather than punish his vassals.

The news of William's landing reached Harold in York, probably on 29 September, to which he responded by marching south to London as quickly as he could. On arrival in the city, Harold confirmed the decision in consultation with his advisers, if he had not decided already, to confront William in Sussex before he could march north – 'rejecting caution', according to William of Jumièges. There has been considerable criticism of Harold for not exploiting the advantages he possessed.[122] According to the traditional understanding of the *fyrd* system, despite the losses in the north, Harold still had access to large numbers of men from across the kingdom who could have been mobilized and brought to bear on William's forces. Edmund Ironside had demonstrated the military capacity of the Anglo-Saxon state in 1016 when, apparently, he raised an army of Englishmen five times in his struggle with Cnut. William would have not wanted a long campaign. He had landed in the autumn, and the waning of the year meant attempts to bring supplies across from Normandy would become increasingly difficult as the weather became more unreliable. The naval power that the English could mobilize meant that there was always the danger of a blockade (the sources suggest that Harold had despatched a fleet to cut the Normans off). The remarkable system William had developed to maintain his army in camp for the previous weeks could not have been easily reconstituted in hostile territory. Many of William's soldiers were serving with the expectation of reward and not through bonds of personal loyalty to the duke, so it seems unlikely that they would have been content if the weeks passed without any decisive result imminent.

There are three potential explanations for Harold's precipitate advance. Most popular amongst historians is the view that he was attempting to repeat the successful stratagem he had carried out at Stamford Bridge by attacking before the enemy was prepared to face him. William of Poitiers, followed later by Orderic Vitalis, claimed there was a possibility of a night attack, implying that surprise was Harold's intent. The geography of Sussex in 1066 was also an important factor. The higher sea levels a millennium ago meant that the area around Hastings formed a peninsula, from which one could only escape by following the ridge that came from Hastings over Blackhorse and Telham Hill and that passes through the modern town of Battle, giving access to paths leading to the rest of southern England. Harold could, therefore, also have been aiming to blockade William in the peninsula by conducting a defensive engagement in the region of his assembly point on Caldbec Hill, or by forcing him, through preventing access to further supplies, to withdraw or come to some arrangement. If the stories of his time in Normandy are to be believed, Harold had first-hand experience of Norman military practices and, as we have already suggested, English aristocrats had deep connections with their neighbours, so undoubtedly had a good understanding of the tactics they would face.

Whether a deal was possible is unclear, though an exchange of envoys between social equals would seem consistent with the parallel codes of honour that were a factor in Normandy and England. The *Carmen* and William of Poitiers both give extensive accounts of discussions that ensued before the battle with Harold's monastic envoy, though the detail is rhetorical imagination and both accounts are carefully presenting William as a good ruler attempting to find a peaceful settlement. William of Poitiers writes that the duke offered Harold an attempt to resolve the matter by single combat to spare unnecessary bloodshed. We are faced here with the problem of William of Poitiers' sources. As a royal chaplain to Duke William for many years, one can assume he had access to top-level information about ducal business, but this is only an assumption. We do not really know much more

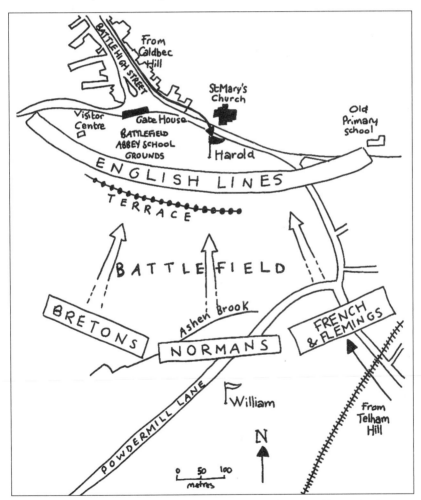

Traditional map of the battle's locations with modern features (illustration by Anne Crofts).

about William's life other than what Orderic tells us, and he appears to be fairly anonymous in the administrative evidence, which implies that he was not especially influential. Like most medieval and ancient historians, when William of Poitiers did not know what was said, but felt that a rhetorical speech was important for the narrative, he would construct one that was appropriate. For Duke William's speech before the battle, William of Poitiers assures us that this 'was undoubtedly a fine one, although it has not come down to us in all its splendour'. Although he claims that his record of the negotiations with Harold's envoy comprises 'the words of the duke ... rather than our own version', the careful presentation of the legal arguments of William's claim and the comparison with Cicero makes one sceptical: that this is a polished presentation of what the duke wanted to say.

As the Anglo-Saxon sources in particular are so circumspect, alongside the Norman tendency to anathematize Harold's posthumous reputation, there is little solid evidence that can be evaluated to reconstruct Harold's decision-making. As Harold lost the battle, historians often focus on explaining this by retrospectively identifying the key reason from a range of possibilities (such as hubris) rather than appreciating how finely balanced the margins of success and failure were in any military adventure. Both Harold and William were undertaking a gamble, but it is only fair in the absence of detailed sources to accept that they had fully explored their options in the light of the belief that they would receive divine aid in return for their faithful patronage of churches (Harold's favour to Waltham Abbey in Essex was shown by his probable eventual burial there). Harold's political position, as we have argued, was not unproblematic, despite his northern success. There is some merit in another comparison with the events of 1016. Although the *Anglo-Saxon Chronicle*'s view of Æthelred's reign is problematic, given it was written with hostile hindsight, it is clearly stated that the king's failure to provide active military leadership in the crisis of Cnut's invasion undermined his vestiges of support. Edmund Ironside's activity was not simply driven by patriotism, but was an attempt to assert his own leadership credentials in a complex succession situation where his father was actively championing the interests of his half-brothers from his second marriage to Emma of Normandy, Edward and Alfred.

The view that Harold should have waited for more men, or was showing his inexperience as a field commander, is not entirely reasonable, either. The Anglo-Saxon military system was increasingly dependent on a relatively limited, elite core of fighting men. The 'nation-at-arms' ideal of the mobilization of all free men existed more as an archaic ideal of the ninth century than a reflection of eleventh-century military reality. There was no bottomless pool of soldiers available, especially after the bloody northern battles. He, therefore, had to ensure a decisive engagement as soon as possible. The *Anglo-Saxon Chronicle*'s Version D states that Harold summoned men to the 'hoary apple tree', which is usually believed to have been on Caldbec Hill, which lies just to the north of the modern town of Battle. There is no clear evidence what the significance of this was, but the usual suggestion is that it was an ancient moot point, which would have been familiar to men in that part of Sussex. Caldbec Hill is at the conjunction of three hundreds, so probably played a customary role in local assemblies. Harold presumably knew this territory well given that he held the estates in the area, and we know from the Bayeux Tapestry that he spent time at Bosham, just down the coast.

PREPARING FOR BATTLE

Whatever Harold's intentions, William's decision to march north on the morning of 14 October was decisive as it appears to have surprised Harold. This finds some support in the accounts of Versions D and E of the *Anglo-Saxon Chronicle*. Version D says that William arrived 'before his [Harold's] army was drawn up in battle array', and Version E recounts that the fight occurred 'before all the army had come'. These could be excuses, of course, but there is logic to this reconstruction given the wider context. The Bayeux Tapestry shows an English scout warning a mounted Harold of the advance of the Norman army after the Norman knight Vital (a rarely named individual in the tapestry, whose significance is obscure) is shown informing William of the English arrival. William of Poitiers records that the Anglo-Saxon army came out of the forest where they had camped the previous night and along the northern road, where they dismounted and formed up on the ridge on which Battle Abbey now stands, which suggests a degree of improvization by Harold. The Normans marched over Telham Hill, with the archers and crossbowmen in the front, the infantry behind them, and the cavalry, with Duke William amongst them, at the back. William's forces then wheeled out of their columns and assembled their forces at the bottom, putting on their armour and then forming into three battle units, with the Bretons on the left wing, William and the Normans in the centre and the other French allies on the right, according to the *Carmen*.

The precise formation that the English took is itself problematic, as on the basis of the Norman sources, it is usually reconstructed as a phalanx of infantry of an unknown depth: anything between three and ten men has been suggested. The Bayeux Tapestry shows the formation with some clarity, but the use of the double-handed axe was not consistent with a shield and fixed formation given the space that was necessary to wield it. This suggests that the unbroken line of shields conjured up by the imagination is only a partial picture. While the position of Harold can be estimated by the later traditions surrounding his standard associated with the altar of Battle Abbey church, we do not know the position of his main lieutenants, particularly Earls Leofwine and Gyrth. It has been suggested that they, with their household troops, held the centre and that they were spread out across the ridge to maintain the integrity of the line. However, this is based on their deaths in the tapestry, which are presented as happening in the same place when this is more probably artistic convention. This, in turn, is accompanied by a view of a heavily armoured front line with the less well-equipped men at the back; but, as we have suggested in Chapter 4, this view is often based on a limited grasp of how the Anglo-Saxon military system had changed by the mid-eleventh century. This was also the origin of the story that the Anglo-Saxons had constructed ditches or a wooden palisade in front of their army, based on a comment in Wace's late-twelfth-century work, the *Roman de Rou*, and repeated by E.A. Freeman. The assumption was that the relative inexperience and training of the English required extra protection. It is probably better to estimate that the different shire and household groups served together and were spread out across the line to give the English the most effective command structure.

THE BATTLE BEGINS

William of Jumièges and John of Worcester say that the battle began at the third hour (9am), and both William of Poitiers and the *Carmen* agree that it began with a Norman assault of archers, crossbowmen and infantry. The initial response from the English army was fierce, responding with the hurling of missiles of various sorts: javelins and rocks attached to sticks, as is clearly shown on the tapestry with the first Norman attacks on the Anglo-Saxon shield-wall position. The *Carmen*, followed later in the twelfth century by Henry of Huntingdon and Wace, say the battle began with the heroic acts of the Norman *jongleur* Tallifer, who rode in front of the two lines singing *The Song of Roland*. An English soldier attempted to strike the singer down, but ultimately died in the attempt as the Norman used the mobility of his horse to cut him down before he himself is killed in turn. This story is one of many that appear in the *Carmen*, which was written in the tradition of the *chanson de geste*, the literary genre through which the heroic deeds of warriors were commemorated by *jongleurs*. This transformation of fact into myth has caused historians endless headaches: isolating the historical kernel of truth within these stories and what has been added as an embellishment is almost impossible to establish with any certainty. The effects can be quite misleading, as can be seen in the two most famous examples of the genre. *The Song of Roland* transforms the massacre of the Frankish rearguard at Ronceveaux in 778 from an act carried out by Christian Basques into one perpetrated by Muslim forces.[123] *The Poem of the Cid*, also set in Spain, transforms Rodrigo Diaz from a pragmatic frontiersman of the late eleventh century who fought for Muslim princes against Christians, into a paradigm of thirteenth-century crusading ideals.[124] This re-interpretation of battles could happen quite quickly. The massacre of Christian Aragonese forces by the Muslim Almoravids at Fraga in 1134 appears only three years later in the account of Orderic Vitalis as a moral victory in which King Alfonso manages to achieve revenge on the Moors (in fact, Alfonso had crawled home to die).[125]

One of the main problems with William of Jumièges' account is his claim that Harold fell in the 'first shock of battle, pierced with fatal wounds', which has caused some consternation given his importance as an early source. There is some illogicality in William's account. He states that the battle began around the third hour (9am) and lasted until nightfall, but that the English only started to flee when they understood that Harold had died. It seems unlikely that Harold's army would be unaware of his death for such a long period of time. This has led some to suggest that William's text has been corrupted in transmission of the Latin text in the manuscript tradition, and the text may read that he fell in the 'first rank' or something similar, but the latest editor has denied that this is possible as the Latin is not faulty.[126] Apart from Orderic Vitalis, who developed the *Gesta Normannorum Ducum* as part of his account, no other contemporary source provides any corroboration for this being Harold's fate, so it is usually dismissed. The Bayeux Tapestry has Harold's death at the end of the battle, as does William of Poitiers and most other accounts. This makes much more sense, given that the consensus in the French and later English sources is that the battle was fought all day. However, the detail does act as a cautionary reminder of how tenuous our information is.

William of Poitiers and the *Carmen* are the main sources of what is, by consensus, portrayed as the decisive part of the battle. After the

Norman infantry failed to make much of an impact and, in turn, the cavalry attack proved ineffective, there appears to have been an attempt at a counter-attack by the English. In William of Poitiers' telling:

> The infantry and Breton mounted warriors both retreated, with all the auxiliary troops who formed the left wing. Almost the whole of the duke's army yielded – in saying this no shame is intended for the unconquered Norman race.

The *Carmen*'s account sees the partial English advance triggered by a feigned retreat of the Norman cavalry, which then gets out of hand as the pressure of the counter-attack intensifies. Crucially, in both accounts it is Duke William's intervention and public assertion of his identity to his men that allows them to rally and restore order to the situation. This story is also found clearly in the Bayeux Tapestry, where William is shown pulling back his helmet, as described in William of Poitiers, and revealing himself to his men, assisted in his efforts by both Odo of Bayeux and Eustace of Boulogne.

Subsequently, in most narratives the narrow window of opportunity for a successful English counter-attack – if that was what this move was – had closed. The Normans and their allies destroyed those English soldiers who had advanced and it appears that Harold's men were forced to remain on the defensive for the rest of the battle. Was it a counter-attack? The traditional view following Charles Oman questioned whether the Anglo-Saxon forces had the capacity to launch any offensive action, but this ignores the evidence from Stamford Bridge and in earlier campaigns that they were perfectly capable of such aggression in fighting. John of Worcester describes a shield-wall advance during the Battle of Sherston (1016), though this account is not without its difficulties, as we shall see below. Harold's position on foot at the rear of the army has also been suggested to have given him no capacity for command and control, unlike the supremely mobile Norman commanders. But this is speculative, and it seems just as likely that both armies had a well-developed system for battlefield communication. This increases the chances that Harold's leading figures served with their individual retinues across the whole of the line. Stephen Morillo has suggested, although this once again can only be guesswork, that the crucial factor in the failure of the advance may have been the simultaneous death of both Leofwine and Gyrth at the moment of attack, which would have led to confusion and a loss of momentum at the crucial moment.[127] Their deaths are shown on the tapestry occurring at the same time, relatively early in the engagement, which may be an attempt at a chronological, rather than positional, statement. Given the importance of co-ordination in an offensive action, any serious incident that disrupts a complex manoeuvre could easily have had major consequences.

Duke William's intervention is perfectly plausible as an explanation for the Norman resilience. He could only have achieved what he did through force of personality and leadership skills. The details of this story are immediately suspicious, however, given the heroic way in which he is portrayed. Alongside the obvious literary conventions of the *chanson de geste*, the other major problem in understanding the events of the battle is the way monastic chroniclers wrote history. The problem is strikingly clear in John of Worcester's account of the Battle of Sherston (1016) alluded to above, which provides numerous details of how Edmund Ironside organized his soldiers. These are absent in the sparse account of the battle in the *Anglo-Saxon Chronicle*, and so has provided useful information for historians attempting to reconstruct eleventh-century battle techniques. Scholars had assumed John's account used sources, such as other versions of the *Anglo-Saxon Chronicle*, which had not survived. However, in the early 1990s, it was demonstrated that John had directly adapted the work of the Roman historian Sallust, who was particularly popular in the eleventh and twelfth century, as can be seen by the number of manuscripts that have survived. John borrowed descriptions of battle scenes directly from two of Sallust's most famous historical works, the *Catiline Conspiracy* and *Jugurthine War*, and grafted them onto the *Anglo-Saxon Chronicle* account. One such example is the description of the advancing shield-wall mentioned above.[128] The consequence of this is stark: not only is there no more data available about the battle itself, it illustrates that much of our information is potentially misleading.

After making allowances for the flattery of the duke, William of Poitiers' military career, which is mentioned by Orderic Vitalis, is often cited as a reason to regard his account of the battle as one fundamentally grounded in realism. The quality of his Latin learning, which he picked up from the schools in western France, is extremely impressive. His text shows a thorough mastery of Caesar's *Gallic War* and *Civil War*, Virgil's *Aeneid*, Cicero, Juvenal, Tacitus's *Agricola* and Suetonius. This would imply that he spent considerable time and investment in education, which he must have started relatively young. However, how much actual military training and experience he had is questionable. The cost and limited availability of books meant that Latin students in the medieval period followed the ancient practice of internalizing long sections of texts when being taught to read and write Latin. Many of these texts re-emerged as templates for the literary construction of important historical set-piece scenes, particularly battles. William of Poitiers' account of the Battle of Hastings is full of classical allusions, comparing Duke William explicitly with Caesar's invasions of Britain in 55BC and 54BC: the range of his learning encompassed the naval expeditions launched by Agamemnon and Xerxes. The claim that the duke conquered England with over 1,000 ships is evoking (and exceeding) the 1,000 ships named in Virgil's *Aeneid*. In the Battle of Hastings, William of Poitiers compares his heroic namesake to the military achievements of Marius, Pompey, Achilles and Aeneas. Unfortunately, these literary allusions make it very difficult for the modern reader to establish if they had been chosen to describe events for which William of Poitiers had received second-hand testimony, and how far they were used to fill out the narrative.

This problem can be most clearly seen in the issue of the feigned retreat. William of Poitiers makes it clear that this was a decisive moment in the battle:

> The Normans and their allies, observing that they could not
> overcome an enemy which was so numerous and so solidly drawn
> up, without severe losses, retreated, simulating flight as a trick ...
> among the barbarians there was a great joy ... some thousands of
> them ... there was great joy ... some thousands of them ... threw
> themselves in pursuit of those whom they believed to be in flight.
> Suddenly the Normans reined in their horses, intercepted and
> surrounded [the enemy] and killed them to the last man.

Acknowledging the success of this action, William goes on to describe two more occasions when the Norman army deployed this tactic to significant effect. The *Carmen's* account is slightly different, as it records one incident of the Norman army retreating and bringing the English away from their lines in pursuit before the horses were wheeled around to cut them to pieces. It was William of Malmesbury's account in the early twelfth century that saw its repeated deployment being unambiguously described as the tactic that secured the Norman victory. While this view became standard for many centuries, in the 1960s historians began to question the veracity of the whole idea of the feigned retreat. Colonel Lemmon, whose book *The Field of Hasting*, proved very influential when it was published in 1956, took the approach of many ex-officers who wrote military history, shaped by recent personal experience, in the mid-twentieth century and denied its veracity.[129] In his view, the level of co-ordination required was impractical, noting the difficulty that modern soldiers faced when changing their direction of attack even when doing so in small numbers. Lemmon believed that the Normans were running away when the Anglo-Saxon counter-attack emerged, and they were fortunate that it did not culminate in a rout. Once again, scepticism in the capacity of medieval armies often substitutes for evidence in much analysis.

As we have already argued, such views are not a fair reflection of the capacity for professional military performance in the eleventh century. Many Norman cavalrymen had been brought up in the *conroi* system to follow their lord's pennon around the battlefield. There are earlier accounts of the Normans using such tactics, firstly at the Battle of Arques in 1054 and again at the Battle of Messina in 1061, which suggests that these tactics were very well known. Walter Giffard, Lord of Longueville, is known to have been present at both Arques and Hastings. Bernard Bachrach argues that the feigned retreat had been a very well-known tactic in the West since antiquity.[130] It was recorded by the Roman writer Arrian as a commonly used tactic by the Alani, a nomadic group found on the Pontic Steppe. In the post-Roman world, the tactic was associated with the Byzantines, the Visigoths, the Magyars and the Huns. In Bachrach's view, the military experience of the eleventh century reflected a long continuity: the Alani who had settled in Gaul during the fifth century AD would have made it more widely accessible. One does not need to invent such a pre-history for the manoeuvre, as it may just as easily have appeared in the mock battles that developed during the Carolingian period and its aftermath during the ninth and tenth centuries.

The problem with our sources using such classical allusions is that they made certain assumptions about ethnicity and cultural practices, of which military practices were a principal example. The association of the 'feigned retreat' with the Normans does not necessarily mean it was a particular practice, more of a stereotype that medieval authors commonly used and whose veracity is hard to establish. In the Mediterranean, the Normans were also famous for their trickery, and the tactic of avoiding scrutiny by sending individuals in coffins, pretending to be dead, is a story that has antecedents going back to use by the Vikings in the tenth century. While Bachrach strongly argues that the use of classical allusion is merely a means by which genuine information is being carried, the dislocation between the world of the eleventh century and the literary models that authors were trained to use when describing them experiences a more serious disjuncture than this allows for.

After this point, the battle becomes enigmatic and we know little of what happened for the majority of it save that, as William of Poitiers says:

> an unusual type of conflict ensured, one side attacking in bursts and in a variety of movements, the other rooted to the ground, putting up with that assault.

The vagueness of his account tends to imply that he too did not really know what had happened. What we can say about the battle was how exceptional it was in many ways, firstly, in the extent of the slaughter. We do not really know the numbers of casualties, but the number of significant English casualties is very telling. This, in turn, relates to the length of the battle. As most authorities on the battle acknowledge, the conflict lasted all day, for about nine hours, which was highly unusual for a medieval battle. The Battle of Tinchenbrai in 1106 was over in an hour, for example, according to an eyewitness.

Several related factors came together at Hastings. The Anglo-Saxons had been used to fighting defensive wars against Scandinavians for the last two hundred years, and so annihilation of the enemy was quite common. This can be seen with the wholesale slaughter of the Vikings at Harold Hardrada and Tostig at Stamford Bridge, which was a grim reminder to William and his men of what they could expect if they lost. Western Frankia had begun the practice of ransom and hostage-taking rather than the practice of killing of opponents that had underpinned the Anglo-Saxon political system. This threat to their lives combined with a vulnerable beachhead and lack of logistical support meant that William and his men simply had to win or die. The level of casualties that can be traced in the English army shows that no quarter was given or expected.

WHY DID THE NORMANS WIN?

We have tended to deny there was much difference in the quality of the armies, which perhaps identifies leadership as the major factor. Harold had not actually fought many conventional battles. The invasion of northern England by Tostig and Hardrada, according to the *Anglo-Saxon Chronicle*, was mainly a naval affair; Tostig was the leader of the land force. Then again, through William he had fought in Normandy, but Hastings was his first of such engagements overseas.

This is not to say that the two men's command was especially hindered by this. The idea of warfare aiming at a decisive engagement is only really relevant to post-Clauwitzian theory, not to the medieval world. Both men knew about warfare and how to achieve your political ends through its prosecution.

The other problem is the way that Hastings was fitted into the framework of the domination of cavalry that came from the battle-oriented analysis of military history through the late nineteenth century and most of the twentieth century. The idea of a cavalry charge by knights against infantry being decisive at Hastings is now rejected by many authors. Was the infantry obsolete in the face of stirrup-wearing horsemen? The 'Norman' victories over the Swabian swordsmen at Civitate in 1053 and the victory at Dyrrhachium (1081) over the axe-wielding Varangians, made up of Englishmen and Scandinavians (which resembles the Battle of Hastings in some ways), are often seen as cavalry victories, yet closer study shows this is a gross simplification. The idea of dismounted horsemen being used to bolster the infantry does appear to be a credible strategy, which may derive from the English army that was assembled at Hastings lacking the coherence and discipline William may have been able to impose with the time he had in camp. Harold dismounted because the tactical situation demanded it. The main problem was that the English did not use their cavalry to pursue the Normans. The lack of decisive cavalry attrition by the Normans of the English infantry is very telling.

The turning point, as found in Wace's account, was that once the Normans managed to gain a foothold on the ridge, they could roll up the English line very effectively. That was the crucial moment. But it was not cavalry but the co-operation of the different units that made the decisive difference in the battle, as at Dyrrhachium. There, it appears that the Varangians succeeded in pushing back the Norman cavalry almost into the sea until the Norman leader Guiscard rallied his horsemen, who pinned down the infantry before his crossbowmen were brought in and they shot the Varangians down, chasing them into a church, which was then set alight. The crucial point with cavalry is that they need effective leadership and control, more so than other units of an army. Wellington often complained that his cavalry would 'get out of hand' in the Peninsula War. Cavalry at Hastings could only make headway against a broken infantry line, and presumably this thinning occurred throughout the day, as the English knights were able to do at the Battle of Falkirk in 1298 when the longbowmen thinned the Scottish lines.

CHAPTER 6

The Arrow in the Eye

While an outline of the main course of the battle has achieved some consensus in the modern accounts, the issue that has sparked the most intense debate is how Harold died. The schism in the authorial church is driven by the question of whether or not Harold was killed by an arrow despatched by Norman archers. Since the beginnings of professional historical study in the nineteenth century and the intense Victorian debates on the Norman Conquest between Freeman and Round, the issue of the 'arrow-in-the-eye' was generally accepted. The doyen of Anglo-Saxon studies in the first half of the twentieth century, Frank Stenton, viewed the matter with some detached scepticism, but observed that:

> Among the stories current about his death, the most probable is that which attributes it to an arrow sent at random into the English lines.[131]

This received wisdom received a sharp challenge by C.H. Gibbs-Smith in his 1957 commentary on the Bayeux Tapestry. Gibbs-Smith argued, for the first time in a mainstream publication, that the arrow story was mistaken.[132] Since then, the views of historians on the arrow story have fluctuated wildly between denial and acceptance, though some attempt a patrician detachment from the question. Almost as much ink has been spilt on debating the matter as with any other famous death in history (save perhaps that of JFK and Tutankhamen).[133] Whether Harold did or did not die this way could be argued to be an excess of pedantry. After all, it was the fact that Harold died that was important at Hastings, not how it occurred. But here we will argue that how Harold died was crucially important, and, again, shapes our understanding of the whole battle.

THE BAYEUX TAPESTRY AS A KEY SOURCE

The image of Harold being struck by an arrow in the eye is burned into the popular imagination because of the vivid scene within the Bayeux Tapestry of the soldier being struck in the eye. Replicated in countless school textbooks and other published material, it is without doubt the most famous mental image people have of the battle. The context of the image is itself significant. It occurs on the penultimate surviving scene of the tapestry, which depicts the Norman cavalry launching one final devastating attack, above which the Latin inscription, which provides a running commentary on the images, reads:

Here the French do battle, and those who were with Harold fell.
Here King Harold was killed, and the English fled.

The crucial scene shows a group of eleven English fighters in full armour, five facing to the left and six looking right (as the viewer sees it). At first, this appears to be confusing: if the English fought in a shield-wall, it makes no sense that two sides of their army would be facing different ways.

What becomes clear, after some initial confusion, is that this scene is testament to the tapestry artists' technical achievement as they overcome the problem of showing cavalrymen attacking a shield-wall up the hill in two dimensions: they show the attack occurring from both sides simultaneously. Below the main scene in the border, the dead are being stripped of their weapons and armour by civilians. Whether these are English or Normans is unclear, though they are presumably Norman camp followers given that the Normans possessed the field after the battle. The tapestry battle narrative is constructed so that Harold's death is the dramatic culmination of the battle. There can be no ambiguity: we are clearly being shown that Harold met his end. This was an event that would resonate strongly with contemporary observers, given that contemporaries believed the altar of the church at Battle Abbey had been placed on the spot where Harold placed his standards before falling, which, despite recent challenges, we can argue is a genuine late eleventh-century tradition.[134]

The group on the right include two men wielding enormous battleaxes, while the figures on the left are fighting under a banner that is traditionally recognized as the 'Æ of Wessex'. The banner's name is a modern term that has no basis in any eleventh-century source, but its identification is based on the testimony found in Henry of Huntingdon, who makes two references to a dragon banner being used as a battle standard in the Anglo-Saxon period. The first is a banner held by the Wessex ealdorman Edelhun, who bore it into battle on behalf of King Cuthred against King Æthelbald of Mercia (the father of the more famous Offa) at the Battle of Burford in 752. The second mention is at the Battle of Ashingdon in 1016, where Edmund Ironside faced Cnut in his fight for control of the English kingdom. There is no explicit evidence that the banner was unique to Wessex. It would be much more likely that Harold was flying it to symbolize his kingship of the English people rather than as an explicitly Wessex military tradition. It is perfectly possible that other English kingdoms had dragons as their standards, given its origin as a Roman military banner. The dragon was a universal image being used by many peoples outside of Europe across the Middle and Far East, as a dragon could symbolize ferociousness and the power of a ruler. Medieval heraldry only developed 'national' symbols in the later Middle Ages. The red cross first emerged as a military badge with the Knights Templars in the mid-twelfth century before being used by the armies of King Richard of England and King Philip of France during the Third Crusade (1191–93). Its use by English soldiers developed under Edward I's wars (1272–1307), though the formal association with St George was developed by his grandson Edward III (1327–77) with the formation of the order of St George in 1348.

The central issue that has divided historians since Gibbs-Smith is over which of two potential figures in this scene on the tapestry is Harold. The first candidate ('Harold A') is the man apparently pulling an arrow out of his eye who stands under the embroidered Latin legend *HAROLD [REX]*. The second ('Harold B') is the warrior beneath the legend *INTERFECTUS EST* ('is killed') who, armed with a battleaxe, is being chopped down by a Norman cavalryman. One strategy to resolve the conundrum is to suggest that the figures have been designed as a sequence of events and, therefore, two scenes, with both figures being Harold: 'Harold A' is being wounded before on the right 'Harold B' is being finished off by the mounted warrior. C.H. Gibbs-Smith strongly argued against this interpretation in the 1950s. He argued that the tapestry typically showed violent death by the character being bent over, prostrate or falling over, and so 'Harold A' could not be Harold, after all. Similarly, given that the two figures are overlapping the horse behind them, they could not be the same person as the tapestry never shows that, either.[135]

Nicholas Brooks and H.E. Walker in 1978 countered this theory by arguing that Gibbs-Smiths' rule on how death was portrayed was arbitrary, and that the portrayal of a single character by two consecutive images was actually a common convention in medieval art. Similarly, the fact that 'Harold A' and 'Harold B' have different clothing and equipment is simply artistic convention: it does not mean that two different people are being depicted. They argued that the tapestry has examples, the principal one being the English messenger who sees the Norman army and warns Harold. Although two figures are shown and the figures have quite different shield and stocking colours, they both wear a belt, which is uncommon when compared to the other mailed characters.[136] It should be noted that Wace, the late twelfth-century canon of Bayeux, whose account is often believed to have used the tapestry, refers to two spies being sent by Harold, which shows that either not all medieval observers understood the rules of art, or that it actually does show two different people.[137] Argument over the minutiae of an oblique art-form that is not fully understood leaves any conclusions tentative and unsatisfactory.

The tapestry is simply too ambiguous. 'Harold A' is below the name *HAROLD*, which has persuaded many that the tapestry artists were clearly trying to communicate that this was the fateful English king. It has been noted that the figure is looking upwards at the 'O' in his name, which has been interpreted as representing an eye. The names of more minor characters in the tapestry do appear directly above their image, as in the cases of Wadard the knight and Turold the dwarf, for instance, but the names of the main characters (Harold, Edward and William) do not always appear with such consistency. In the first three scenes of the tapestry, for instance, Harold is always clearly identifiable as part of a wider group of people, yet his name appears to the left of his embroidered figure. By this rationale, the falling man is just as likely to be Harold as the figure to the left of the falling man.

Despite this, one cannot escape from the importance of the Bayeux Tapestry. It is probably the earliest evidence for the arrow story and historians who champion this interpretation rely heavily upon it. The artist is reflecting contemporary beliefs that archery was a decisive factor in the battle. Two scenes before Harold's death, twenty-two archers are depicted in the lower border. They are firing towards the English army, several of whom are shown with arrows stuck in their shields and bodies (two figures who appear in a group before Harold's death have been hit in the eye). Earlier in the narrative, two Norman archers are shown in the main narrative, moving amongst advancing cavalry who are attacking a section of shield-wall. The English hold shields peppered with arrows, with a man (presumably an Anglo-Saxon) lying dead in the lower border, two arrows protruding from his body. The scene is introduced by the inscription:

Here Duke William exhorts his troops to prepare themselves
manfully and wisely for the battle against the army of the English.[138]

The precise meaning of this phrase is unclear, but it may be alluding to
William's tactical wisdom in using his archers alongside the cavalry.
William of Poitiers comments on the effectiveness of the Norman
army's archers and the damage they inflicted, indicating that this
tradition emerged quite rapidly after the battle.

If it could be proven that any of the later written accounts derived
their information from viewing the Bayeux Tapestry, it would
demonstrate that those who saw the embroidery believed that it
showed Harold with an arrow in his eye. The most important textual
source that appears to directly support the arrow story is Baudri (also
known as Baldric), the abbot of the monastery at Bourgeoil (1089–
1107). He was a prolific author who composed a poem in honour
of William's daughter, Adela, at some point before 1102. Adela was
a formidable woman, who clearly viewed her father as a model of
appropriate aristocratic conduct. Her husband Count Stephen of Blois
went on the First Crusade in 1096, before abandoning the enterprise at
Antioch in 1098 in despair of its future. Stephen's impeccable timing
saw Antioch fall soon after he left, and when the Crusade ultimately
triumphed in July 1099 with the capture of Jerusalem, the news was
enthusiastically celebrated across Europe. Stephen was humiliated.
Orderic Vitalis records Adela's contempt for her husband's failure
to live up to her father's standards, describing her as admonishing
Stephen for his cowardice while giving him his conjugal rights![139]

Baudri's poem refers to the scenes on tapestries that hang on the
four walls of Adela's chambers. These are described as being worked
in silks, gold and silver threads and decorated with pearls and jewels.
One of the tapestry scenes he describes apparently deals with the
Battle of Hastings, and in his poem he mentions Harold's death:

At last, lest the celestial omens proved false
The merciful deity inclines to the Normans
A shaft pierces Harold with deadly doom
He is the end of the war: he was also its cause.[140]

Baudri describes a tapestry that has numerous parallels with the
Bayeux version, but the crucial issue is the extent both shared common
details. There is a description of the portentous comet; Harold's oath
to William is mentioned; and the duke's anger at receiving the news
of Harold's coronation. There are indications, however, that the

narrative in Adela's tapestry was different: there is no mention of any incidents from the first half of the tapestry, such as Harold's journey to Normandy or the time he spends as William's guest. Nor does the list of William's military triumphs Baudri refers to obviously parallel the visual imagery of the Bayeux Tapestry.

Most studies now acknowledge that Baudri's poem is not a literal account of Adela's chambers at all, but a literary exercise that creatively draws on a variety of different sources. There is a debate over whether Baudri had seen the Bayeux Tapestry and drew on its imagery for his own descriptions.[141] If that is the case, then this provides good evidence that contemporaries read the 'arrow-in-the-eye' figure as Harold. As a deeply learned contemporary, Baudri's reading of the tapestry would have far more authority than any twenty-first-century observer. Such speculative arguments are unconvincing, however. It is just as likely that the work was a product of Baudri's imagination, and the phrase 'if you could believe that this weaving really existed, you would read true things on it', strongly suggests this possibility. The reference to the arrow just says that it pierces Harold: there is no precise location of which part. Its generic description has strong overtones of Virgil's *Aeneid*.[142] While there is a clear reference to Harold's perjury being the *casus belli* (he is described as *perjurus*), Harold's behaviour is so firmly embedded in our sources by the end of the eleventh century that it is impossible to make any specific identification of Baudri's source. As we have already discussed in Chapter 1, William took every opportunity to broadcast his central claim to legitimacy. Baudri's reference is not proof of a specific reference to the tapestry.

At the very least, Baudri's poem is independent testimony for the existence of a tradition from the end of the eleventh century that Harold had been struck by an arrow. The tradition continued to evolve in the first half of the twelfth century. William of Malmesbury, writing around 1125, reports that Harold fell ('his brain pierced with an arrow') before having his thigh slashed by a knight. Malmesbury's history often conflates the sources he uses, such as William of Poitiers and Eadmer, while selecting and adding his own details to enhance the narrative. This description is so close to what the tapestry appears to show that many argue that Malmesbury must have seen it. Other details that William uses support this contention, such as Harold's departure from Bosham.[143] Henry of Huntingdon's history was written soon after William of Malmesbury (*c.* 1130–40) also talks of 'death-bearing clouds of arrows', before a particular shower of Norman arrows fell around Harold and 'he himself sank to the ground, struck in the eye' before the wounded Harold was finished off by the horsemen.

Wace, who composed the *Roman de Rou* in the 1170s, also incorporated the arrow tradition into his work. He conflated all the earlier traditions we have already discussed and elaborated them even further. He describes how the Norman archers launched volleys of arrows to limited effect, but then altered the angle of their trajectory of fire. By shooting higher, the arrows dropped down onto English heads and:

> It happened in this way that an arrow that had fallen from the sky
> struck Harold right in the eye, removing one of his eyes.

For Wace, this is not simply incidental as 'the man who took out Harold's eye greatly increased the Norman's pride'. The description of the battle continues for 600 lines before culminating with Harold's death. Standing by the standard and 'suffering great pain from his eye as it had been put out', Harold was attacked by Norman knights and cut down by unknown individuals. Wace's account is particularly significant because as a canon of Bayeux he probably knew the tapestry. The 1476 account in which the tapestry is first explicitly recorded states that it was displayed annually at the feast and octave of the relics. How far back this went is unknown, but the tradition could plausibly date back to the twelfth century.[144]

Brooks and Walker emphasize that Wace's account refers to Harold being hit in his *right* eye, which, they argue, is a detail closely supported by the figure depicted on the Bayeux Tapestry. As he is represented in profile, the image only shows his left eye. The arrow disappears out of view behind the nose-guard of the helmet, which would indicate that he is being struck in the right eye.[145] However, this is not what Wace is saying: the translation of *dreit* as meaning his 'right' eye makes no sense given the next phrase when he says 'one' of Harold's eyes was removed. Wace would only have needed to say that the same eye was removed. The consistency with the tapestry is also weakened by the discrepancy in Wace's account of the battle where there is a considerable time lag between the arrow striking Harold and his death. This could simply mean that he was certainly not recording the tapestry's narrative slavishly, which he was perfectly entitled to do, but it does make a positive attribution more difficult.

We have established that our ability to trace the development of the story of the 'arrow-in-the-eye' from the Bayeux Tapestry into the written accounts of the twelfth century is impossible to prove with any certainty. Even if we could, it would not necessarily inform us what the artists' originally intended. A more plausible interpretation is that we are seeing a series of distinct traditions developing over time. Baudri, whose poem is not believed to have been widely read, was probably not the common source for the other accounts. Even Wace, who had the best opportunity to view the tapestry, cannot be proven to have used it in his account. Multiple traditions for a story could arguably make it more credible. But it is also important to acknowledge how the story appears to have accumulated increasingly elaborate rhetorical embellishments over time, which undermines any capacity to isolate any genuine contemporary information.[146] By the end of the twelfth century, Gerald of Wales could claim that not only had Harold been severely wounded in the left eye, but had actually survived the battle!

The joker in the pack is the testimony of the Norman author Amatus of Montecassino, who wrote his *History of the Normans* between 1078 and 1082 in Italy, where the Normans were successfully carving out a series of lordships for themselves at the expense of Byzantine, Muslim and Lombard domains.[147] Amatus mentions that William fought with Harold and, 'gouged out his eye with an arrow'. At face value, this evidence is potentially crucial as it is early and apparently independent of the Anglo-Norman/Blois traditions, but once again considerable doubts can be cast over the validity of this evidence. Amatus' work only survives in an early fourteenth-century French translation from the original Latin. Study of the sections of Amatus' original work that were incorporated verbatim into the *Chronicle of Monte Cassino* show that the Old French translations are generally quite faithful to the original Latin. However, to make the text more comprehensible to his readers, the French translator omitted, summarized or paraphrased some of the sections as well as expanding or commenting on other parts that had particular resonance to a French reader of the period.[148] Therefore, we cannot ascertain for sure whether the comments on the arrow preserved in the manuscript are original or a later interpolation by a translator reflecting that the arrow story had become accepted by his time and which he felt should have been added to the original text.

The textual evidence for the 'arrow-in-the-eye' account really tells us no more than the story became widely believed in the twelfth century: it tells us nothing concrete about what happened to Harold at Hastings in 1066. It is always possible in medieval historiography for accounts of different battles to become confused. Harald Hardrada was killed by an arrow in the throat, according to the *Helmskringla*, written in the late twelfth or early thirteenth century by the Icelandic poet and historian, Snorri Sturluson. Perhaps the two stories were elided together? This occurred in accounts of the Battle of Tours (sometimes called the Battle of Poitiers), which took place c. 733. At this battle, the Frankish warlord Charles Martel famously defeated a Muslim Umayyad army that had been raiding from its base in Spain. An earlier victory against the Muslim armies had been won at Toulouse in 720 by Count Eudo, a rival of Martel. The number of casualties recorded in a contemporary account of the Toulouse engagement, *The Book of Popes* (*Liber Pontificalis*), was soon being attributed to Charles Martel by later authors who wished to denigrate Eudo and praise Martel.[149]

The other explicit tradition contained in the sources about Harold's death is that he was killed by Norman or French knights, which would be consistent with the portrayal of the second figure in the tapestry. This view has a much more solid textual tradition in support of it. The *Carmen de Hastingae Proelio* describes how William and three knightly companions, including Eustace of Boulogne, charged bravely through the mêlée to attack and finish off Harold in a gruesomely described action:

> The first, cleaving his breast through the shield with his point, drenched the earth with a torrent of blood; the second smote off his head below the protection of the helmet, and the third pierced the innards of his belly with his lance; the fourth hewed off his thigh and bore away the severed limb; the ground held the body thus destroyed.

There is an enormous split on the fundamental reliability of the *Carmen*. It was traditionally believed to have been written by Bishop Guy of Amiens straight after the battle, but R.H.C. Davis famously argued that it was a literary exercise written in northern France between 1125 and 1140; the death of Harold is one of the main reasons for his scepticism because of its inherent incredibility.[150] Others have resolutely defended the authenticity of the source.[151] Whatever the precise format, the basic outline of this event is also supported by William of Malmesbury in particular, who says that a knight Harold sliced at his thigh, which is what the tapestry appears to show (though, in this account Harold was already dead). Henry of Huntingdon describes twenty knights pledging themselves to seize Harold's standard, which they do, before a 'host of knights' break through and kill the wounded Harold. Wace describes how intensive fighting around the standard saw the wounded Harold knocked to the ground by an 'armed man'. Then a knight struck him to the thigh before the English banner fell and Harold was killed, though Wace admits, 'I cannot say who killed him'. Given that there is a stronger consensus amongst scholars that 'Harold B' shows the king, this tradition would appear to be more reliably authentic than the arrow story.

We have argued the evidence that the tapestry is the key source of the arrow tradition, the ambiguity of its testimony is only strengthened by the argument that the arrow scene is not authentic, but a product of over-zealous restoration. This is a result of the tapestry's eventful history, which is almost as dramatic as the narrative on which it is embroidered![152] It is traditionally believed that the clergy of Bayeux Cathedral displayed it every year around the walls of the church from the early twelfth century, though its existence does not explicitly appear in any written records until 1476. The tapestry managed to survive the sack of the cathedral in 1562 by the Huguenots thanks to some smart thinking by the local clergy – having learned of a possible attack, they had stored it safely with the municipal authorities.

The tapestry first came to the attention of the learned public when drawings of the first section were found in the papers of Nicolas-Joseph Foucault, a royal administrator and bibliophile, who had served for a time in Normandy. When he died in 1721, his work was bequeathed to the Bibliothéque du Roi in Paris, where it was found by the antiquarian scholar Antoine Lancelot (1675–1740). Lancelot published an article containing the image, though he had no real notion of what he was publishing. The great Benedictine historian Bernard de Montfaucon (1655–1741) was intrigued by the drawing, and used his local contacts in Bayeux to locate the tapestry. Montfaucon published the Lancelot picture in 1729 before sending the leading draughtsman Antone Benôit to produce an accurate copy of the tapestry. This engraving was published in 1732 in Montfaucon's *Monuments de la Monarchie Française*, the first time that the whole tapestry had appeared in print.

These images are priceless in allowing us to understand what the tapestry looked like at the moment of its re-discovery. Despite the various holes, tears and lost stitches it had suffered over the seven and a half-centuries since its production, the whole piece had been remarkably well preserved save for the mutilated last section and the last 30ft or so of the lower border, which had become unstitched. The two ends were the most damaged as they had been wound and unwound repeatedly over the centuries. Crucially, these engravings

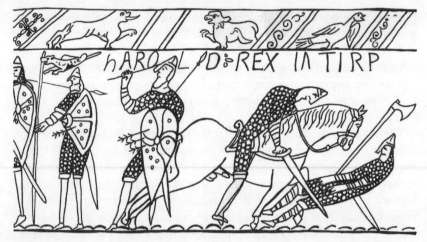

The Montfaucon engraving of King Harold II of 1732 (illustration by Anne Crofts).

show that there is no arrow in the eye of the figure of 'Harold A'. Instead, Harold appears to be holding an extended line above his head, which is much longer than the arrow that can be seen today. This is much more plausibly interpreted as being the shaft of a spear rather than an arrow, especially when compared with the images of Anglo-Saxon warriors using them as javelins on the tapestry, including the warrior two figures to the left of 'Harold A'. These publications meant that the tapestry became a subject of increasing academic interest and a steady stream of visitors headed to Bayeux, including several from England, asking to see it. It was in response to this increased demand that the cathedral clergy first initiated a restoration programme in 1742.

The tapestry's vicissitudes were not over. In 1792, the Revolutionary Government of France proclaimed that all artworks reflecting the monarchic period and its history were to be destroyed. Fortunately, awareness of the tapestry was limited to a narrow circle of academics, which saved it from hostile attention during the first wave of this iconoclasm. It nearly suffered a fatal catastrophe in the same year, however. When the Bayeux militia were called up to fight in the Franco-Prussian War that began the Revolutionary Wars (not to be confused with the later Franco-Prussian War of 1870–1), the tapestry was seized as a protective covering for one of the supply wagons accompanying the militia to the front. Fortunately, the local police commissioner heard what had happened and recovered the tapestry, replacing it with a more suitable material. The tapestry was given legitimacy as a national heritage object in 1803 when it was exhibited in Paris as part of the preparations for Napoleon's invasion of England. The propaganda value was not lost on the First Consul, who spent some time studying the story, and numerous observers noted the parallels with 1066 when a comet appeared across France and southern England in November 1803. After its return to Bayeux, the tapestry was exhibited in the Hôtel de Ville from 1812 to satisfy the increased demand from visitors who wished to view it.

The century between the tapestry's first publication and its placement on public display caused considerable damage. The increasing demands for viewing accelerated the natural process of deterioration. Aware of this imminent threat, in 1816 the eminent British artist Charles Stothard was commissioned by the Society of Antiquaries in London to produce a full-size, colour reproduction. Stothard carefully studied the original engravings and the needle-holes and thread traces in the material to create a reconstruction of how he believed the tapestry would have originally appeared. It is with his watercolour in 1819 that the fletched arrow in the eye of the 'Harold' character can be seen for the first time. Another contemporary drawing by the French antiquarian Le Thieuillier in 1824 has a long, dotted line, which is

The Stothard engraving of King Harold II of 1819 (illustration by Anne Crofts).

more plausibly a javelin than a fletched arrow. It is not entirely clear whether Stothard was using his imagination in his reconstruction or reflecting the actions of those involved in its restoration since the eighteenth century. Le Thieuillier could have been using the published work of his predecessors as his guide rather than how the tapestry appeared at the time of his publication.

What we can say is that at some point the arrow in the eye of the 'Harold A' character was altered into the form that can be seen today. The modern stitching actually lowers the angle of the line as it runs behind the warrior's head. It is quite possible that the conservators altered the textile's content to bring the images into line with the written sources that mention the arrow. During the nineteenth century, some scholars believed that the tapestry dated to the twelfth century and that Wace's account was the source used by the embroiderers. The tapestry has numerous arrows protruding from the shields and bodies of several figures, but these were added subsequently: the modern arrows are notably longer than the original ones.[153]

This discrepancy in the visual record is the main basis of the arrow-denier position, and it is very difficult to ignore its coherence. Despite this, many authors continue to claim that the interpretation is still valid and that the pre-Stothard illustrations themselves contain simple errors, or are based on the damaged tapestry and are, therefore, misleading. David Bernstein has argued that the falling 'Harold B' figure has seventeen stitches in a line coming out of his eye, which could originally have been an arrow.[154] Bernstein also suggests that the arrow was subsequently removed to fit in with Wace's story of Harold pulling the arrow out of his eye before he was killed.[155] This is compatible with the argument that Harold is portrayed twice in the tapestry, or that he is only shown as 'Harold B'. Martin Foys acknowledges that the holes exist, but argues against Bernstein's interpretation that they were not part of the original eleventh-century design; rather they were the result of nineteenth-century restorations.[156] The problem with both approaches is that they are built on different layers of supposition about the actions of the conservators in the eighteenth and nineteenth century, which are now irrecoverable. The tapestry as we see it today is a composite of centuries of alteration and interpolation. As a result, our ability to understand the original design is severely impaired.

AN ALTERNATIVE DEATH FOR HAROLD?

Ultimately, the arrow argument is unresolvable, given the current state of knowledge, but there are even more important contextual conclusions that we can make about Harold's death that are perhaps more significant than the traditional debate recognizes. It is important to reflect how cursorily many of our sources treat the matter of Harold's death. Versions D and E of the *Anglo-Saxon Chronicle* both simply state that Harold was killed with his brothers Gyrth and Leofwine, without any elaboration. William of Jumièges says that Harold fell 'pierced with fatal wounds'. William of Poitiers does not mention the nature of Harold's death, just noting that it was the knowledge of the fate of the king and his brothers that led the English army to flee the field. The other twelfth-century authors who discuss Harold's death, apart from those already discussed here, all tend to follow the line of William of Poitiers. John of Worcester simply says that Harold fell at dusk, while the *Brevis Relatio*, an account dated to 1114–20 and written by a monk of Battle Abbey, merely declares that he was killed in the battle. The *Chronicle of Battle Abbey*, which you would expect would want to elaborate on the fate of the English king, given the importance of his fate to the foundation of the institution, merely states that Harold was killed by chance.

There are also strong hints that the story of Harold's death was more complex than often appears. Some scholars have theorized extensively on the basis of hints in the tapestry that there is something more significant going on with the narrative than at first appears. Andrew Bridgeford has argued that the role of Count Eustace of Boulogne in the creation of the tapestry was far more important than has been traditionally argued, as the debate on who commissioned it usually focuses on Bishop Odo of Bayeux.[157] Eustace plays a prominent role in the text, being generally acknowledged as the figure pointing at William as William is tipping back his helmet to show his face. 'Eustace' is shown holding a banner, which, as we have discussed in Chapter 1, is probably a Boulogne family symbol and not the papal *vexillum* said to have been granted to William. It was Charles Stothard who read the damaged legend in the upper border above the figure *E ...TVS* as *EVSTATIVS* ('Eustace'). The enormous moustache would appear to confirm the identification: Eustace was known as *algernons* (moustachioed).

The *Carmen* focuses on the Frankish, rather than the Norman role in the battle, and records Eustace as one of the three knights who fight their way through the English army to kill Harold. Eustace was the knight who is mentioned after William in the text underlining his importance. Bridgeford argues that Eustace is the knight shown killing Harold in the tapestry. The lettering of the legend *HAROLD*

INTERFECTVS EST is spread out so that the last six letters (*TVS—EVS*) are isolated. A golden sword appears out of nowhere directed at the *EVS*, while the knight's head is bowed at a strange angle, ensuring that the point of his helmet directs the viewer's eye to the *TVS*. If the two triplets are reversed, it then reads *EVS—TVS*, which is an abbreviation of *EUSTATIVS* ('Eustace'). The suggestion would be that the tapestry was making an esoteric reference to the man who actually killed Harold.[158]

Much of this is unconvincing. The 'golden sword' that appears from nowhere can easily be interpreted as being held by the second soldier from the left in the group of six shown on the right of Harold 'B'. The reconstruction of the letters is purely speculative. Bridgeford's approach to the tapestry draws heavily on David Bernstein's work, which suggests that the embroidery is full of biblical allusions hostile to the Normans and sympathetic to the English. His overall thesis has been criticized, as his metaphorical reading can easily be interpreted as being as critical of the English as it can be of the Normans. The broader point that Bernstein makes can be treated more sympathetically: medieval artwork is full of symbolism and allegory. He argues that the tapestry artist is showing Harold's right eye being pierced as this was a symbol of the punishment for perjury.[159] The whole Norman case against Harold was based on his breaking of the oath he swore to William, and there is a body of stories current in the eleventh century showing this as divine punishment for this and related sins. The *Psychomachia* of Prudentius, a popular medieval book, makes the connection between blindness and avarice. A legend of St Christopher has a pagan king bind the saint and have him shot at with arrows, but when he questions the existence of the Christian God an arrow transfixes the king in the eye. Harold's oath breaking was not the sole factor why he was criticized by the Normans: he could also be receiving divine justice for Alfred *Ætheling*'s blinding in 1036 (literally, an eye for an eye). Even the knight cutting at the thigh of 'Harold B' could be read as a symbolic castration – further divine retribution for his perfidy.

Allusions and symbols were designed to add layers of interpretation to the narrative for the discerning observer. The series of fables that adorn the lower border of the opening scenes can all be seen to be reflecting Harold's moral failings. The fox and crow relates the tale whereby the foolish bird loses what it has when enticed to sing by the animal's flattery. The tale of the pregnant bitch related themes of broken faith and ingratitude towards another creature who failed to give help when a favour was needed, which culminated in verbal and physical conflict over possession. Even if we reject Bernstein's specific interpretations, in general terms his argument is persuasive. Such moral speculation was typical for authors in the medieval period, especially in our period when they were almost exclusively clergy who saw history as the unfolding of God's purpose for mankind. The principal contingency that determined the outcome of events was human behaviour, which could bring divine blessing or curse, depending on what the actions deserved.

It could be argued that the variety of traditions that appeared on the matter of Harold's death tell us as much about the lack of certainty about what happened to Harold as they do about how he actually died. The reticence of William of Poitiers and William of Jumièges to discuss Harold's death in battle suggests that this actually caused Duke William problems. On one level, it was a positive result as it removed a major rival from the power struggle William had embarked upon. However, as we have seen in Chapter 1, William's wish for legitimacy was a paramount concern. Killing an anointed ruler was a sacrilegious act that complicated his relationship with the Church, and so Harold's killing was a potential political minefield. The death of King Edward Martyr in 978, which had probably been carried out by the close family of the ultimate beneficiary Æthelred II, continued to plague the new king's administration. His subsequent travails were seen by many as divine punishment for the crime that had permitted his accession. As the author of the *Anglo-Saxon Chronicle* 'E' recension wrote: 'His [Edward's] earthly relatives would not avenge him, but his Heavenly Father has much avenged him.'

WILLIAM'S DILEMMA ON VICTORY

Throughout history, there have been numerous examples of communities that have sought the removal of a ruler who had no rightful claim or who behaved as a tyrant by acting in an oppressive way that challenged established custom. When this was achieved, the deposition was always controversial as it represented the smashing of the communal consensus that had been symbolized by a ruler's enthronement. As a result, such a conflicted act often led to violence against the fallen ruler as a form of catharsis: one thinks of the Emperor Commodus' body being dragged with hooks through the streets of Rome while people shouted at it.[160] The Ancient Greek ceremony of *aikia* saw the expulsion and destruction of an enemy's body to deprive him of power; instead of washing and anointing the body, it was desecrated. There are some parallels that show something similar operated in late Anglo-Saxon England. When Harold Harefoot died in 1040, his half-brother Harthacnut had his body exhumed and dumped in a fen. Later sources criticize Harthacnut for his actions, but he clearly saw political benefit in trying to erase the memory of his half-brother as a legitimate and honourable ruler through desecrating his body.

The cutting of Harold Harefoot's body to pieces, particularly in the manner that it is described in the *Carmen de Hastingae Proelio*, can be interpreted in a similar light. The *Carmen*'s more straightforward lionizing of its protagonists' martial virtues presents a broader Frankish view of the battle than simply considering the Normans. Despite his argument that Harold's perfidious behaviour had brought the English into rebellion, William could not convincingly argue that the local community had rejected Harold. William of Poitiers shapes his account to emphasize William's sadness at events and lay the blame squarely with Harold: 'His greed was the cause of so many others lying unburied'. There is a strong sense of this developing ambivalence towards Harold's fate in the tradition recorded by William of Malmesbury, where the duke punished the knight who slashed at Harold's body after his death:

> For which shameful and cowardly action he was branded with
> ignominy by William and expelled from the army. The imperatives
> of seizing power are very different from those needed to keep it.

This ambiguity over Harold's death also appears in the lack of consensus over where Harold was buried. According to William of Poitiers, Harold's mother Gytha offered Duke William her son's body's weight in gold if she could have him returned to her for burial. He refused and instead Harold was buried by the seashore in a mocking gesture:

> To leave him as the keeper of the shore and sea which he had so
> recently sought to defend in his insanity.

The *Carmen* records the same outline story except that Harold is placed in a purple cloth and an epitaph, in a similar mocking tone to that recorded by William of Poitiers, was carved on a stone for Harold's cliff-top grave. On the other hand, William of Malmesbury preserves a different tradition, saying that William did restore Harold's body to his mother, who then buried it in Waltham Abbey in Essex, where a stone marks his tomb today. These differing stories about Harold's final interment that emerged in the following decades indicate that there was no public funeral and that he was not entombed in any of the locations previous English kings had established for royal burials (e.g. Winchester). This suggests that he was buried in non-consecrated ground, the treatment for criminals: a description entirely consistent with how the Normans portrayed Harold.

The disappearance of Harold's body was undoubtedly convenient for William in the short term. The lack of clarity over the English king's fate meant that any continued English resistance to the Norman incursion would inevitably lack coherence over whether they were still loyal to Harold or were supposed to rally around a successor. However, in ceremonial terms, Harold's reign never received closure. Despite William's attempts to emphasize Edward the Confessor as his immediate predecessor, there was a gap in the collective memory that needed explanation and so invited the opportunity for alternative explanations to emerge.[161] Such developments were quite common. There is evidence that a cult grew up around the murdered Alfred Ætheling, which is recorded in the *Encomium Emmae Reginae* written only a few years after his death. This seems to have caused considerable embarrassment for the Godwin family, given the role of Godwin in Alfred's murder.

Nicole Marafioti has shown that the succession in the English kingdom had become closely intertwined with the interment of the previous king, as this could be used to associate and disassociate the ruler from his predecessor, as appropriate.[162] Cnut had managed the legitimacy of his conquest by burying Edmund Ironside with suitable propriety, but choosing Glastonbury Abbey as his burial place. This was a site where earlier kings had been interred, but was some distance from the key political centres of the kingdom, thus ensuring that Edmund's memory was not a focus for resistance to Cnut. All previous instances of desecration had bad precedent and William's attempts to compensate for his deficit in symbolic power probably explains his sole church construction at Battle Abbey. He was attempting to control the symbolism of the battlefield and prevent it from attracting sympathy for Harold's legacy.

As George Garnett has argued, William's treatment of Harold became more problematic with the passage of time, as the legal arguments he had made for the Conquest became the basis for his reign. In William's earliest writs and within the Bayeux Tapestry, Harold is acknowledged as *rex* ('king'); by the time of Domesday Book, Harold's royal title has disappeared and he is referred to simply as 'Earl Harold', again. It is only with the early twelfth century that dissident views of the Norman Conquest begin to emerge in the written record for the first time.[163] This conscious attempt to shape the presentation of William's legal right to rule can be paralleled by the obfuscation of Harold's death, which later began to fragment with the passage of time into a variety of different traditions.

We can, therefore, argue that the 'arrow-in-the-eye' debate has essentially been based on a misunderstanding. Officially, Harold's fate was obscured. The uncertainty over how to deal with Harold's body and the embarrassment over the death of an anointed king meant that it was much safer to say nothing. However, in the absence of official clarity, speculation was inevitable and, in the continued debate over the battle and its aftermath, Harold's death became a leitmotif in historical accounts of Hastings. It became the very essence of myth. The arrow story could well have originated in clerical moralizing about divine punishment for sin, while the story of Harold being chopped down by mounted warriors probably developed in the heroic stories that celebrated the martial prowess of those who participated. One of the key details of the battle is lost to us and the matter will remain unresolved unless Harold's skeleton is successfully exhumed from its supposed resting place at Waltham Abbey.

CHAPTER 7

The Lost Battlefield

Battlefields have always been a source of fascination. The image of bones of the slain lying where they fell, bleached by the sun, has an ancient pedigree in historical writing. Orderic Vitalis claimed that the bones of the slain of the Battle of Stamford Bridge were still visible in his day, over fifty years later. This motif has its origins in the Latin literary tradition, as can be seen in Tacitus' description of Varus' legions, destroyed in AD9 at the Battle of the Teutoburg Forest:

> In the centre of the field were the whitening bones of men, as they had fled or stood their ground, strewn everywhere or piled in heaps.

Generations of young men (and sometimes women) in medieval Europe were instructed in Latin through Virgil's *Aeneid* and they would have learned by rote his description of the region of Latium as being made up of 'great plains that grow, white with bones'. It is a powerful, almost primal, image accentuating the paradoxical image of an author, sitting peaceably and quietly at his desk, writing about the consequences of visceral, bloody combat.

With the development of the nation-state, nineteenth-century Europe saw a flurry of 'memorialization' as national monuments were constructed, national traditions were collated and national rituals devised or 'rediscovered'. National history began to be taught in schools. Battlefields were a natural part of this focus on a collective historical consciousness, given that it was believed that history was shaped by the actions of great men who usually proved their worth through martial exploits. British battlefields had attracted serious visitor interest from the educated elites since the seventeenth and eighteenth centuries. The noted traveller Celia Fiennes visited Bosworth in her 1698 tour of England and wrote:

Over ye ground where was ye battle between King Richard who lost his life by ye hand of ye Earle of Richmond afterwards, King Henry ye Seventh, who was crown'd in this Bosworth field with ye crown taken off from King Richard's head, who being dead was ignominiously cast across a horse and carried to Leicester and buried there as a just judgment of God for killing his two nephews and reigning in their stead.

The vision of the battle as the crucible that defined an individual's moral worth may seem old-fashioned to us, but the rituals that still surround contemporary British society suggest that conflict still produces collective emotional responses, even in a time of unprecedented peace. Festivals of Remembrance every November focus on bravery and sacrifice. The proliferation of protected heritage sites over the last fifty years around famous battlefields, and the explanatory panels erected to explain and interpret these sites for visitors, illustrates how important battlefields are as frameworks for national memory, even when the precise location is disputed or unknown.[164]

USING BATTLE ABBEY AS EVIDENCE

St Martin's Abbey at Battle lies at the centre of one of the most famous battlefield sites in Britain. Its fame is a product of the perceived importance of the Norman Conquest and the belief that it represents the actual location of the engagement between King Harold II and Duke William on 14 October 1066. Visitors today enter the site through the abbey's gateway and follow a walking route that proceeds around the site. A series of interpretative panels outline the traditional narrative of the battle, with the key moments being highlighted: William raising his helmet to rally his forces; the failed Anglo-Saxon counter-attack; the feigned retreats. Although the English Heritage website strongly defends the traditional location of the battle, one could argue that there are vested interests in ensuring people believe the site to be the genuine battlefield: otherwise, the site would just be a rather typical Benedictine abbey. The abbey ruins are pleasant enough, but hardly unique in the British landscape. English Heritage has made their strategy for their Battle site perfectly clear: they want it to be self-funding as far as possible.[165]

In 2016, English Heritage announced that it was moving the memorial stone erected in the early 1980s to mark the traditional location of Harold's death. This often has flowers laid on it by people who see the death of Harold as an event that still deserves acknowledgment: a romantic attachment to the notion of the last true English king. Since the early twelfth century, it was believed that the church's high altar was built on the site where Harold had fallen. William of Malmesbury wrote that the church was built 'on the very spot where, according to tradition, among the piled heaps of corpses Harold was found.' John of Worcester states that the altar was 'where the body of Harold (slain for the love of his country) was found'. After the suppression of Battle Abbey in 1538 during the Dissolution of the Monasteries, the site became an ornamental garden and the location of the high altar was lost. It lay undiscovered until 1817 when excavations revealed the crypt, and the association re-emerged. It was only in 1929, with the excavation of the church, that conservators understood that the church had been extended in the thirteenth century and, as the crypt lay 27 yards from the east end, the altar could be more accurately placed. Recent research showing that Romanesque churches placed their high altar on the chord of the apse, where the semi-circular end of the church began to curve, rather than in the centre, meant that English Heritage felt the memorial stone had to be moved 20 feet to the east to make the experience of visitors more authentic.

The timing of the move was significant, and was most likely chosen in conjunction with the 950th anniversary of the battle to raise the site's media profile. The move leaves several questions unanswered about the rationale behind it. How much consideration was given to the likelihood that a commemorative monument from the medieval period accurately reflected the location of a grave? Battle monuments are well attested at the sites of several medieval conflicts. In Sweden, the battlefield at Visby (1361) has a large stone cross that dominates the site of the graves of those who died in the battle. The Battle of Neville's Cross (1346) took its name from the monument that stood on the site, but in England most crosses that are found in battlefield contexts are believed to have been associated with the death of an individual. The cross associated with the death of Lord Audley at Blore Heath in 1459 is a good example, and the only visible marker of the battle itself. However, such monuments have often been moved from their original context, which makes their usefulness in locating sites ambiguous at best. For instance, the cross erected to commemorate the Battle of Boroughbridge (1322) was moved two-thirds of a mile away into the centre of nearby Aldborough in 1852. Studies have shown that the cross traditionally believed to have been erected to commemorate the death of James, Earl Douglas, at the Battle of Otterburn (1388) was moved several hundred yards in the nineteenth century as a result of a road realignment. This cross was originally dated to 1777, though

Armstrong's map of Northumberland (1769) shows a 'battle cross' existed there eight years earlier, which may indicate that the cross was replaced later. The lacuna of 381 years between the battle and the illustration of the map means that we cannot confidently use the cross as a secure guide to the location of the battle. The memorial stone in Battle Abbey church is, therefore, not a firm indication of anything except as that the site was where, for several hundred years, people have believed that Harold was killed.

The increased public awareness of the capacity of archaeology to help confirm or deny traditional locations of battlefields probably explains why English Heritage is keen to place its attribution on the basis of solid research rather than mere tradition. Certainly, the last twenty years have seen intensifying arguments and doubts over the veracity of the traditional location of the battle. The events of 14 October 1066 are traditionally believed to have occurred on the ridge where the abbey now sits. This is based on the testimony of the *Chronicle of Battle Abbey*, written in the late twelfth century. 'The English had already occupied the hill where the church now stands, in an impenetrable formation around their king.' The text is traditionally dated on palaeographical grounds and the internal evidence of events that the narrative refers to, the latest of which are in the 1180s. The author claims to have collected together disparate written accounts and oral traditions into one volume to explain the circumstances of the abbey's foundation for posterity. In reality, the *Chronicle* is a compilation of two documents: a shorter outline of the circumstances surrounding the abbey's foundation and a longer account that elaborates on the origin story before outlining the institution's claims to independence from episcopal oversight. The order of composition of the two pieces is unclear. Searle, the most recent editor, argues that the shorter account was written first, but there have been dissenters, and the matter is unlikely to be resolved.[166]

The *Chronicle*'s main concern is the precise context for the abbey's foundation. The first part consists of a detailed narrative that describes how, as the Norman army was advancing to intercept Harold's forces, soldiers were hurriedly preparing themselves by putting on their armour. In the midst of this chaotic clamour, Duke William was handed a hauberk the wrong way around. Several soldiers are alarmed at what they believe to be a bad omen for the battle but, with impeccable timing, William's steward steps in to explain that the incident means the opposite: it shows that William would turn a bad situation around – a fine example of 'spin', which could almost have been lifted from the modern media manager's handbook!

William then makes a speech to those present that demonstrates his piety and clear sense of purpose. In the *Chronicle of Battle Abbey*, William rejects the significance of oaths and soothsayers, and instead proclaims his belief that God will determine his fate. William then makes a solemn oath:

> To strengthen the hands and hearts of you who are about to fight for me, I make a vow that on this very battlefield I shall found a monastery for the salvation of all, and especially for those who fall hereby, to honour God and of all his saints, where servants of God may be supported: a fitting monastery, with a worthy liberty. Let it be an atonement: a haven for all, as free as the one I conquer for myself.

The author is clearly suggesting that William's oath was a crucial factor in the Norman victory, a claim repeated in one the abbey's forged charters produced in the 1150s where William says 'that [the oath] which gave me my crown and the means by which my rule flourishes.' Although the second section of the document does not repeat all the traditions mentioned in the first part, it repeats the story of the pre-battle oath to construct a monastery on the site of Harold's death, which underlines the role that this gesture played in Norman success.

The modern reader can see this account is a stylized, literary set-piece using ecclesiastical models of how secular rulers should behave regarding their spiritual obligations. As we have discussed already, William's bequests to churches demonstrates that he was a genuinely pious individual, even by the standards of his contemporaries in the eleventh century. However, the portrayal of William as an opponent of superstition and champion of orthodox Christian understanding of the divine role in human affairs is implausible. Anecdotes associating William with a series of soothsayers and witches appear in many of our sources, even though they all tended to come to unsavoury ends (such as the witch he used to try to bring Hereward the Wake's rebellion to an end); but this cannot conceal the fact that William used them, as any eleventh-century leader would have done. Medieval religious belief did not adhere to the tightly defined ideas of religious orthodoxy defined by the Scriptures and Church Fathers. The Christianity found in the *Chronicle* represents the views of a tiny clerical elite.[167]

> The line between magic and religion is one which it is impossible to draw in many primitive societies; it is equally difficult to recognize in medieval England.[168]

The whole episode of the pre-battle oath is, therefore, almost certainly an invented tradition, which makes perfect sense when taken in the context of the document's composition.[169] In the second half of the twelfth century, the abbey came into dispute with the diocese of Chichester over the monks' autonomy, which the monks fiercely defended against the bishop's attempt to extend his authority over them. The dispute culminated in the excommunication of Abbot Walter de Luci (1139–71) by the bishop, which led to the case being brought before the recently crowned Angevin King Henry II. The twelfth century was an axial period in European history, as the written record was coming to replace oral traditions as the basis of testimony. Ecclesiastical and royal courts now required a paper trail to confirm past claims to land or jurisdiction over natural resources. It was in the context of the legal dispute of the 1150s the monks followed what was often standard practice in the medieval world by forging documents to prove the original grant by the king. This was not necessarily an act of desperate cynicism, as the forgers would argue that their act was merely presenting a perfectly valid tradition in a form that was admissible in court. Clearly aware of the weakness of the monastery's reliance on the forged charters, the author tries to subtly emphasize more reliable evidence for the monastery's claims. The work lists the properties that the monastery held as endowments, and the second section is a history of the monastery's legal disputes.

The *Chronicle*'s purpose was to explain a major discrepancy in the case. If William had made the oath to construct the abbey (with the attendant privileges) before the battle, why did it take so long to fulfil these wishes? The author's story was that William was distracted by the various rebellions and other affairs that followed the Conquest and so was unable to finalize the details until later. At this point, the text launches into an encomium on William's rule, representing him as the ideal king:

> Outstanding in goodness, open-handed in generosity, notable for clemency, admirable in his abilities, constant in spirit, vigorous in arms, great-hearted in his undertakings.

With this fresh in the reader's mind, the author then raises the issue of William's apparent absent-mindedness, clearly hoping the impression he has created obscures the holes in his story. William's 'conscience was urging him from within', but the crucial agent was William the Smith, a monk from Marmoutier, a famous Benedictine house based just outside Tours (hence the abbey's connection with St Martin). The monk had accompanied William in 1066 in search of reward. He then lobbied the king repeatedly until William 'committed the building of the abbey to him as he had wished', and instructed William of Marmoutier to, 'fetch some brothers from his own church and set speedily in hand the establishment of a suitable monastery on the battlefield.'

The first section of the *Chronicle* adds extra rhetorical weight by adding a tradition about what happened when the monks moved to Battle:

> They studied the battlefield and decided that it seemed hardly
> suitable for so outstanding a building. They therefore chose a fit
> place for settling, a site located not far off.

Water and stone were in short supply on the site of the battlefield, while the other site was much more convenient. On learning this, William:

> ordered them to lay the foundations of the church speedily on the
> very spot where his enemy had fallen and the victory had been won.

He then provided them with the necessary resources, such as Caen limestone, before, miraculously, sufficient stone supplies were found within easy reach of the site, after all. 'It was quite apparent that the Lord had laid up a treasure of stone ... for the predestined work.'

The first half of the twelfth century produced some excellent Anglo-Norman historians, such as William of Malmesbury and Orderic Vitalis, who carried out considerable research while writing histories of some analytical depth and narrative skill. The *Chronicle* does not fit into this genre: it is an extended written submission aimed at supporting the monastery's rear-guard action against legal challenges to its autonomy, threatened as it was by the circling vultures of rival ecclesiastical powers. The story of the oath's significance in the battle's outcome, and the tale of the miraculous discovery of the necessary resources for building the abbey were traditions the author deployed to support their argument that William had granted the institution extraordinary privileges and 'liberties' in perpetuity and had promised their exemption from various financial and administrative exactions. Freedom from the Bishop of Chichester's jurisdiction is explicitly referred to several times in the text. Ecclesiastical politics in the twelfth century was dominated by the issues of authority, property and rights. These may seem excessively materialistic to us, but they were inalienable from how religious specialists of the period saw their function. As a result, the *Chronicle*'s reliability as a guide to the story of the battle's location is potentially seriously compromised.

If we cannot rely on the *Chronicle*, how likely is it that the abbey church was built on the actual battlefield? Considerable insight can be gained by placing the building in its wider chronological and cultural context. Chapels are important monuments for locating battlefields in Britain before the English Civil War period. They were a popular means of commemorating victory as well as solving a practical issue of achieving absolution of sins for those who had killed and those who had died in a battle (there is some ambiguity in the surviving textual accounts about which of these two aspects was more important). Provision for the souls of those who had died in battle had been a key part of the military culture of Western Europe during the early Middle Ages, especially from the Carolingian period onwards.[170] A variety of strategies were available, such as priests praying over the dead, or monks being given property in return for putting the names of specific deceased into their devotions. Building churches was the most powerful of these symbolic acts, and was common practice amongst William's contemporaries, as it was a way of demonstrating their concern for those who fought for them, in the context of a militarized warrior culture that was also deeply pious. This attitude appears contradictory or cynical to modern eyes but, as we have argued already, the culture of Western Europe in the Middle Ages is impossible to comprehend unless we accept that was the way things were at that time. Count Fulk Nerra of Anjou founded an abbey at Loches after his victory at Conquereuil in 992, while Count Robert I of Flanders (1070–93) founded a series of abbeys after his final conquest of Flanders in 1072.

Churches were constructed either *de novo*, as occurred at Battle Abbey, or existing chapels were modified. The earliest documented chapel in England built by the victor was constructed by King Cnut to commemorate his victory in 1016 at the Battle of Assandun. This chapel, according to William of Malmesbury, was said to have been constructed to benefit the souls of those who died. Similarly, a collegiate church was constructed at Shrewsbury in 1403 after the victory of Henry IV and Prince Henry's victory over the rebellious Percy family. Lesser chapels are documented as being constructed in association with the battles at Wakefield (1460), Towton (1461), Barnet (1471) and – probably – Evesham (1265). Arguments over whether these buildings were simply commemorative or explicitly penitential in nature is probably too abstruse. Only a few sophisticated theologians in senior Church positions would have concerned themselves with such distinctions. These churches were declarations of divine favour demonstrated by the granting of victory in the field, so it was entirely appropriate that gratitude should be expressed in the fabric of buildings dedicated to divine services.

Using churches as direct evidence for battlefield locations is not entirely straightforward, however. The church at Wakefield is still in situ to the north of the battlefield, but most of the others are more elusive. The location of the church at *Assandun* is still controversial, with the site being identified with both Ashdon and Hadstock near Saffron Walden (where there is a church that was built by Cnut in 1020) and Ashington in south-east Essex. Towton Chapel has been associated with the present hall, though the famous battlefield grave was exhumed next to Chapel Hill, which suggests a close connection with the location of the conflict. Barnet's chapel has been identified using documentary evidence, but its relationship to the battlefield is unclear. The well or spring associated with the death of Simon de Montfort at the Battle of Evesham became associated with miracles and a popular pilgrimage destination, but attempts to trace the existence of the chapel have so far been fruitless.

Rather than being a result of a pre-battle oath, as suggested by the testimony of the *Chronicle of Battle Abbey*, the abbey's construction makes more sense in relation to William's need for ecclesiastical absolution for the events of 1066. Clerical attitudes to violence were undergoing a transformation in the eleventh century, which would see violence against heretics and schismatics being justified by theologians close to the papacy in the 1080s, a process that culminated in the First Crusade where violence became an act of penance in itself.[171] However, these views emerged in the context of the Investiture Crisis, which boiled over for several decades from the late 1070s and comes after the period we are examining. The official view in the period of the Norman Conquest was that the killing of fellow Christians required priestly absolution and subsequently a penitential act to ensure true repentance. The theology of penance was another area undergoing forensic analysis and systemization in the eleventh century and this explains why considerable attention was being given to it by the clerical elite.[172]

Bishop Ermenfrid of Sion issued a penitential ordinance for all those who fought in the 'great battle', which was confirmed by the papal legate in 1070. The document stands as a useful insight into the interest that the Church leadership was also giving to matters relating to conflict and its regulation, particularly concerning those clergy who were involved (the fact that clergy were forbidden to fight was emphasized by the document). The motivation of the individuals who participated is brought under particular scrutiny in the document, reflecting the ideas of Just War articulated by St Augustine of Hippo in the early fifth century AD: those who fought for material gain were considered to have committed homicide, while those who fought legitimately due to their social and military obligations to their lord were treated more leniently. The range of punishment varied according to the level of violence. A year's penance was ordered for every man killed. Wounding with no knowledge of the ultimate consequence was reckoned at forty days penance per incident. Those ignorant of how many people they had killed were instructed to do penance one day a week for the rest of their lives. However, in line with common beliefs on the efficacy of monastic prayers in matters of obtaining divine grace, penance could be redeemed by 'a perpetual alms either by building or endowing a church'.[173] Therefore, it makes much more sense that William had the abbey of St Martin's constructed in response to the demands for penance from the Church hierarchy after the battle rather than believing the story of the pre-battle oath and the subsequent delay in its construction, as recounted by the *Chronicle*. Enough progress had been made by 1076 to allow the venue to be suitable for Abbot Gausbert's blessing before the altar of St Martin. But even if many of the traditions in the *Chronicle* can be questioned, this is not necessarily proof that the story of the church being located on the actual battlefield is untrue.

The question of the reliability of the *Chronicle*'s account has been central in the challenges made on the traditional location of the battle that have appeared between the 940th and 950th anniversaries. The first challenge came in 2010 from Nick Austin, who argued that the battle actually occurred 2 miles away from Battle to the south-west at Crowhurst.[174] This is part of his wider contention that William did not land at Pevensey at all, but at the old Hastings port, which is further west than the present town, at a site known as Bulverhythe. William's march to meet Harold would, therefore, have naturally brought him to meet Harold at Crowhurst. His argument hangs on his interpretation of the account in the *Chronicle*, which he argues, originally says that the monks were building the abbey on the original battlefield before they abandoned that building and then moved to the current site.

Austin believes that the first section of the *Chronicle* was written much earlier than the second and was based on a first-hand account of the construction. The original meaning of the text was lost when the monks in the late twelfth century copied the document as part of their argument in defence of their traditional privileges. The current manuscript, therefore, has additions inserted by a later editor to obscure the original statement that the building was constructed on the battlefield, and so the order of events was switched with the account being rewritten to say that they started on the wrong site before moving back to the battlefield. Not only did this strengthen the monks' case, given the widespread acceptance of the tradition that the abbey had been built on the battlefield, they probably could not comprehend that it was actually different from the original intended site, which would explain the garbled transmission of the original story in the twelfth-century version. There was no-one around by the time that the original accounts were written down and, therefore, no-one would have dissented. Even William never actually visited his abbey to point out their error. Many of our early twelfth-century chroniclers, John of Worcester, William of Malmesbury, Orderic Vitalis and Henry of Huntingdon, all repeat the traditional story of Battle Abbey being sited where William fought Harold. Austin argues that they are merely repeating the later tradition, but his identification of the original meaning is crucial as it provides contemporary first-hand testimony, which is more valuable than these later authors.

Austin's argument rests on his reading of the crucial text in the first section of the *Chronicle*. Currently, the standard version in print was edited by Deborah Searle and published in 1980.

Qui memoratum bellilo cum considerates cum ad tam insignem fabrium minus idoneum, ut videbatur, arbitrarentur in humiliori non procul loco, versus eiusdem collis occidentalim plagam, aptum habitandi locum eligentes ibidem ne nil operis agree viderentur manisiunculas quasdam fabricaverunt. Qui locus, hucusque Herste cognominatus, quondam habet spinam in huius rei monimentum.

They studied the battlefield and decided that it seemed hardly a suitable for so outstanding a building. They therefore chose a fit place for settling, a site located not far off, but somewhat lower down, towards the western slope of the ridge. There, lest they seem to be doing nothing, they built themselves some little huts. This place, still called Herste, has a low wall to mark this. (Translated by Searle)

Austin prefers the translation proposed by Neil Wright of Cambridge:

> The monks, inspecting the said battlefield judged it unsuitable, as
> it seemed, for so important a structure and chose a suitable living
> site on [or towards] the western side of the same hill; and, lest they
> seemed to be making no progress, built small dwellings there. This
> place, still called *Herste*, has a column as a memorial of this.

Austin suggests that *spinam* is better translated to say that the church
was constructed on the west side of 'the hill' rather than 'the ridge',
as Searle renders it. Austin also argues that *monimentum* should be
translated as 'monument' and that this would only make sense if this
were marking the death of someone important. Searle and Wright's
translations are written on their understanding that the traditional
battlefield is the correct site. But if the battle site were at Crowhurst,
then the original text makes much more sense. Austin has argued
more recently that a recent resistivity survey he has carried out reveals
a series of significant building foundations beneath the present Court
Lodge and laid out in a similar pattern to Battle Abbey.[175] Resistivity is
a form of geophysical survey where electrical current is passed through
the ground at regular points on a survey grid. Electrical resistance
in the soil varies, and is affected by the presence of archaeological
features. Austin argues that this represents the original buildings of
the monastery and the monument built to mark Harold's death, which
were then later altered when the monastery was moved to its present
site.

Austin's argument has not established much traction, though
he continues to push it through his website and challenge English
Heritage to prove him wrong. While he may well have discovered
building foundations, only careful examination will be able to
show whether they are, in fact, an original attempt by the monks
to construct a church. Even if such buildings are discovered, these
do not necessarily contradict the *Chronicle*'s account that the first
building activity took place away from the later abbey site: the point
is that this was not where William and Harold fought! Part of the
weakness of his case is the series of assumptions he makes, including
that the name of the location of the first building site in the text
'Herste' is a corrupted rendering of the term 'Crurst', which he argues
is the original local dialect for Crowhurst. He may be correct, but
being able to confidently trace a place name through a millennium of
linguistic evolution is a brave argument to make. The *Chronicle* does
refer to land the abbey holds in Crowhurst ('Croherste') in two other
places in the text, which somewhat weakens his case.

Austin's reading of the text has also been accused of idiosyncrasy, given that the narrative of the *Chronicle* consistently focuses on the establishment of the abbey on the spot where Harold fell.[176] The idea that monks started construction on the battlefield before moving to a site more suitable for a monastery is completely at odds with the structure of the entire work: there are no obvious discrepancies in the account. Austin's proposal that the document was amended later makes sense in terms of the circumstantial evidence of the abbey's later legal disputes, but the text he removes in support of his reading is chosen arbitrarily to suit his theory rather than being based on a close study of the manuscript tradition. His view is that the *Chronicle* in its original unedited form is a genuine contemporary document. However, the version that survives is unreliable and a later fabrication. This may have some superficial logic, but ultimately is a case of circular reasoning.

Systematic archaeological surveys were carried out in the abbey site in the late 1970s and early 1980s to try to understand the different phases of its existence.[177] The amount of levelling and terracing that can be traced beneath the monastery buildings is strong evidence for the considerable investment required to make the site viable for construction. The abbey church was built off the natural summit of the hill and other buildings, such as the putative thirteenth-century infirmary south-east of the church, required artificial platforms. The east of the church had extensive terracing to allow it to be built on a level surface. The surviving thirteenth-century dormitory range of the abbey, which was built southwards from the heart of the claustral buildings, had to come over the slope of the ridge. To construct a continuous first floor of 164 feet in the refectory, a huge undercroft was constructed to counteract the fall of the ground. The difficulty of managing the water on the site, for example, explains why evidence suggests that the latrines were cleaned out by hand. The *Chronicle* accounts of the monks' complaints about the suitability of the site for the construction of the abbey certainly gain credibility, given the amount of investment that was put into making the terrain suitable.

There was a functional aspect to the development of Benedictine architecture. The cloisters were constructed on the side of the church to provide a means by which the community could operate within a sealed environment to allow them to maintain a separation from the world, while maximizing the internal space for the community to carry out its liturgical and practical tasks. The landscape was also an important consideration for monasteries when they were being constructed, with streams and valleys being the optimal choice of location for most communities. Not only could these provide isolation, as one appreciates when visiting former Cistercian monasteries, such as Rievaulx Abbey, dotted all over the British landscape, but they also allowed easy access to running water and productive terrain. However, monastery construction was primarily driven by ideological factors. They were deeply symbolic buildings that expressed theological and cosmological ideas: the garth, or central garden, reflected notions of paradise, and a monastery could be a metaphor for a mountain, a key aspect of medieval cosmology.[178] The evidence strongly suggests that symbolic considerations were more important in the choice of site at Battle Abbey than the practical ones, which undermines Austin's explanation of why the monks would have moved away from the battlefield.

Austin also uses circumstantial evidence in the Domesday survey to support his view. He argues that the records show Crowhurst as the most significantly damaged of all the manors in England, which can only be explained if the battle itself was fought here. Harold had held Crowhurst in 1066, when its hide assessment was 6 hides and was worth £8; in 1086, when the survey was carried out, the land was assessed as being worth 100s. A virgate of land in Crowhurst was held by the abbot of Battle in 1086, which was worth 12d. Domesday is unequivocal about what happened to Crowhurst in the autumn of 1066: 'It was laid waste [*wastata*]'. Wilting's comparable devastation is argued by Austin to show the Normans landed in September 1066 at Bulverhythe, 3 miles to the west of the modern town of Hastings, rather than at Pevensey, which has been the traditional landing-place. Thus, Crowhurst was the logical point for Harold to intercept William's advance north.

Austin's argument is weakened by his selective focus on Crowhurst and Wilting: Netherfield to the north of Battle was worth 100s, but this had dropped to 50s in 1086, a fall of 50 per cent compared with the effect in Crowhurst, which was worth 62.5 per cent of its pre-Conquest value. The term *wastata* that appears in the context of 2,000 sites in Domesday Book is also complicated by the fact that the term was related to the land's tax assessment, and the surveyors were not really interested in describing why a site was *wastata*. Most entries are glossed with an explanatory comment. 'King Gruffydd and Bleddyn laid waste this land in the time of King Edward so it is not known what it was like at this time,' explains the situation that confronted the commissioners at Archenfield in Herefordshire, but this is an exception. The term could cover several different scenarios explaining why there was no longer a tax assessment, and the ambiguity has led to some revisionist approaches to conclusions drawn from the data about the effects of the Norman Conquest, such as the 'Harrying of the North' in 1069–70 (traditionally used to explain the large number of waste sites across the north of England in 1086). Developing earlier observations that the areas laid waste were often in upland areas, whereas the more fertile, valley settlements appeared to be untouched, W.E. Wightman argued that *wastata* was actually an accounting device showing when a manor was no longer in use after its resources had been transferred to a neighbouring site.[179]

In turn, this approach has been criticized as not being representative of the whole evidence, and the argument continues, but it is hard to argue that the estates in Sussex were affected by anything other than damage in war. The word *wastata* is used consistently in circuit 1 of the Domesday survey to describe the situation after Edward's death in early 1066, and the concentration of sites around Sussex is incontrovertibly due to Norman invasion, given how central the destruction of property was to the method of early Medieval warfare – in England, it was common practice as a strategy for dispute resolution.[180] Tying these records to particular events is far more complex, however. There is nothing novel in Austin's approach. The Domesday *wastata* entries have been used to attempt to reconstruct the movements of armies in 1066 since the late eighteenth century when the Sussex antiquary William Hayley argued that wasted manors were the key to understanding Harold's route. F.H. Baring made a systematic study of the wasted manors in relation to our contemporary accounts to track William's movements in 1898.[181]

Subsequent examinations have argued that the information of Domesday is too imprecise to support such speculative reconstructions. The land in the manors could be spread out over a considerable distance from the estate centre, and we just do not know enough about the particulars of the land to make any judgement on the nature of the original events. The twenty intervening years between wasting and survey were an opportunity for a wide range of factors to impact on the cultivation of the land, of which we are completely ignorant. If one wants to highlight Crowhurst's fate as significant, it is much simpler to suggest that it was targeted by the Normans in 1066 because it was Harold's land, rather than because the battle was fought there. A group of manors around Dover, which was burned late in 1066, have lower intermediate values that suggest a connection with events, but Wallingford, which was also burned and ravaged by William's armies, has no comparative effects.[182] Austin's circumstantial evidence is as problematic as his direct evidence.

THE CASE FOR AND AGAINST CALDBEC HILL

Another candidate for the battlefield is Caldbec Hill, a few miles to the north-east of Telham and Blackhorse Hills. This site was suggested by Jim Bradbury in 1998 as a better location than Battle Hill.[183] Bradbury's argument rested on the traditional identification's reliance on the *Chronicle of Battle Abbey*. Once this is taken out of consideration, the other written accounts are more ambiguous. Version D of the *Anglo-Saxon Chronicle* talks about Harold assembling an army in response to William's army and then coming 'against him [William] at the hoary apple tree'. The location of the tree is subject to an unusual degree of consensus amongst writers as being on Caldbec Hill. At the conjunction of three hundreds, it would be an entirely appropriate landmark for the assembly of the fyrd. Given Harold held land in the area, and his family's long-standing connections with Sussex, he would have known it well. Most authors then argue that Harold moved down onto the hill where the abbey now sits. Bradbury dissents and points out that the account in the *Carmen* mentions that the English army came out of a wood before taking up its position on a hill, a detail also supported in William of Poitiers' account. This fits the situation of the traditional hill on which Battle Abbey sits, as well as Caldbec Hill. Orderic Vitalis was the first writer to identify the name of the hill as being *Senlac* and this name, meaning 'sand-lake', seems to sit at odds with the landscape if the battle was fought at the traditional site. Bradbury points out that there was a pool at Oakwood Gill, increasing the probability that Caldbec Hill was the site of the battle.

However, Bradbury refused to nail his speculative colours to the mast, using the suggestion more as a didactic exercise on the lack of certainty of any conclusion drawn from sources that constantly undermine attempts to reconstruct the events of 14 October 1066. The suggestion was renewed and developed with conviction by John Grehan and Martin Mace in 2012.[184] They take an even more jaundiced view of the *Chronicle of Battle Abbey* than Austin, and reject it as a source that is completely unreliable. They argue that as none of the other sources actually specify the abbey as being on the site of the battle, the traditional location is a product of *a priori* reasoning. As Bradbury argued, several accounts allude to the English army assembling near woods, which better suits the geography of Caldbec Hill. The question of the *Malfosse* could be explained if the English had dug a ditch to protect themselves, something again that Grehan and Mace suggest is best suited to the gradients of Caldbec. They also argue that the Bayeux Tapestry presents a realistic depiction of the fighting and argue that the Englishman who spots the Norman forces is peering through lush foliage, a situation unlikely to fit the landscape at Battle Hill. The scenes of the fighting portray an undulating landscape and a confused series of hand-to-hand engagements between Normans and Englishmen. This does not fit the traditional narrative of a series of attacks up a slope. If the fighting took place on the conical-shaped Caldbec Hill, the English would have been deployed around the hill and the fighting would have taken place all across the slopes, which makes better sense of the images on the tapestry.

Grehan and Mace's argument also presents wider contextual evidence on old English military tactics that would make the battle more likely to have occurred on Caldbec Hill. They stress that the English shield-wall was not deployed at Hastings because it was the only way the English knew how to fight. The shield-wall could be used as an aggressive tactic, as it was at the Battle of Sherston in 1016. They push the argument, already discussed within Chapter 4, that the English were perfectly capable of using horses in warfare, yet at Hastings did not because they were too tired after the previous fortnight's physical exertions. Grehan and Mace also reason that the English army failed to be more offensive with the Normans because of the terrain they were based on, which would better fit the steeper sides of Caldbec Hill than those of Battle Hill. The English had a good defensive position, which they may have been forced to adopt if we accept the evidence from the sources that Harold was surprised by the Normans.

Furthermore, Grehan and Mace argue, the ridge on Caldbec Hill is narrower than that on Battle Hill, and this would have permitted the English to create a much longer and more effective line of defence. The fact that the battle appears to have lasted all day could only have resulted from the Norman attacks being consistently rendered ineffective through exhaustion from having to ascend the more considerable gradients of Caldbec. The slope on Battle Hill is simply too gentle to explain the length of the battle. One of the issues that puzzle those wishing to understand the battle is why William did not simply flank the English shield-wall, using the mobility of his cavalry. The fact that he does not appear to have done so would make much more sense if the fighting occurred on a hill with steeper sides. If the English were on Caldbec, they would also have been able to create an encirclement to provide an all-round defence of their position, which the Normans would have had enormous difficulties in dealing with. This could also make Harold's behaviour appear more strategically sensible. When Edmund Ironside faced Cnut in 1016, he was able to raise a series of armies, and so a single defeat did not cost him the war. One major military reverse would have meant Cnut's invasion failed. By creating a solid defensive position on Caldbec Hill, Harold ensured that the Normans could not advance further inland with Harold and his army in their rear separating them from their ships. By blockading the Normans in, Harold could wait on reinforcements and then force a decision. What happened, however, was once the English army had been weakened by the end of the day, the Norman cavalry was able to get a foothold on the ridge, and this would have ensured the fighting would have been brought to a swift end.

As with the Crowhurst argument, the weakness of the case for Caldbec Hill is that it is entirely negative and very selective in its approach to the evidence, dismissing those details that do not support the authors' thesis. While there is no doubt that the traditions of the monastery's foundations were exploited in the later legal dispute, this does not meant that there is no kernel of truth in the basic details. None of the earlier twelfth-century accounts report that there was any doubt or debate over the matter. Even if these are dismissed as not being direct witnesses, more weight can be placed on the *Brevis Relatio*, an account written by a monk of Battle Abbey during the abbacy of Abbot Ralph (1107–24) and dated to 1114–20 due to its references to William Adelin, the son of King Henry I who died in the White Ship disaster of 1120. This account of the life of William the Conqueror was written within fifty-four years of the battle and related the personal experiences of Abbot Ralph, who had come to England in 1070 as a royal chaplain and who thus knew the Conqueror personally. The text makes no mention of the battlefield oath that appears in the *Chronicle of Battle Abbey*, but uses the same basic framework for its narrative, repeating the mistake made with Duke William's hauberk and the duke's speech about not trusting soothsayers. This text is clear that Harold and his soldiers arrived at a place 'now called Battle', and his standard was raised in the centre of his retinue 'on the site where afterwards William had an abbey built'. The Abbey was built 'to the memory of this victory and for the absolution of the sins of all those who had been slain there'.[185]

Finally, Version E of the *Anglo-Saxon Chronicle*, which was written in the early 1120s, makes a reference that is probably even earlier. The manuscript was initially copied from an earlier manuscript from Christ Church in Canterbury to replace the earlier Peterborough copy that had been destroyed in a fire in 1116. The entry for the year 1086 contains a brief obituary for William I, which is a slight chronological error, given that he died in 1087. The obituary notes that:

In the same place where God permitted him to conquer England, he
set up a famous monastery and appointed monks for it.

The text mentions William's three sons and notes that Robert Curthose
inherited Normandy while William Rufus took the crown of England;
the text goes on to record that 'the third was called Henry, and his
father bequeathed to him incalculable treasures'. The fact that the
chronicler does not mention Henry becoming king would imply that
the text is written before August 1100, so gives a testimony to the
tradition from between twenty and thirty-four years after the events
it describes.

While the oath is probably an invention and other details were
undoubtedly shaped to serve the legal cases that form the context of
the creation of the *Chronicle of Battle Abbey*, the monks' case was
probably based on a genuine belief of a very early tradition: the case
failed because it had not been written down, not because it was not
true.

The burden of proof surely falls on those who argue for the battlefield
being elsewhere to demonstrate that the abbey was not the location of
the engagement of October 1066. Austin's arguments are unconvincing
in their detail and, given the unsuitability of the terrain for infantry
defence against cavalry, fail the law of military feasibility. Grehan
and Mace's approach to this problem is to suggest that the abbey was
built as part of a defensive strategy under William to prevent anyone
successfully repeating his successful endeavour. William divided
Sussex into five strips of land called *rapes*, running north to south:
compact lordships based around castles to defend against invasion.
The Count of Eu who held the Hastings *rape* was asked to accept the
independence of Battle Abbey as a separate entity within his estates.
Grehan and Mace develop the argument that these freedoms were
part of a deliberate strategy aimed at attracting settlers to re-populate
the area, as the investment necessary in building a monastery would
produce considerable economic activity. Such practices were often
used in medieval Europe to encourage settlement, given that shortage
of labour was a major impediment to the development of aristocratic
estates. It is also true, as the authors write, that monastery buildings
were used as defensive locations that gave refuge to local people,
and abbots were important community leaders who had defensive
responsibilities in times of crisis and invasion. Grehan and Mace,
however, push this argument beyond what is sustainable by arguing
that the strategic location of Battle Hill was so important that the
monastery was built with defence as a major consideration. This

seems implausible: if one was primarily concerned with defence, one would build a castle. These played the some role as a monastery in organizing labour for the land: a monastery's defensive role was a subsidiary benefit. Thus, it cannot have been the major reason for its construction and is not a solid basis for denying the tradition that Battle Abbey stood where the battle was fought.

While the democratization of the media through the internet and television documentaries is undoubtedly a good thing, it also perpetuates the myth of the plucky amateur who comes across evidence that challenges the group-think of the professional academic establishment, who have a vested interest in defending the *status quo*.[186] This is a human story we all buy into, as it reflects a combination of specific features of the culture of the post-industrial West in the late twentieth and early twenty-first centuries: distrust of the Establishment, traditional institutions and elites, the profusion of mass media, etc. This is not the occasion to unhelpfully generalize in a pseudo-sociological manner about why the conspiratorial mind-set is so prevalent, except to note that, as we have mentioned, there is a sharp contrast between what we think we know about Hastings and what can be proved with the evidence that survives. Archaeology can be a slow and complex discipline that gives up its secrets only through careful and painstaking research. Impatience is a perfectly natural response, but pseudo-archaeology of the sort we have outlined in this chapter does not really answer any questions.

CHAPTER 8

Locating the Battlefield

THE PROBLEMS WITH IDENTIFYING
THE SITE OF A BATTLE

The crucial link underpinning the case for those who challenge the traditional location of the battlefield is the lack of evidence from the battlefield itself: given that this was the most famous battle of the British Middle Ages, would not there have been considerable amounts of metalwork or mass graves excavated by now? The deficiency of information is not due to lack of effort. Major excavations of the eastern site of the ridge on which Battle Abbey was constructed were undertaken between 1976 and 1984, and the exhaustive survey by J.N. Hare of these works records a huge range of material, but none of this is recognizably from a battlefield.[187] Grehan and Mace argue that there are sufficient finds in other areas that mark this discrepancy as more than coincidence. An axe-head found in the 1950s on Marley Lane between Battle and Caldbec Hills, and an arrow discovered on the abbey site in 2004, dated to between the eleventh and fourteenth centuries and assessed as hunting gear, show that metalwork does survive from the relevant periods. Grehan and Mace also cite the discoveries of metalwork associated with the Battle of Fulford Gate in York, as well as graves showing evidence of death in battle from nearby St Andrew's Fishergate, to highlight the Battle lacuna.

The discovery of burials at Ocklynge, near Eastbourne, in the 1820s and again in 1909, which were identified as being for victims of combat, and the existence of mass burials associated with the Battle of Lewes (1264), indicate that war graves do exist in Sussex. One of the excavated skeletons found in 1993 at Lewes medieval hospital was originally believed to have originated from the thirteenth century, until carbon-dating results from the University of York surprised everyone by confirming the remains to be even earlier – actually, mid-eleventh century. The six extensive wounds that skeleton 180 suffered at the back of the skull, probably inflicted by a sword, would explain the individual's demise.[188] This led to extensive press coverage in 2014 reporting that the first victim of the Battle of Hastings had been discovered.[189] This association, while plausible chronologically, is far too casual to permit any such conclusion. Merely accumulating a mass of circumstantial evidence does not an argument make, and the critical discussions of the archaeological evidence all fail to approach the evidence systematically enough.

As a rule of thumb, the further a battle recedes into the past, the more tenuous is the knowledge of its location. The process of identifying where an engagement actually occurred is far less straightforward than is suggested by the large number of commemorative features that litter the landscape of England or the many crossed swords marked on an Ordnance Survey map. Whereas many of the battlefield sites of the Wars of the Roses (1455–87) can, in most cases, be located with some degree of certainty, those from the earlier periods are far more elusive. The only battlefield from before 1066 that is generally understood is the Battle of Maldon (AD991). All other putative locations are pure speculation. The debates over the location of the Battle of Brunanburh in 937, at which King Æthelstan defeated a coalition of northern rulers (Norse, Scots and British), stands as extreme testimony to the complex nature of the problem. Seven different locations have been suggested, with the debate relying on arguments over place names (e.g. Bromborough in the Wirral) or speculation over the strategic concerns of tenth-century rulers, with potential sites being identified from Sheffield to the borders of Scotland.[190] Even at sites where the general location of the battle is understood, there can be problems in assessing the finer detail: three possible sites have been suggested for where Maldon was fought.[191] At Bannockburn, there are nine existing potential reconstructions of the battle across the landscape that surrounds Stirling Castle: a detail the wonderfully entertaining computer-based interactive reconstruction at the visitor centre somewhat glosses over![192]

Some of the problems that complicate a positive identification of a medieval battlefield are structural. Medieval written accounts are a major impediment to clarity as authors rarely give clear topographical detail, which makes linking a textual description to the features in modern landscapes almost impossible for most engagements that occurred before at least the sixteenth century. In most cases, these writers, many of whom were monastic scribes, had never seen the battlefield they were describing and were following literary traditions (especially from Latin literature) that provided models for the description of conflict, in which reconstruction of 'what really happened' was not a primary consideration. In our Introduction and Chapter 5, we have already seen how William of Poitiers' testimony is compromised by his use of classical allusions designed to make William of Normandy appear as a new Caesar. The amount of written material is also a problem. In many cases, the relative paucity of information is a major issue, while in others it is the capacity of the sources to provide misleading or conflicting details, either through ignorance or through deliberately manipulating information. We have seen this problem already in the difficulties of achieving any consensus from the relatively abundant sources for Hastings. Tony Sutherland has argued that accounts of the Battle of Towton were manipulated by the Yorkist victors, leading to considerable confusion over how many actual distinct engagements there had been.[193]

Accurately locating battlefields from later periods is not a precise science. Two sites have claims as the location for the Battle of Braddock Down (1643), for instance.[194] This makes the obstacles facing identification of earlier sites even more daunting. Besides the paucity of documentation, the smaller size of armies during the medieval period makes the probability of conflict detritus by archaeologists much smaller. Although, as we have seen in Chapter 4, the actual number of soldiers at Hastings is unknown, it can be estimated to be, at most, about 15,000. This was less than half the number that fought at Marston Moor in 1644. The increased use of gunpowder weapons from the fifteenth century onwards makes finding artefacts with a clear military origin much more straightforward, allowing for the collation of more comprehensive datasets. Objects from medieval battles are much more elusive and there is an unknowable issue of how much equipment would have remained on the field afterwards. The increasing high status of the warrior class across Europe in the eleventh century meant that their weapons, armour and fittings were very high value investments that could not afford to be left strewn around a battlefield, no matter what the fate of their owner. The scenes of warriors being stripped of their armour on the Bayeux Tapestry emphasizes the amount of recycling that would occur on a medieval battlefield after the fighting had ended, leaving doubts about how much war paraphernalia remains for the archaeologist to find.

Like all branches of archaeology, assessing the material evidence of battlefields requires a viable and scientifically applied methodology. The value of the Ocklynge warrior graves in East Sussex is severely compromised by the lack of care in the recording of the contextual information. The only war graves associated with a battlefield that have been excavated with sufficient care to allow comprehensive recording and skeletal analysis were the Towton graves in 1996, which were extracted in a rapid, rescue excavation.[195] The absence of war graves at Battle are not proof of anything. While a concentration of bodies can be anticipated near the main engagement, this is not always the case. A large proportion of the casualties during medieval battles would occur in the rout at the end of the battle when formations broke up and men became vulnerable, which makes the burials just as likely to appear in the surrounding landscape as on the battlefield itself. The mass grave from East Stoke (1487) seems to lie close to the ancient enclosures, which would have impeded the movements of the fleeing troops and facilitated their being cut down. The grave pits at Lewes have turned up around 2,000 skeletons since the early nineteenth century, and their position at the west of the town is explained by their encountering an area of settlement that would have impeded their passage.

HOW ARCHAEOLOGY CAN HELP

Developments in archaeological science over the past thirty years have led to a more robust methodology being applied to the material evidence to allow the reconstruction and understanding of battlefield sites.[196] Technological advances have also assisted this progress, though the most important tool has been one that has existed for over a century: metal detectors. Traditionally, archaeologists have been suspicious of the use of these; their easy availability to the amateur has afforded considerable opportunities for treasure hunters to locate valuable artefacts for monetary gain, which are usually then excavated without any care or systematic recording, thus destroying the valuable contextual information that allows individual finds to be properly evaluated and understood. 'Nighthawks' who use the cover of darkness to illegally excavate archaeological sites, are a particular bugbear to the academic community and, given the high probability of locating metal objects, battlefields are a prime target for chancers. The alarm was raised at the battlefield at Towton in the early twenty-first century where Tim Sutherland, the director of the Towton Battlefield Archaeology Survey, claimed that 'bucketloads' of artefacts were being removed to be sold off.[197] Despite this institutional hostility, over the last couple of decades professional archaeologists have increasingly recognized the potential of the humble metal detector in facilitating systematic exploration of battlefields.

This acceptance was triggered by two innovative studies in the 1980s, which produced spectacular results. The first was in Montana, USA, at the site of the Battle of Little Bighorn (1876). In 1983, a prairie fire exposed the surface, allowing for a systematic survey of artefacts the following year. Initially, metal-detectors had followed behind individuals scanning the surface for finds, but soon it became clear that the technology was producing the greater number of finds, and so the detectors were placed in front of the surveyors. Little Bighorn was an ideal site for such a survey, given that it had been relatively untouched since the late nineteenth century and, marking where individual soldiers had fallen, there were graves that could be studied to better understand their fate.[198] Combined with the enormous documentary record that had been created by the mythical discourse surrounding the battle, there was enormous potential for invaluable inter-disciplinary work that could enrich understanding of the whole event. The carefully managed survey of the surface area and thorough recording methods, combined with modern forensic firearms analysis, allowed a huge advance in understanding of the progress of the battle across the terrain and revealed how Custer's men had been comprehensively outgunned by their Lakota and Cheyenne opponents.[199]

The second study that demonstrated the merits of the metal detector in reconstructing battlefields from their material remains was the identification of the site of the Battle of Teutoburg Forest (AD9), a battle that saw the destruction of three Roman legions by local Germanic tribesmen led by their chief Arminius. This battle was of enormous significance and effectively brought major Roman expansionist policies in north-west Europe to an end.[200] Westphalian archaeologist Wilhelm Winklemann summed up the state of research on the battle in 1983 when he described '700 theories, but none of them leading to the battlefield'.[201] Antiquarian interest in the battlefield had begun in the seventeenth century, and coins of the period that were found by farmers in the nineteenth century increased the intensity of the debate, but nothing had been established for certain. Major Tony Clunn, a British soldier stationed in northern Germany who had read of the advances in America, began surveying some of the proposed locations in 1987 with his metal detector, and soon revealed large numbers of coins and sling shots in areas that have subsequently revealed large numbers of bodies.[202] Subsequent excavation not only uncovered considerable numbers of casualties and artefacts, but the ambush context that the German tribesmen used to lure the legions into a terrain that allowed them to trap the Romans and annihilate them.[203]

These developments in conflict archaeology have increasingly been deployed in Britain over the last few decades and have led to a more intense, scientific interest in analysing battlefield sites. The excavation of the Towton battlefield in the 1990s saw important advances in developing a multi-disciplinary approach to battlefield excavation. Fought in 1461, the site of what is claimed to be the largest ever battle in England had been studied by antiquarians in previous centuries and in more recent times has become a magnet for amateur metal detectors. Tony Sutherland, a leading battlefield archaeologist, developed a professional research project for the battlefield that employed a range of techniques: documentary analysis, field-walking with metal detectors, geophysical survey and excavation. Sutherland worked closely with an amateur metal detector who had spent a considerable time in the 1980s surveying the site and making basic recordings of his finds. One of their innovations was the use of a GPS system to record the position of finds more accurately.

This systematic approach compensated somewhat for the more haphazard collection by earlier enthusiasts who had removed large numbers of artefacts from the site without leaving any written records to allow researchers a chance to understand how their finds related to the bigger picture. The concentration of arrows that were located in certain areas, for instance, was an important development in understanding how and where the battle was fought.[204] Geophysical surveys targeted sites that had been traditionally associated with the battle, and found that virtually every site that was thought to have a connection with the battle contained no evidence relating to it at all. Careful analysis of previous recordings of grave finds, and the discovery of errors in transmission, also revealed several war graves, which were analysed using modern osteology methods, and clear evidence of the trauma injuries of victims of the conflict were identified, greatly enhancing understanding of the battle.[205]

The Battlefield Trust's *UK Fields of Conflict* project, which ran between 2006 and 2010, attempted to create a database of sites across Britain and place them into a more systematic research framework, which involved issues such as clarifying definitions of 'battles' as opposed to 'skirmishes' and 'sieges'.[206] This stimulated more research, and the most spectacular result was at Bosworth, where, in 2009, the archaeologist Glenn Foard was able to demonstrate that the battle took place several miles from the traditionally understood location, which had hosted a visitor centre since 1974. This was due to the discovery of thirty-four lead cannonballs from the late fifteenth century, which are only explicable if they were fired in August 1485.[207] Interestingly, these discoveries have had no detrimental impact on visitor interest at Bosworth. Added to the discovery of Richard III in the Leicester city car park in 2012, the resulting publicity has helped numbers to increase over the last ten years and the new findings have been incorporated into the site through an extended walk.[208] The discovery of new battlefields continues to grab the public imagination. Nick Arnold's claims to have identified the site of the 1069 battle, which saw King Harold II's sons Godwine and Edmund defeated by Count Brian of Brittany (dubbed a 'Hastings re-match' by the media), in a field between the villages of Northam and Appledore in Devon was widely reported in the national media in the spring of 2016.[209]

Deployment of systematic metal-detecting techniques is ultimately the best means of locating where the Battle of Hastings was fought. Each battlefield has its own distinctive 'signature' of artefacts, depending on the period in which the fighting occurred (*see* Table 2). There is a considerable advantage in surveying battlefields from the sixteenth century onwards. The increasing deployment of firearms means that significant numbers of lead bullets can be unearthed – often in such numbers that the battlefield's location can be almost proven beyond doubt. This is not an option for an eleventh-century battlefield, where the majority of projectiles would have been arrows and personal objects from participants will often have a non-military nature (e.g. as clothes fasteners, buckles, strap ends and brooches). This complicates attributing them to a combat context. The best understood examples of comparison for our purpose are those of the Wars of the Roses, some of which have been well studied. The site where the Battle of Towton was fought in 1461 has seen large numbers of arrows and other artefacts being found, the majority having a non-military component. Plotting the concentrations on the ground allowed a series of trenches to be dug, the excavation of which allowed the location of human remains associated with the battle and a rich vein of new evidence to be opened up.

Unlike the lead that was used in firearms projectiles, a significant obstacle to locating ferrous objects on a battlefield is their poor preservation. The soils at Towton are particularly favourable to preservation due to the limestone base that exists below the site. Even then, most arrowheads that were excavated had deteriorated to such a degree that their ferrous content had largely been mineralized. The chances of survival are even poorer in the acidic soils that make up the High Weald, where Battle is located. Technology is not always reliable, either: known locations of arrowheads at Towton could not be located by the fluxgate gradiometers used to create a geophysical analysis of the site. This was due to the natural replacement over time of the arrows' ferrous component by mineralized products. Not only is the site's geology crucial, but the way the soil has been managed

Table 2: Summary of weapons technology by period[210]

Period	Technology	Examples
Roman	Ferrous metal technology	Fragments or complete pieces of metal alloy or ferrous artefacts: • Roman militaria, e.g. fragments of Roman armour and possible weapons • fragments of native British equipment and weapons • collection of *ballista* (large crossbow) bolts, apparently aimed at a large roundhouse in the Iron Age hillfort at Hod Hill, Dorset, by the besieging Roman army • Roman *ballista* bolt in the spine of a skeleton buried in Maiden Castle, Dorset
Medieval	Ferrous metal technology	• fragments of clothing fasteners, badges, buckles and arrowheads
Post-medieval	Early firearms technology	• lead round shot from muskets and pistols and cannon balls
Modern	Modern firearms technology	• cylindrical or rifled shot, e.g. Minié balls • bombs and shells or fragments of each

is important. Regularly ploughed soil is particularly effective for locating finds as the process allows artefacts to rise into the top layers and be accessible to metal detectors. This also means artefacts are more likely to be degraded or exposed to the attentions of amateur treasure hunters, and thus prone to disappear from the historical record. Unploughed soil used for meadow or pasture will preserve artefacts better, but they are also much more difficult to locate with a metal detector and worm sorting of the soil can lead to the objects to 'sink' lower down the soil profile.

English Heritage responded to the challenges made against Battle Abbey being the genuine battlefield by asking the battlefield archaeologist Glenn Foard to assess the site. Grehan, Mace and Austin had all emphasized the failure to produce any recognizable eleventh-century artefacts associated with the battle as being a major criticism for the traditional view that the abbey had been built on the site of the battle. For Battle, Foard carried out two pilot excavations in 2011 and 2013 to assess the effectiveness of the methodology that he developed at Bosworth. The topsoil was removed and metal detectors were then used to locate any artefacts that could be associated with the battle from the earlier medieval layers within the soil. The problem with attempting to survey an eleventh-century battlefield is that no-one knows what such a site would look like. The extent to which ferrous objects at Towton (1461) had degraded suggests that objects from 400 years earlier are even less likely to have survived in any recognizable form.

The excavations did not produce any finds, nor did the brief surveys of Caldbec Hill. This was not at all surprising to Foard from his experience. The survey area probably only covered the English counter-attack, which would have left very limited traces in the first place. Most of the battlefield, with the vast majority of any surviving artefactual evidence, is still probably under the abbey and, therefore, only accessible through complex excavations. The field-walking survey that yielded such spectacular results at Towton and Bosworth was not equivalent to that carried out at Battle owing to the difference in terrain. Rather than being used for ploughing, the area that is called the battlefield today was laid out as gardens in the early nineteenth century under the fifth baronet of Battle Abbey, Godfrey Webster. This work saw the fish ponds being dug. The current land-use also precludes any sufficiently extensive surveying. For any effective results, battlefield surveys need to occur on a large scale, given that one needs to test an extensive area to prove absence of evidence. English Heritage discussed funding a large scale project that had been intended to follow the preliminary excavations, but this is no longer happening as English Heritage withdrew funding.[211]

When investigating the challenges to the traditional location of the site, the Channel 4 archaeology programme *Time Team* came up with its own hypothesis, based on its use of an aerial LIDAR survey that it commissioned for the battlefield in 2013. LIDAR is a portmanteau word combining 'laser' and 'radar'. The technology sends out beams of light across a surface area and records the beam reflection, the variations being equivalent to differences in the height of the landscape and other features. The quality of the surveys has continually improved since the technology, first developed for NASA in the 1970s, was first used for terrestrial surveying purposes in the late 1990s. Between 1999 and 2014, LIDAR technology improved its power, and advanced from firing 3,000 pulses per second to 20,000 per second. This allows the production of highly detailed and accurate models of the land surface at metre and sub-metre resolution. This provides archaeologists with the capability to recognize and record features otherwise hard to detect.

The *Time Team* survey suggested that the location of the battle was, in fact, slightly to the east of the current location and, therefore, proposed a 45-degree re-orientation of the battlefield. The survey's reconstruction of sea levels in the eleventh century shows that the area between Hastings and Battle was a peninsula at that time, which makes Harold's decision to engage the Normans at this point more comprehensible: he was trying to keep them bottled up. The LIDAR survey also suggested that in 1066 the traditional battlefield would have been too boggy for cavalry to operate. *Time Team*'s conclusion, much publicized in the aftermath of the programme, was that the battle would have been fought to the eastern end of the ridge, which, in line with the earlier re-orientation of the battle, would suggest that Harold's shield-wall would have been placed on a line perpendicular to the present A2100 road, and speculates that he was killed on a site presently occupied by a mini-roundabout.

Roy Porter, the chief curator for English Heritage, was quick to downplay the significance of the LIDAR survey, arguing that it did not really provide a rupture with past convention as the traditional battlefield included this area. The new location was, after all, only a couple of hundred yards from the abbey precinct, and the fighting would have occurred across the whole of the ridge. There is also a question how far the LIDAR analysis had taken into account the changes in land use around the abbey. Their analysis is, therefore, arguably overly simplistic. Archaeologists and landscape historians have attempted to reconstruct historical landscapes over the last thirty years and, as a result, the evolution of the British landscape is now far better understood. We now know how the development of open-field farming in the central belt of England, from Northumbria to Hampshire, was the dominant feature of land organization from the Middle Ages until the eighteenth and nineteenth centuries. This was then replaced by the large scale enclosure of previously open land, though these patterns had developed earlier in places like East Anglia. The consequences of these changes are also vitally important to appreciate: they often led to a radical alteration of the landscape, which makes it very difficult to translate modern landscapes onto the past.

Crucially, for the *Time Team* conclusion, the LIDAR survey did not sufficiently take into account what remains of undisturbed slopes amongst the extensive terracing that occurred in the construction of the abbey and town; nor did it consider the slight changes that have occurred in the relief across the top of the ridge over the past centuries. Excavation has shown how the southern side of the slope was reduced in severity over time with an accumulation of 8 feet to the north of the reredorter (communal latrine). When this is combined with the post-suppression changes in the level to the courtyard to the west of the claustral ranges, it is clear that the topography of the site has been greatly altered between the eleventh and the sixteenth centuries. The traditional battlefield was much steeper than it is now. This undermines the Caldbec Hill theory, given how it relies on the sharper gradient of the slopes in its interpretation of the battle. As yet, since the largely unreferenced work in the earlier twentieth century, there has been no serious attempt to assess all the medieval and early modern documentary evidence for the landscape to see what significance this can add. Whether any soil or pollen evidence is recoverable from the valley below the abbey to inform on early land use is also in doubt, owing to the various ponds created there subsequently, but it is a potential source of information that would allow more precision than is possible at the moment.

Ultimately all the alternative candidates for the battle site are speculative and rely on negative evidence. All future excavations in the abbey precinct ought to have a metal-detecting component, but when this might ever happen is the question. The regular re-enactments that have occurred since 1984 continue to potentially contaminate the artefact record by depositing modern replicas of earlier metalwork. Battle is ultimately a site where it is too soon to try to firmly answer the question: was the battle actually fought there?

CHAPTER 9

Mythologizing the Battle

WHAT MAKES A MYTH?

Conflict – and battles, in particular – have long played an important role in how different societies remember their past. Violent traumatic events are especially memorable. This is not exclusive to Western civilization: other cultural traditions, too, use such events to shape their understanding of the present. In early Islamic historiography, which developed during the eighth and ninth centuries AD, the earlier seventh-century Arab conquests in the Middle East were partly presented as a series of key battles, most notably at Yarmouk and al-Qadisiyyah, both traditionally dated to the year 636 (15 AH). The 'decisive battle' paradigm, which suggests human history advances through a series of crucial military engagements, is a very popular approach amongst authors and is used extensively in television documentaries. It can allow the complexity of history to be seen through the lens of a conflict between two sides, with clear winners and losers. Its domination of military history writing in the English-speaking world has its origins in Victorian Britain, with the publication of Edmund Creasy's *Fifteen Decisive Battles of the World*, which became a bestseller rivalling other epoch-defining works such as Darwin's *Origin of the Species*.[212] For Creasy, battles were occasions for social improvement and subsequently validated the importance of their study by historians on the grounds that 'they decide things, they improve things'.[213]

Most people in contemporary Britain, even those who profess complete ignorance of the medieval period, will know *something* about the Battle of Hastings, however basic or clichéd. One such 'fact' will be that the battle was decisive. The numerous jokes based on Harold taking an 'arrow in the eye' in cartoons and comedy, and the significant number of newspaper references to the Norman Conquest and the year 1066, only work because a large proportion of the audience understands these references. However, the 'decisive battle' concept is fraught with difficulties. While reducing Hastings to a conflict between 'the English and the Normans' is attractive as a way of making the battle comprehensible, it does not adequately reflect the realities of the mid-eleventh century, as outlined in Chapter 2. At the regular re-enactments that have taken place at Hastings since the 1980s, the most recent events have typically seen the crowd express spontaneous support for Harold and the Anglo-Saxons: this reaction reveals a binary view of the battle between 'us' and the Normans, who represent 'them'. In reality, modern attitudes are far more complex: when surveyed about the battle, contemporary Britons can express sympathy for the English, the Normans, or even neither.[214]

The fashion amongst historians to explain events as the result of long-term structural changes has seen the concept drop out of fashion over the past few decades. To argue that Harold's death at Hastings was the cause of the Norman Conquest appears to many scholars to be a crude simplification. It is what occurs *after* a battle that makes it important, rather than the decisiveness of the engagement itself. Many clear victories on the battlefield had little effect on the evolution of historical progress. Therefore, we can suggest that the idea of a 'decisive battle' is not a universal concept, but one built on a series of social and cultural assumptions. It has functioned as a mechanism through which societies can help construct a common past that can be used to build a sense of group identity – an 'imagined community' – whether that be in belonging to a tribe, region, nation, or a broad cultural tradition such as 'Western civilization'.

We prefer to see history as a series of facts about events in the past that can be reconstructed from the surviving evidence. Of course, this factual approach should ideally inform a society's 'collective memory', a commonly shared pool of knowledge about its past. This objective approach is subject to intense academic scrutiny, however, by those who would argue that our understanding of historical events is a function of present concerns and, thus, logically, there is no 'past' independent of contemporary perspectives and concerns. This 'constructionist' approach can be modified by pointing out that there is a difference between establishing if an event ever happened as a concrete reality, and then acknowledging how that event is actually interpreted.

As already discussed in the introduction to this book, the past is one of the most powerful tools for legitimizing the present. Typically, theorists of a constructionist mind-set have argued that 'facts' are usually produced by those in power wishing to consolidate that power and to legitimize the *status quo* by claiming that they are following tradition. While such a theory is attractive, in reality establishing this is more difficult and, of course, it is a fallacy that 'collective memory' represents a monolithic entity. Raphael Samuel, the British social historian, argued:

> History is not the prerogative of the historian ... it is rather a social form of knowledge, the work in any given instance, of a thousand different hands.[215]

Therefore, at any one time we must deal with diversity and conflicting views of the past that exist simultaneously.

Thus, while the idea that the Battle of Hastings is a significant event cannot seriously be questioned, explaining *why* it is significant is far less straightforward. One could argue that it was a national tragedy, or that it was a necessary stage in the path to national greatness: an individual's perspective would depend on how their knowledge of the event has been mediated to them. The diversity involved in remembering the past can be seen in way that battlefields have been preserved and presented to the public. By way of comparison to the site at Battle, which we have already discussed in some depth in Chapter 8, Scotland provides an excellent example – the site associated with the Battle of Bannockburn. It would be valid to argue that Bannockburn was, in some aspects, a civil war, given that Scots fought on both sides. Nevertheless, in the grounds dedicated to the battle, there is a conscious celebration of Scottish national identity, where the plucky, outnumbered Scots demonstrated the quality of their leadership, ingenuity and spirit (often expressed in egalitarian terms) against the socially and politically divided English army. A triumphant equestrian statue of Robert the Bruce, constructed in the 1960s, stands in the park surrounding the visitor centre, inscribed with references to Robert Burns' celebratory poem *Scots Wha Hae Wi' Wallace Bled*, which he wrote in 1793. The centre was refurbished in 2013, ahead of the much anticipated 700th anniversary of the battle (1314). Information about the battle is more consciously balanced in its presentation of the complex political situation of the Anglo-Scottish wars of the late thirteenth and fourteenth centuries and the ambiguous position of the protagonists.

Such contradictions are an integral part of memory and, arguably, are why we often see the creation of 'historical myths'. The word 'myth' has so many different meanings that it is often used without a clear definition. I would argue that 'myth' is best understood as a narrative that develops around an historical event or process when that narrative has a particular symbolic resonance for a group or society facing particular challenges. By creating and renewing a social group's 'collective memory' and imbuing it with mythical qualities, these problems can be tackled with a degree of unity – whether imposed or consensual. As the French anthropologist Claude Levi-Strauss has argued, the creation of myths is a defining aspect of what makes us human. Myths emerge as a way of creatively resolving social tensions by providing a coherent way of understanding the present in terms of the past: a past that simultaneously appears to be familiar and alien. Myths allow us to understand why the world is the way that it is.

Thus, myths form a key component in the creation of collective memory, as they can produce a popular understanding of the past that is deeply held, but are predicated on an unreflective acceptance of a partial or incomplete interpretation of the facts. For many historians, myth is simply a misleading 'untruth', whether deliberately fabricated or inadvertently misunderstood – an 'invented' history, as it were. For example, Henry Kamen's recent work *Imagining Spain: historical myth and national identity* argues that Spain's understanding of its fifteenth- and sixteenth-century history is riddled with misleading untruths, many of which were produced by the political struggles of the nineteenth and twentieth centuries. In *The Myth of Nations: the medieval origins of Europe*, Patrick Geary similarly argues that modern European nationalists' search for their nations' origins in the migrations that accompanied the collapse of the Western Roman Empire have led to specious reconstructions of the realities of Late Antiquity. Both Kamen and Geary argue that the mythical perspectives can be challenged and corrected by a more accurate reading of the historical record. This is certainly an important task, and one that this book has attempted to address, but, as an approach, it is limited as myths can provide us with important insights about the situation that led to their creation. The commitment to a mythical past cannot be denied: myths can have considerable power.

We can illustrate this better through two concrete examples. Two battles, whose transformation into 'myths' have been studied recently, are the siege of Masada in AD73 and the Battle of Kosovo in 1389. Masada was recorded by the Jewish historian Josephus Flavius, and became well known through several publications in Israel and across the West in the second half of the twentieth century. I learned about it at school through a library book. The story was typically presented in this way: Jewish freedom fighters (typically called 'zealots'), fleeing the sack of Jerusalem in AD70, hole up in the mountain fortress constructed by Herod the Great in the Dead Sea region and proceed to resist a besieging Roman army; the Romans spend several years building a ramp up the side of the mountain; with the ramp's imminent completion, the Jewish defenders realize that there is no escape, so, to avoid slavery and humiliation, they draw lots and ten men are chosen to kill all 960 defenders, including women and children, before killing themselves.

The site of Masada was identified by scholars in the 1830s, but only fully excavated between 1963 and 1965 by the Israeli archaeologist Yigal Yadin, with government support. Among the large numbers of structures excavated were two palaces, storerooms and a synagogue. There was plenty of evidence for fighting, such as sling stones and arrow-heads; several skeletons were also found and these were interpreted as Jews who had been killed in the fighting. A group found in a cave was identified as being from one family, and they were given a traditional Jewish re-burial in 1969. These excavations transfixed the Israeli public, many of whom volunteered in the excavations, and the apparent confirmation of Josephus' version led the story to become a key part of modern Israeli identity. Masada symbolized resistance in the face of persecution. 'Never again would Masada fall', became a key slogan for the Israeli Defence Force (IDF), and Moshe Dayan, one of the major Israeli military figures of the period, had all new armoured-unit recruits perform their swearing-in ceremony on top of the Masada massif.

Further research revealed inconsistencies in the evidence.[216] Josephus only mentioned one palace in his account, while the excavations showed that there were two at Masada, putting some doubt on the text's reliability. An omission in most narratives published from the 1930s onwards, including the famous account by Yigal Yadin himself, was that the defenders were a group called the *Sicarii* ('knife-men'), an extremist group that had fallen out with the Zealots, the main resistance movement in Judea at the time. The *Sicarii* were responsible for raids on local Jewish villages, including the slaughter of 700 women and children at Ein Gedi – a fact that had disappeared from Yadin's narrative. Closer study showed that Josephus' account was not at all sympathetic to the Jews, nor were the accounts of most of his contemporaries. The siege by the Roman Xth Legion probably lasted only a few months; the great siege ramp was largely made up of a naturally occurring spur of rock, and so not quite such an impressive feat of engineering legend, after all. Recent re-examination of the finds has also indicated that the twenty-eight bodies found by Yadin were probably not even Jewish. Even the 'family group' found in the cave appears now to have been made up of unrelated individuals, and may even have been Roman soldiers.

However, the 'Masada myth' did give Israelis of the post-1948 state a collective memory that provided a degree of cohesion and social integration amongst a disparate population with no tradition of political unity. Israel was a new country. The reason the excavations in the 1960s had such a resonance with the public was partly due to the nationalism that was being forged amongst Israelis in the 1950s onwards by political leaders such as David Ben-Gurion. Ben-Gurion was the Israeli prime minister (1955–63) and president (1948); he founded the IDF. The IDF's primary interest in Masada lay in how it could be used to legitimize arguments in favour of using violence in a secular Zionist context, as well as its relevance to Jewish religious identity, which stressed the continuity of the modern Israel from the biblical kingdoms. That such a respected scholar as Yadin could become a champion of this 'mythical' reading of the past is a striking illustration of the power of 'living history'. Indeed, this can also find strong parallels in the memory of the Battle of Kosovo (1389) for the Serbs.

The Battle of Kosovo was a major reason why Kosovo's fate became such a destabilizing factor in the Balkans during the late twentieth century, with political recognition for the Albanian majority being an anathema to the Serbian minority, given the importance of the site to the Serbian sense of nationhood. In 1999, a 53-year-old Serbian resident was quoted as saying, 'This is Serbian holy land. Our churches and our graves are like a stop sign to us, they don't let us leave here.'[217]

Kosovo not only became the last significant conflict of the civil wars that led to the collapse of Yugoslavia in the 1990s and culminated in military intervention by NATO in 1999, it was the location where Slobodan Milošević had first broken the post-war taboos laid down by the Yugoslavian President Tito and incited Serbian nationalist feelings as a way of manoeuvring himself into power.

The myth of Kosovo is particularly interesting, as the historical complexities of the actual battle are dwarfed by the subsequent myth that developed. The battle's religious overtones were bolstered by the description in later accounts of the Serbian warlord 'Prince Lazar' having faced defeat and death at the hands of the Turks in return for an eternity in the heavenly kingdom, thus underwriting Serbian nationhood forever. The cult of the dead leader was preserved in ten cycles of folk ballads created between 1390 and 1419. His bones were also preserved and, as late as 1988, were carried in a religious procession from one holy site to another in Serbia before being deposited in time for the 600th anniversary of the Battle of Kosovo, in the great Gračanica Monastery adjacent to the plain where the battle had been fought.

The representation of the battle as a catastrophic defeat for the Serbs by the Turks is rather misleading. The Serbs managed to avoid direct incorporation into Ottoman imperial structures until 1459. Some scholars have suggested that an earlier defeat in battle in 1371 was more significant strategically. What precisely occurred on the 'Field of the Blackbirds' has been drowned out by the poems and songs that emerged in the decades after the defeat, sustained by the support of the Serbian Orthodox Church. This culminated in the emergence of the 'Kosovo Covenant' during the nineteenth century, when the story was invested with Christian overtones. The battle also came to illustrate loyalty and betrayal in the contrasting roles of Miloš Obilić (or Kobilić) and Vuk Branković. Having been accused of planning to betray Lazar at a banquet before the battle, Obilić showed his commitment to the Serb cause by killing Sultan Murad in his tent after pretending to join the Ottoman side, thus condemning himself to death. Branković changed sides and betrayed the Serbian cause, establishing a reputation that sees him even today in Serbia represent an archetype as a 'negative character, a slanderer, defiler and traitor'. The Christianization of the battle has led to portrayals of Lazar's banquet to assume features of the Last Supper of Christ and for Branković to become viewed as a Judas figure.

These mythical narratives have a range of common features. Their religious symbolism ensures that the stories contain a strong sense of the sacred. They are also didactic: myths provide moral lessons for the society or community they serve, demanding a response from the recipient. Masada (and Kosovo) taught Israelis (and Serbs) that their nascent state in the twentieth century was highly vulnerable; as such, the state would need considerable personal commitment from its people if their divinely ordained traditions were to be preserved and their ancestors had not died in vain. Both myths were given additional power by being associated with a specific site: Masada, for Israelis; Kosovo, for Serbs. These myths also take a consciously selective approach to the way the main events are presented, with inconvenient details disregarded and the broader historical context largely ignored. In both the Israeli and Serbian cases, the narratives are morally simplified, with the two sides involved representing 'good' and 'evil'.

In comparison, the Battle of Hastings seems less impressive as a myth. Avishai Margalit has argued that the battle should not be compared with Kosovo at all, given that it plays a marginal role in

British history and its existence is confined to the history books.[218] Margalit points out that while Kosovo and Hastings were both major defeats, the implications for England were far less serious than they were for Serbia. Hastings was:

> more a war of succession to a childless king than a conquest by an alien force – much like the ascension of William of Orange [to the British throne] in 1688.[219]

Margalit goes on to argue that the consequences of the Norman Conquest were actually beneficial for the English in terms of 'better institutions, more law and order and an end to internal strife'. Russell Hardin, when discussing social identity and the way this is formed by notions of a collective memory, noted that 'the English seem to be exempt from the effects of the dreadful memories of Hastings'.[220]

I completely disagree with Margalit and would argue that the Battle of Hastings is as mythical as Kosovo, if in a less visceral way. Leaving aside the question of how much value exists in a crudely comparative approach, the differences between Hastings and the two examples of Masada and Kosovo can be explained by the relatively recent creation of the Israeli and Serb states. As new countries emerging out of complex post-colonial situations, it was inevitable that they would reach back to a distant past to avoid the problematic issue that in more recent centuries their populations existed in different, multi-cultural, political contexts. England's relatively stable history and the time that has passed since 1066 means that the Hastings myth has become less intense as the trauma of the event recedes into the past.

It should also be noted that the views of Margalit and Hardin reflect the concerns of the 1990s, when these authors were writing. As such, both reflect the optimistic liberal consensus that emerged in the aftermath of the Cold War. This predicted that nationalism and the nation state were becoming obsolete and would be replaced by supranational political bodies and a globalized economy. Subsequent events have proved this to be Panglossian. Ultimately, in the long term, the liberal consensus may, indeed, be correct in its predictions, but in the short term, the future is less predictable.

The persistence of the Battle of Hastings' mythical qualities were shown when it re-emerged from the school-books into the national debate via newspapers during the rancorous preliminaries and bitter aftermath of the Brexit referendum (23 June 2016). At a moment when Britain's geographical, class and cultural divisions were being starkly exposed, Hastings became a lens through which contemporary society sought to understand and justify its future direction by referencing the past. Ed West, writing in *The Spectator* in October that year, reflected the conservative magazine's perspective by explicitly comparing the Normans with the stereotype of those who supported the 'Remain' position: economically sophisticated and civilized, but ultimately entitled, privileged and thus remote from the deeper, integral aspects of 'English' character such as notions of freedom.[221]

Daniel Hannan, a leading theorist of the movement that wished to leave the European Union, argued in the *Daily Telegraph* that the Battle of Hastings should not be commemorated at all, given the destructive consequences for Britain of the arrival of an exploitative and oppressive foreign aristocracy that destroyed the Anglo-Saxon achievements of liberty and equality before the law.[222] For those who had argued that Britain's future lay with remaining within the European Union, the notion that Brexit represented a redress for the Battle of Hastings could be rejected as an illusion. Stewart Lee, a satirical comedian and journalist, responded to Hannan's arguments by suggesting (rather caustically) that this narrow focus on the insular origins of England and Britain was yet another re-writing of the past in the articulation of a new 'origin myth' for a post-Brexit world, in which outside influences (in this case, French) would be cast as detrimental.[223] Ironically, this occurred exactly fifty years earlier when the famous medievalist Sir Richard Southern had linked 1066 to England's anticipated entry into the then Common Market, in his famous Creighton Lecture.

This has been a re-articulation of an older aspect of the 'Hastings myth', which is to reflect and explain the state of Anglo-European or, more specifically, Anglo-French, relations. This can be traced to the first half of the fourteenth century when tensions grew between France and England in the run-up to the Hundred Years War and English chroniclers began to present Hastings as a national tragedy that was never to be repeated. Robert Mannyng, writing between 1327 and 1338, bewailed the oppressive government that would once again befall England if William the Conqueror's victory at Hastings were to happen again. This was in the context of royal demands for parliamentary taxation to pay for Edward III's military expeditions to France and a perceived threat of French invasion. During the English Reformation of the sixteenth century, writers such as William Tyndale came to present William of Normandy's victory at Hastings, under a papal banner, as being symbolic of the imposition of papal authority onto the Anglo-Saxon Church. This unwarranted alien interference, according to the historical revisionism that accompanied Henry VIII's break with Rome, represented the destruction of an ecclesiastical apostolic tradition that had practised Erastianism (state control of the clergy) and, thus, was an historical outrage in need of correction. In 2008, there were for calls for the Bayeux Tapestry to be returned to England on the grounds that the embroiderers were from Canterbury, something that is suspected but not proven. Thus, Duke William and his Norman followers have a venerable tradition of being portrayed as the 'them' in an 'us-and-them' mentality.

However, myths can also be contradictory and, while they must be internally coherent, different myths can co-exist. Changing circumstances can also allow society to reconcile itself with a new reality that requires a fresh narrative. William's victory at Hastings has not always been seen in antagonistic terms, but it has become integral to a notion of Englishness and a positive aspect of British history. The mid-thirteenth-century chronicler of St Alban's, Matthew Paris, had no problem seeing 1066 as a positive part of his English identity and portraying Harold as the problem: describing him as being rash, untrustworthy and self-confident in contrast to William, who was 'great-hearted in the business of war, circumspect, faithful to his word, sociable and cheerful in peace'. Similarly, during the Renaissance, English authors maintained this view. Polydore Vergil, an Italian writing in an English milieu, presented William as a law-giver and the Saxons as being rebellious and inimical to good order. In 1520, during the negotiations at the Field of Cloth of Gold between King Henry VIII of England and King Francis II of France, the English delegation put forward a proposal to canonize William the Conqueror as a way of symbolizing the two countries' diplomatic rapprochement. The importance of Hastings has been enshrined in the History national curriculum for English and Welsh secondary schools since its introduction in the 1980s, which is quite remarkable given the bitter debates that emerged over which historical events should be included, why history was being taught, and its relationship to enshrine 'British values'.[224]

It is important to acknowledge that the Battle of Hastings' mythical nature is also deeply intertwined with the broader issues of the Norman Conquest itself. The most famous 'myth' that developed around the Conquest was the 'Norman Yoke'.[225] Derived from phrases used by the twelfth-century historians Orderic Vitalis and Geoffrey of Monmouth when referring to the subjection of the English by their conquerors, this myth reached its most powerful expression during the English Civil War in the seventeenth century. The political challenges to the 'tyranny' of the Stuart monarchy by groups such as the Levellers were based on the argument that Anglo-Saxon England had been a proto-democratic society and that Englishmen (women were generally absent from these debates) had lost their freedoms to an oppressive system of 'feudal' government introduced by the victorious Normans. Although this view is now largely discredited, the power of the myth still percolates debates about the past today, in terms of whether the Conquest was a 'good' or a 'bad' thing.

While Margalit is correct to suggest that the debates over the Battle of Hastings and the Norman Conquest lost their visceral political significance after the eighteenth century, they remain a key part of mythical cultural notions of 'Englishness'. The creation of professional historical study in the nineteenth century helped to transform the discussion into a more technical debate over the relative strengths and weaknesses of the Norman and Anglo-Saxon societies, as discussed in Chapter 2. However, there was a strong element of whether Hastings was a 'Norman triumph' or an 'English tragedy'. E.A. Freeman's famous account of the battle, published in 1873, was written as a panegyric to the bravery and skill of King Harold and his English soldiers and their embodiment of ancient Teutonic warrior traditions and individual valour, while crediting underhand Norman tactics and bad luck for the result.[226] Freeman's views were eventually discredited in the 1890s by J.H. Round, who challenged his antagonist's reconstruction of the battle and sympathies. For Round, the English defeat was partly self-inflicted by:

> anarchical excess of liberty, the want of a strong centralized
> system, the absorption in party strife, the belief that politics are
> statesmanship, and that oratory will save a people.[227]

From our vantage point in the twenty-first century, we can see that such debates probably reflect the tensions of Victorian Britain as it dealt with the reverberations of social and economic change created by the Industrial Revolution and its political legacy in the enfranchisement of the new working class and the creation of mass participation in politics. As so often, these arguments led to the creation of a 'mythical' past.

This did not necessarily mean that the twentieth-century debate became more sober and restrained: the Battle of Hastings could also act as a proxy for contemporary concerns, deeply tinged by national and class anxieties. It could easily be suggested that the elite Norman mounted warrior, who had embraced the new cultural and technological world of chivalry, was destined to triumph over the obsolete infantry tactics of the plucky, democratic, but tradition-obsessed, English. For some, the battle was more a tragedy, as England lost many of its unique cultural attributes in a single cataclysm. The experience of World War II and the threat of invasion by Germany in 1940 also helped to revive the battle's memory. Hastings became important because it symbolized the last successful invasion of England, and was compared to 1588 and 1805 as years when Britain stood up to the invasion of a European power. The year 1066 became a symbol of the longevity of Britain's invulnerability. This re-emergence of the Hastings myth can be seen on the monument that stands in the British war cemetery at Bayeux, which contains the remains of those soldiers who fell during the Battle of Normandy in 1944. The monument has the following Latin inscription:

NOS A GULIELMO VICTI VICTORIS PATRIAM
LIBERAVIMVS
We, who were conquered by William, have liberated the homeland
of the Conqueror

The popularity of the battlefield at Battle Abbey demonstrates how the site has become a monument to England's national history (*see* Table 3). The recent 950th anniversary of Hastings saw an upturn in interest, and it remains one of English Heritage's most popular sites, entirely on the basis of its historical significance – there is nothing spectacular to see! Recent challenges to the accuracy of its location could be said to be an expression of a wider cultural phenomenon increasingly common throughout the second half of the twentieth and twenty-first centuries: an increasing rejection of the authority of established authorities, and a challenge to the 'myths' those authorities have perpetuated. Nick Austin has been particularly vocal in his belief that English Heritage has arrogantly refused to engage with his objections. Certainly, the desire to challenge popular misconceptions as 'myths' is a method beloved by scholars over the same period: the challenge to the 'Masada myth' was part of a wider movement of revisionist Israeli historians working in the 1990s onwards who challenged previous generations' understanding of the past. While this book has tried to show that the arguments against the traditional location of the Battle of Hastings are essentially negative and based on the absence of any conclusive material evidence for fighting at the traditional site, these alternative views have received extensive media coverage as they resonate so strongly with the public. The quest to find the 'authentic' site is evidence for the persistent strength of the

Table 3 Visitor numbers at Battle Abbey and battlefield site
(Source: English Heritage)

Year	Visitor numbers
2012/13	117,289
2013/14	113,650
2014/15	112,425
2015/16	108,834
2016/17	134,590

'Hastings myth', not its weakness. Austin used his arguments for the battle having been fought at Crowhurst as part of his opposition to the extension of the A259 link road around Hastings, arguing that the work would destroy valuable evidence of such an important battle.[228]

While much of our engagement with the Battle of Hastings is shaped by the myths that have emerged across the centuries, it is also important to emphasize how early the myth developed and how fundamentally this has shaped the information with which we engage in an attempt to understand the battle. The first generation of English that lived through the immediate aftermath of the battle and its consequences were so traumatized by the event that they marginalized its memory. This can be seen in the way that Hastings is almost ignored in the *Anglo-Saxon Chronicle*, where we find only a few terse comments about what occurred. It is difficult to be certain about when these were written. Version D was updated until 1100, while Version E continued to be compiled at Peterborough Abbey until 1154; nevertheless, there is a good chance that both versions' comments on Hastings were composed in the immediate aftermath of the Norman victory. The one English source we know that is strictly contemporary with the battle is the *Vita Ædwardi* ('Life of King Edward'), which was written for Edward's widow, Queen Edith, who lost three brothers (including Harold) and whose family was ruined – even so, remarkably the event is only vaguely hinted at in the work.

On the other hand, the Normans living in the aftermath of 1066 wrote from a position of triumph, while also having to deal with a major deficit of legitimacy. As we have argued, William launched an aggressive invasion of conquest, for which he sought clerical support by claiming a 'just war' on account of Harold's moral failings, most clearly illustrated by Harold's supposed perjury in breaking his oath. As a result of his invasion, William had killed an anointed monarch and been responsible for a degree of slaughter that had shocked contemporaries. The first decade of the Conquest had seen a series of rebellions put down with occasional brutality and the death, exile and execution of what remained of the Anglo-Saxon aristocracy, such as the earls Edwin, Morcar and Waltheof. In the midst of this, great swathes of land had been seized by William's followers through a mixture of royal grants of dispossessed estates, extortion and intimidation. To put the legacy of conquest into some form of legal and moral order, William had to ensure that the past was re-ordered. There can be no doubt that William believed in the divine justification of his cause, as was 'proved' by his spectacular victory against the odds at Hastings.

This led to a systematic campaign of quasi-legal arguments over Harold's behaviour that shaped his entire reign. The legal uncertainty of William's position is revealed by the way both William of Jumièges and William of Poitiers present the story of Harold's perjury and his ignoring of Edward the Confessor's wishes, which serves only to emphasize William's justification for his claim to the English throne. George Garnett has shown how this claim underpinned the whole conquest and the subsequent land-holding of the new aristocracy that almost completely replaced the old Anglo-Saxon elite, which explains the attempt to present the battle as a rightful king taking his inheritance in the face of rebellion.[229] This culminated in Domesday Book, where a new chronological framework was created: the time of King Edward (*tempus regis Edwardi*). The Domesday commissioners surveyed England and collected information relating to the landowner situation on the death of King Edward (6 January 1066), which was used to compare with the situation in 1086. Harold's kingship by this stage had disappeared from the historical record: he was now simply Earl Harold. Our view of the battle from the Norman perspective is thus entirely shaped by William's narrative of legitimate succession.

This absence of any detailed contemporary accounts of the battle in the English sources endured for several decades until a second generation emerged at the turn of the twelfth century. These authors saw the beginning of a cultural and, in some cases, genetic fusion between English and Norman identities. Monastic authors, such as Eadmer, John of Worcester and William of Malmesbury, began to try to salvage what they could of their Anglo-Saxon heritage and this took the form of additions to the earlier entries to the *Anglo-Saxon Chronicle*. They took a theological approach and rationalized Hastings as being divine punishment for English sins.[230] This moralizing approach was a crucial aspect of the construction of the battle's history and its mythology, giving it a sacred and didactic role.

Some forty or so years after the Battle of Hastings, Eadmer, a monk of Anglo-Saxon descent based at Canterbury, wrote in his *Historia novorum in Anglia* ('A History of Recent Events in England'):

> Of that battle [Hastings] the French who took part in it do to this day declare that, although fortune swayed now on this side and now on that, yet of the Normans so many were slain or put to flight that the victory which they had gained is truly and without any doubt to be attributed to nothing else than the miraculous intervention of God, who, by so punishing Harold's wicked perjury, showed that He is not a God who has any pleasure in wickedness.

This view became firmly established in the next generation, as can be seen in the works of authors such as Henry of Huntingdon. Henry, an English priest of Norman descent, wrote his *Historia Anglorum* ('History of the English') in the 1120s and 1130s:

> In the year of grace 1066, the Lord, the ruler, brought to completion what he had long planned for the English nation. He delivered them up for destruction by the violent men and cunning Norman people.

For all their spiritual virtues, these gloomy accounts failed to add much detail about the battle. Elisabeth van Houts has commented on the significance of a failure of this generation of monastic authors to focus in any detail on the fallen at Hastings (aside from Harold and his two brothers).[231] As already noted in Chapter 3, we are shockingly ill-informed about the identities of the Anglo-Saxon army, given that monasteries were typically scrupulous in recording the names of the deceased for liturgical commemoration, especially from the elite landowning class who made up the Church's key patrons and who would have formed the bulk of Harold's army. This would appear to hint at a feeling of loss and shame, which had personal, institutional and national dimensions. By seeing the battle as an act of divine punishment for national sins, it was possible for this generation of authors to de-personalize this feeling and, to some extent, anaesthetize the trauma that was still being felt.

Around the 1120s, the emotional resonance surrounding the Battle of Hastings changed as the last living witnesses to the events of 1066 died, leading many literate members of society to become aware of the need to preserve oral traditions in the written record. We can see this in works such as the *Brevis Relatio*, which deals with the foundation story of Battle Abbey, or the slightly later *Waltham Abbey Chronicle* (written *c.* 1177), which records the story of Harold's burial in the abbey church. The author of the *Waltham Abbey Chronicle* based his recollections on earlier conversations with the 80-year-old Turkill, who had been sacristan of the abbey in 1066. Significantly, the treatment of the battle's memory moved beyond narrow monastic concerns and became a matter of interest to the secular descendants of the French aristocracy, now busy forging a new sense of English past for themselves, prompting the memory of Hastings to become a burning topic for many of the historians of the twelfth century. Accounts of the battle become more detailed in some cases than those found within the *Carmen de Hastingae Proelio* and the works of William of Poitiers. The writing of the history of 1066 in Old French rather than Latin by authors such as Gaimar and Wace show the secular and vernacular forging of a new English identity. Wace's *Roman de Rou*, written during the 1170s, suggests an increased interest in the history of the Battle of Hastings, albeit in the Cotentin region of Normandy; this illustrates how the memory of the battle was becoming less emotionally charged and more a matter of military interest.

This different context saw the myths that surrounded Hastings change – most strikingly, in the transformation of Harold's reputation. The first generation of Normans ensured that he was first vilified as the usurper and perjurer whose defeat was clear proof of William's divine favour. The English sources were less hostile, though there were mixed feelings about Harold, and he was judged through the consequences of his actions. As discussed in Chapter 6, the official silence surrounding Harold's fate led to several contradictory accounts emerging, though the construction of Battle Abbey's altar on the spot where he fell seems to reflect a semi-official approval. The story of the 'arrow in the eye' emerged from this polemical tradition. However, from the mid-twelfth century onwards, a more favourable interpretation of Harold emerges in several works. This consciously favourable view of Harold can be seen in the *Waltham Abbey Chronicle*:

> Elected king by unanimous consent, for there was no one in the
> land more knowledgeable, more vigorous in arms, wiser in the laws
> of the land or more highly regarded for his prowess of every kind.
> So those who had been his chief enemies up to this time could not
> oppose this election, for England had not given birth to a man as
> distinguished as he in all respects to undertake such a task.

This favourable treatment of Harold is perhaps no surprise, given the patronage that Harold lavished on the Church, but it does show how his reputation had recovered by the late twelfth century in parts of the English consciousness.

More surprisingly, is the positive portrayal of Harold in Gaimar's *Estoire des Engleis*, which was written at some point in the late 1130s in Old French vernacular. Unlike the earlier ecclesiastical contexts of history writing, Gaimar's history was written for an Anglo-Norman secular aristocratic milieu in the form of his patron, Constance de Vertuz. Constance had family connections on both sides of the English Channel. Normans and English are not distinguished in Gaimar's account, as is appropriate for an audience for whom a dual identity was now accepted. In Gaimar's telling, Harold becomes a tragic figure whose problem at Hastings was caused by the losses at Fulford Gate and Stamford Bridge. Rather than re-packaging the Norman propaganda of William of Poitiers that Harold was being punished for his perfidy, Gaimar saw Harold as an instrument of divine justice. His account of Hastings also reads as almost an epic of Harold, who dominates the narrative (whereas William scarcely gets a mention). The brave fighting defeat of Harold and his brothers is strongly resonant of the *Song of Roland*, the great medieval *chanson de geste* beloved by the medieval aristocracy. In this epic poem, the eponymous hero fights a brave rearguard action against his Muslim foes, alongside his heroic companions Oliver and Archbishop Turpin, before his glorious death sees his soul transported to Heaven.

Gaimar's ambiguity over the fate of Harold is another strange feature of the work. While Gyrth and Leofwine's death are explicitly mentioned, Harold's is not. There is a parallel with the tales of King Arthur, which gained popularity at the same time (most famously in the work of Geoffrey of Monmouth): Arthur was believed to be in a state of immortal sleep, waiting to be awoken when his country needed him. This ambiguity surrounding Harold's fate is also present in the famous *Life of Harold*, written around 1205 and again associated with Waltham Abbey.[232] This famously records that Harold survived Hastings, was cured by a Saracen woman and, after a fruitless attempt to build an alliance against William in Scandinavia, converted to a religious life, embarking on several pilgrimages to the tombs of the apostles before returning to England to live as a hermit, first at Dover and then on the Welsh border. Harold throughout is portrayed as a holy individual: his conversion is not the result of his fate at Hastings, nor was the battle a punishment for the English king – these events were all part of God's mysterious will. This was the most complete expression of a tradition that had emerged in the twelfth century. The Cistercian abbot Ailred of Rievaulx, writing a life of Edward the Confessor in the early 1160s, wrote:

> In that same year, Harold himself, despoiled of the English realm, either died wretchedly or, as some people think, fled to live in penitence.

While this is undoubtedly legendary, with no basis in truth, this was the reverse of the tradition expressed most clearly by William of Malmesbury, who presented Harold's death as a just punishment for the moral decline that ensued after his seizure of the throne. Harold's death by arrow was part of a moralizing trajectory in Malmesbury's narrative, explicitly contrasted with Duke William, who was pointedly untouched by anything despite the hail of missiles – a clear sign of divine protection. While it seems to be drawn from a different mind-set to that of William of Malmesbury, the *Life of Harold* actually shares many crucial attitudes. Harold does not survive to lead a guerrilla war of resistance or national liberation, but accepts God's judgment and becomes a hermit, a common figure in the medieval English landscape. *The Life of Harold* shows that while Harold did not physically die at Hastings, though he was *semi necem* ('half-dead'), he experienced a political death, which is best symbolized by his broken standard, an obvious sign that the old English power was broken at this battle. The story of Harold's survival and acceptance of God's judgment is, therefore, an example of a myth of reconciliation, in that Harold became one of the means by which the peoples from across both sides of the channel could forge a common identity: local saints.[233]

While William of Malmesbury's account of Harold's fate remains the central myth of Hastings, given that the 'arrow in the eye' is one of the most commonly recognizable aspects of the battle amongst the general public, there is a contradictory tradition that has continued to re-emerge to challenge William's 'semi-official' version. During the twelfth century, there was some suggestion that Harold had been transformed into a saint – a claim developed by Harold's monastic foundation at Waltham Abbey in Essex. Since 2004, King Harold Day, a medieval festival aimed at highlighting the king's links with Waltham, has been held annually on the nearest Saturday to the anniversary of the battle. Harold's myth still has legs. With the discovery of Richard III in a Leicester car park, a quest for other English kings began. Peter Burke, a local historian in Waltham, claimed that the *Vita*

Haroldi's account was true, and the king had escaped the battle. After performing a geophysical scan in 2014 revealed an unmarked grave, Burke worked with a documentary crew the next year to try to obtain permission to exhume the body and prove that another man had been placed in Harold's grave.[234] This not the first time that Harold's tomb has been 'discovered': in 1954, the remains of a wealthy and physically elderly man from the eleventh century were located at Holy Trinity Church in Bosham. These remains have been attributed to Harold on the grounds that Harold had close family links with the town and would have worshipped at the church. Permission has not been granted at the point of writing, and is unlikely to be (according to locals), but in some ways the continuing mystery probably serves the story better.

Thus, the Battle of Hastings has continued to be fought over and over again ever since that fateful evening of 14 October 1066. A series of myths developed in the immediate aftermath of the battle, which, while they have changed over the centuries, have never completely lost their symbolic and didactic power.

CHAPTER 10

Conclusion

In Britain, on 5 June 1956, a television programme was broadcast about the Battle of Hastings. The programme included members of the Surrey Walking Society dressed like members of the Saxon *fyrd* during their 20-mile march across the Fosseway. Various re-enactments have occurred on the site since 1984. In 1989, there were only a few hundred participants, but the event has become more and more popular over the last two decades. In 2016, over 2,000 re-enactors took part at the event held on the 950th anniversary of the battle. The international flavour was much broader than the original battle, with an Antipodean William the Conqueror and participants from Russia, America, Poland, Australia, France and the Czech Republic, amongst others. The re-enactment is the largest and most important event in the medieval re-enactment calendar because the battle continues to be treated as such an iconic event.

This illustrates how the story of the battle continues to exert a strong control over the collective memory as an event of national importance. The obscurity of what happened at the battle has also created considerable space in which alternative narratives can be created and aspirations can be projected onto the battle. The enthusiasm of the re-enactors is primarily channelled into the attempt to achieve authenticity, and political opinions are seen as having little place in the experience. It has been suggested that those who choose to fight as Anglo-Saxons have a degree of romanticized enthusiasm for the losing side. Then again, if a re-enactor owns a horse, they will be asked to join the Norman side. The fact that the crowds at the Hastings re-enactment cheer for the Anglo-Saxons and have to be prompted to acknowledge William's victory, albeit with grudging enthusiasm, shows how the views of the battle continue to be shaped by present notions of national identity and how these are transposed on the past.

The year 1066 was a defining date in English history, but this is much to do with how it has been remembered as with historical reality. Harold is often referred to as 'the last English king', and his death at Hastings is usually a chronological *caesura*: when we discuss the royal dynasties of England, it usually runs from King William I to Queen Elizabeth II. The defeat at Hastings saw the end of a dominant Anglo-Danish aristocracy and its replacement by a northern French elite. The centre of cultural gravity moved from Scandinavia to mainland Europe. The problem is that this view of decisive turning points is also deeply misleading. Referring to Harold as an 'Anglo-Saxon' is to use a term that would have made no sense to the man himself, and encourages a belief that 'English' history begins in 1066 when, of course, it most certainly did not. Many of the linguistic features of Middle English, whose distinction from Old English is often attributed to what happened at Hastings, were actually present beforehand. The great expansion of western Frankish culture across the rest of Western Europe, both in England before Hastings and across the continent afterwards without conquest (such as Iceland, where the written sagas were heavily shaped by French models), shows that the trajectory of English history would not necessarily have been that different if Harold had won. Both armies that faced each other on that October morning were products of similar social developments.

In the introduction, we outlined the problems of establishing 'exactly what happened' in the past. This book has tried to show how many aspects of the Battle of Hastings remain fundamentally uncertain and even unknowable. Many aspects were hidden, such as Harold's fate, which encouraged speculation and editorializing to fill the information vacuum on such an important manner, as it does today whenever we cannot know what we want to. William himself, in his attempts to justify his conquest in the court of contemporary opinion as well as posterity, encouraged a partial reading of events, which may be fabrication or wishful thinking on his part. The problem is that the concern for 'truth' in terms of knowing 'what happened' has only really been a concern of historians since the nineteenth century: it was not as much of an issue for medieval historians, for whom a 'deeper truth' was more important. History was the working out of God's plan for mankind, thus human events were as much a matter for theological speculation as historical explanation. Later generations took the little information that survived and have tried to re-arrange it in a way that suited their particular interpretational agendas, leaving us hopelessly removed from being able to understand what really occurred. However, this has not been a crude exercise in nihilistic reductionism. One of the most interesting aspects of studying the past is not simply uncovering facts, but understanding the complex ways how we remember it. The debate over the battlefield shows how the myth persists and the debate goes on, each generation imposing its own concerns onto this powerful story.

Notes

INTRODUCTION

1. Brownlie, S., *Memory and Myths of the Norman Conquest* (2013), pp. 37–8.
2. Ritchie, R.L.G., *The Normans in Scotland* (1954), pp. v, 177, 179.
3. Brownlie, *Memory and Myths of the Norman Conquest*, pp. 39–40.
4. Given-Wilson, C., *Chronicles: the Writing of History in Medieval England* (2004), pp. 2–3.
5. *See*, for example, the range of recent books: Pastan, E.C., White, S.D. & Gilbert, K. (eds), *The Bayeux Tapestry and its Contexts: a reassessment* (Boydell Press, 2014); Lewis, M.J., Owen-Crocker, G.R. & Terkla, D. (eds), *The Bayeux Tapestry: new approaches: proceedings of a conference at the British Museum* (Oxbow, 2011); Foys, M.K., Overbey, K.E. & Terkla, D. (eds), *The Bayeux Tapestry: new interpretations* (2009).

CHAPTER 1: DEFENDING THE CHURCH

6. This analogy is explicitly used by Ian Sharman in *News, Propaganda and Spin in Medieval England* (Dovecote Renaissance, 2000).
7. Croce's dictum that 'All history is modern history' can be taken too far!
8. See Habermas, J., *The Structural Transformation of the Public Sphere: An Inquiry into a Category of Bourgeois Society* (Polity Press, 1989). Habermas argues that 'public sphere' is the informal voluntary public space in civil society where private middle-class individuals join in groups and become involved in 'critical' and 'reasoned' discourse about common issues, and formulate conceptions of the common good in order to influence the process of state decision-making. Habermas believes this was historically specific to developing Capitalist, democratic societies in the West during the eighteenth and nineteenth centuries.
9. *See*, for example, the Roman emperor Augustus, as outlined in Clark, M.D.H., *Augustus, First Roman Emperor: Power, Propaganda and the Politics of Survival: Power and Propaganda in Augustan Rome* (Bristol Phoenix Press, 2010).
10. *See*, for example, Carlson, D.R., *John Gower: poetry and propaganda in fourteenth-century England* (Boydell & Brewer, 2012).
11. Leyser, K., 'The Polemics of the Papal Revolution', in Leyser, K., *Medieval Germany and its Neighbours 900–1250* (1982), pp. 138–160.
12. Lifshitz, F., 'The *Encomium Emmae Reginae*: A Political Pamphlet of the Eleventh Century?' *Haskins Society Journal* 1 (1989), pp. 39–51.
13. Jowett, G. & O'Donnell, V., *Propaganda and Persuasion*, 4th edn (Sage, 2006).

14. Glassner, J.-J., *Mesopotamian Chronicles* (Society of Biblical Literature, 2004), pp. 108–9.

15. Barlow, F., *Edward the Confessor* (Yale University Press, 1997), pp. 48–9.

16. Whitelock, D., Douglas, D.C., Tucker, S. (eds), *The Anglo-Saxon Chronicle: A Revised Translation* (Eyre and Spottiswoode, 1961), pp. 120–1.

17. In Douglas, D.C., *William the Conqueror* (Yale University Press, 1964), pp. 55–69, Douglas argues that William was too busy, but Sten Körner argues that, on the contrary, William would have had time: *see* Körner, S., *The Battle of Hastings, England and Europe, 1035–1066* (CWK Gleerup, 1964), pp. 158–65.

18. Both Frank Barlow, in Barlow, F., *Edward the Confessor* (1997), and Pauline Stafford, in Stafford, P., *Unification & Conquest: a political & social history of England in the tenth & eleventh centuries* (Edward Arnold, 1989) are very sceptical. Eric John argues that Edward did intend to make William his heir: *see* John, E., 'Edward the Confessor and the Norman Succession', *The English Historical Review* Vol. 94, No. 371 (Apr, 1979), pp. 241–67.

19. Baxter, S., 'Edward the Confessor and the Succession Question', in Mortimer, R. (ed.), *Edward the Confessor, The Man and the Legend* (2009), pp. 77–118.

20. Darlington, R.R. & McGurk, P. (eds), Bray, J. & McGurk, P. (tr.), *The Chronicle of John of Worcester* (Clarendon Press, 1995), pp. 600–1.

21. Grierson, P., 'A visit of Earl Harold to Flanders in 1056', *English Historical Review*, LI (1936), pp. 90–7.

22. Douglas, D.C., *William the Conqueror: the Norman Impact upon England* (1999).

23. Bachrach, D.S., *Religion and the Conduct of War, c. 300–1215* (2003), p. 66.

24. Maylis, B., 'Norman Architecture around the year 1000: its place in the art of Western Europe', *Anglo-Norman Studies XXII* (1999), pp. 1–28.

25. Douglas, *William the Conqueror: the Norman impact upon England*, pp. 153–4.

26. Leyser, K., 'The Polemics of the Papal Revolution', in Leyser, *Medieval Germany and its Neighbours 900–1250*, pp. 138–60.

27. An example of this is Sigebert of Gembloux, whose 'Apology against those who challenge the masses of married priests' was written after 1075 where Pope Gregory VII's Lenten synod argued that people should not accept the offices of married clergy. This was hugely controversial, especially as the definition of simony that Gregory used was much more extreme than most conventional clergy were prepared to accept. The text implies the debate occurred amongst other lower social classes and not just amongst the literate elite: 'What else is talked about in women's spinning rooms and the artisans' workshops than the confusion of all human laws ... sudden unrest amongst the populace, new treacheries of servants against their masters and masters' mistrust of their servants, abject breaches of faith among friends and equals, conspiracies against the power ordained by God? And all this backed by authority by those who are called the leaders of Christendom.'

28. *See*, for example, Dudley, L., *Information Revolutions in the History of the West* (Edward Elgar, 2008), p. 61.

29. In Crouch, D., *The Image of the Aristocracy in Britain 1000–1300* (Routledge, 1992), p. 138, David Crouch expresses some passing scepticism: 'The papal banner supposedly sent to William the Conqueror on the eve of his expedition to England.'

30. Bennett, M., 'Poetry as history? The Roman de Rou of Wace as a source for the Norman Conquest', *Anglo-Norman Studies* 5 (1983), p. 28.

31. Crisp, C., 'Hastings and Jerusalem', *The Coat of Arms* 1 (1975), pp. 148–9.

32. *See* Chapter 6 'The Arrow in the Eye' for further discussion.

33. Morton, C., 'Pope Alexander II and the Norman Conquest', *Latomus* xxxiv (1975), pp. 362–8.

34. Stroll, M., *Popes and Antipopes: the politics of eleventh-century Church reform* (2011), p. 121.

35. Daniell, C., *From Norman Conquest to Magna Carta: England 1066–1215* (Routledge, 2003), pp. 136–7.

36. Smith, M.F., 'Archbishop Stigand and the Eye of the Needle', *Anglo Norman Studies* XVI (1993), pp. 199–220.

37. Cowdrey, H.E.J., *Pope Gregory VII* (Clarendon Press, 1998), p. 650.

38. 'Not that I desired the destruction or planned the death of any of the Normans or of any men, but that those who do not dread the judgements of heaven might at least come to their senses through the fear of men.' Anonymous, *The Life of Pope Leo IX* II.20 in Robinson, I.S., *The Papal Reform of the Eleventh Century: Lives of Pope Leo IX and Pope Gregory VII* (Manchester University Press: Manchester, 2004) p. 150.

39. Southern, R.W., *Western Society and the Church in the Middle Ages* (Penguin, 1970), p. 41.

40. Tyerman, C., *God's War* (Penguin, 2007), pp. 59–61.

41. van Houts, E.M.C., 'The Norman Conquest Through European Eyes', *The English Historical Review* 110 (1995), pp. 832–53.

42. Gillingham, J., 'William the Bastard at War', in Harper-Bill, C., *et al.* (eds), *Studies in Medieval History Presented to R. Allen Brown* (Boydell Press, 1989), pp. 141–58.

43. Morillo, S., 'Contrary Winds: Theories of History and the Limits of Sachkritik,' in M. Ragnow (ed.), *The Medieval Way of War Festschrift for Bernard Bachrach* (2015), pp. 205–22.

CHAPTER 2: THERE'LL ALWAYS BE AN ENGLAND

44. Anderson, B., *Imagined Communities* (Verso, 1991).

45. Gellner, E., *Nations and Nationalism* (Blackwell, 1983).

46. Gat, A., *Nations: the long history and deep roots of political ethnicity and nationalism* (Cambridge University Press, 2013).

47. Fukuyama, F., *The End of History and the Last Man* (1992).

48. Breuilly, J., 'Dating the Nation: How Old is an Old Nation?', in Ichijo, A. & Uzelac, G. (eds), *When is the Nation: Towards an Understanding of Theories of Nationalism* (2005), pp. 15–39.

49. Wormald, P., 'Bede, the Bretwaldas and the origins of the *gens anglorum*', in Wormald, P. (ed.), *Ideal and Reality in the Frankish World* (Blackwell, 1983), pp. 99–129.

50. *See* a charter of Burgred of Mercia dated 855 by which he granted the minster at Blockley to the church of Worcester, freeing it from various obligations including that of lodging all mounted men of the English race (*& ealra angelcynnes monna*) and foreigners.

51. Foot, S., 'The Making of Angelcynn: English identity before the Norman Conquest', *Transactions of the Royal Historical Society*, Vol. 6 (1996), pp. 25–49.

52. Stafford, P., *Unification & Conquest: a political & social history of England in the tenth & eleventh centuries*.

53. For an outline of the debate, *see* Richards, J., *The Blood of the Vikings* (Hodder & Stoughton, 2001). Stenton, F., 'The Danes in England', *Proceedings of the British Academy*, 13 (1927) is the classic statement on the settlement thesis, while Sawyer, P., *The Age of the Vikings* (Edward Arnold, 1962) goes for the elite takeover view.

54. The evidence is mixed. A survey by *Britain's DNA* in 2014 indicated that the Viking impact was greater than people had thought from earlier surveys. Key findings from the research include that men from the Shetland (29.2 per cent) and Orkney (25.2 per cent) islands, heavily populated by the Northmen in the Viking Age, are most likely to have Viking in their bloodlines. South of the Scottish border, Yorkshire (5.6 per cent) and northern England (4 per cent) are the most prominent areas of the country for Norse Viking ancestry, with more than 300,000 northern men able to claim direct descent – accounting for almost a third of descendants. Further south, the percentage of Viking descendants dropped significantly, with South-West England being home to as few as 40,000 father-line descendants. Another survey by the Wellcome Trust in 2015 came to a different conclusion from the survey of 2014. The team analysed the genomes of 6,209 people from continental Europe to understand their ancestors' contributions to Britons' ancestry. This confirmed the flow of Anglo-Saxons from present-day Germany into Britain after the departure of the Romans in 410. They interbred with local residents instead of replacing them wholly, as some historians and archaeologists have suggested. Danish Vikings, who occupied Britain between the 700s and 1100s, in contrast, left little signature in most Britons' genomes.

55. Lang, J.T., 'The Hogback: a Viking colonial monument', *Anglo-Saxon Studies* 3 (1984), pp. 85–176.

56. Campbell, J., *The Anglo-Saxon State* (Hambledon, 2000); Wormald, P., '*Engla Land*: the making of an allegiance', *Journal of Historical Sociology* 7 (1994), pp. 1–24.

57. Molyneux, G., *The Formation of the English Kingdom in the Tenth Century* (2015).

58. Rees Davies, R., 'The Medieval State: The Tyranny of a Concept', *Journal of Historical Sociology* 16 (2003), pp. 280–300.

59. Marten, L., 'The Shiring of East Anglia', *Historical Research* (2008), 81, pp. 1–27.

60. Fletcher, R., *Bloodfeud: murder and revenge in Anglo-Saxon England* (Allen Lane, 2002), pp. 1–12.

61. Fletcher, *Bloodfeud: murder and revenge in Anglo-Saxon England*, pp. 1–12.

62. Freeman, E.A., *The History of the Norman Conquest of England: its causes and results* (1867), Vol. I, p. 1.

63. Carlyle, T., *History of Frederick the Great* (1858), p. 415.

CHAPTER 3: AN ENGLISH ARMY?

64. Freeman, E.A., *The History of the Norman Conquest of England: its causes and results* (1873), Vol. III, pp. 301–7.

65. Baxter, S., *The Earls of Mercia* (Oxford University Press, 2007) strongly criticizes the 'over-mighty subject' argument in Fleming, R., *Kings and Lords in Conquest England* (Cambridge University Press, 1991).

66. Stenton, F., *Anglo-Saxon England* (Clarendon Press, 1971), p. 579.

67. Sawyer, P., *The Wealth of Anglo-Saxon England* (2013).

68. Moore, R.I., *The First European Revolution c.975–1215* (2000).

69. John, E., *Reassessing Anglo-Saxon England* (Manchester University Press, 1996), pp. 175–7.

70. Barlow, F., *Edward the Confessor*, p. 214.

71. Kapelle, W., *Norman Conquest of the North* (Croom Helm, 1979), p. 98.

72. For a criticism of Kapelle, *see* Aird, W., 'St Cuthbert, the Scots and the Normans', *Anglo-Norman Studies XVI; Proceedings of the XVI Battle Conference on Anglo-Norman Studies* (1994), pp. 1–20. For the role of saints, especially St Columba, *see* Driscoll, S.T., *Alba: the Gaelic Kingdom of Scotland AD800–1124* (2002).

73. *Vita Wulfstani*, Winterbottom, M. & Thomson, K.M. (tr.) *William of Malmesbury: Saints Lives* (Clarendon Press, 2002), p. 57.

74. Herman of Bury St Edmunds, *Miracles of St Edmund in van Houts*, E.M. C. (tr.), *The Normans in Europe* (2000), p. 17.

75. Higham, N.J., 'Harold Godwinson: the Construction of Kingship', in Owen-Crocker, G.R. (ed.), *King Harold II and the Bayeux Tapestry* (Boydell Press, 2005), p. 31.

76. Stenton, F., *Anglo-Saxon England* (1973), p. 581.

77. Stenton, F., *Anglo-Saxon England* (1973), p. 589.

CHAPTER 4: DECONSTRUCTING THE ARMIES

78. Oman, C., *A History of the Art of War in the Middle Ages*, 2nd edn (Methuen, 1924), p. 165.

79. Fuller, J.F.C., *The Decisive Battles of the Western World, and their Influence upon History* (Eyre & Spottiswoode, 1954), I.374–82.

80. Brown, R.A., 'The Battle of Hastings', *Proceedings of the Battle Conference on Anglo-Norman Studies* 3 (1980), pp. 1–21.

81. Bartlett, R., *The Making of Europe: conquest, colonization and cultural change, 950–1350* (1993).

82. White, L., *Medieval Technology and Social Change* (Clarendon Press, 1964).

83. For Goltho, *see* Beresford, G., *Goltho: development of a medieval manor c.850–1150* (1987); for Sulgrave, *see* Davidson, B.K., 'Excavations at Sulgrave, Northamptonshire', *Archaeological Journal* CXXXIV (1977), pp. 105–114.

84. Williams, A., 'A bell-house and a *burh-geat*: lordly residences in England before the Conquest', *Medieval Knighthood IV: papers from the fifth Strawberry

Hill conference, Harper-Bill, C. & Harvey, R. (eds) (Boydell & Brewer, 1992), pp. 221–40.

85. Brown, R.A., *English Castles*, 3rd rev edn (Batsford, 1976).

86. Douglas, D.C., 'Companions of the Conqueror', *History* 28, No. 108 (1943), pp. 129–47.

87. Bachrach, B., 'Some aspects of the military administration of the Norman Conquest', *Anglo-Norman Studies* 8 (1986), pp. 1–26.

88. Verbruggen, J.F., 'The Role of Cavalry in Medieval Warfare', *Journal of Medieval History* 3 (2005), pp. 49–71.

89. Gillingham, J., 'William the Bastard at War', in Harper-Bill, C., *et al.* (eds), *Studies in Medieval History Presented to R. Allen Brown*, pp. 141–58.

90. Haskins, C.H., *Norman Institutions* (Harvard University Press, 1918).

91. Chibnall, M., 'Military Service in Normandy before 1066', *Anglo-Norman Studies* 5 (1982), pp. 65–77.

92. Strickland, M., *War and Chivalry: the conduct and perception of war in England and Normandy 1066–1217* (Cambridge University Press, 1996), pp. 1–7.

93. Körner, S., *The Battle of Hastings, England and Europe 1035–1066*, pp. 218–37.

94. Abels, R., 'Bookland and *Fyrd* Service in Late Anglo-Saxon England', *Anglo-Norman Studies* 7 (1984), pp. 1–25.

95. Hollister, C.W., *Anglo-Norman Military Institutions* (1962), pp. 174–8.

96. Gillingham, J., 'Thegns and Knights in Eleventh Century England: who then was the gentleman?' *Transactions of the Royal Historical Society* 5 (1995), pp. 129–53.

97. Howarth, D., *1066: The Year of Conquest* (Penguin, 1981), p. 80.

98. Poyntz Wright, P., *Hastings* (Windrush, 1996), p. 85.

99. Tetlow, E., *The Enigma of Hastings* (2008), p. 113.

100. Grehan, J. & Mace, M., *The Battle of Hastings 1066: the uncomfortable truth* (Pen & Sword, 2012), p. 46.

101. Hollister, *Anglo-Saxon Military Institutions*, pp. 12, 18.

102. Larson, L.M., *The King's Household in England before the Norman Conquest* (Madison, 1904).

103. '*Familie sue militibus quos lingua Danorum Housecarles vocant*', Osbern's account of the translation of Ælfheah's relics from London to Canterbury 8–11 June 1023 *Translatio Sancti Ælfegi Cantuariensis archiepiscopi et martiris*, in Alexander Rumble (ed.), *The Reign of Cnut: King of England, Denmark and Norway* (Leicester University Press, 1994), pp. 302–3.

104. Whitelock, Douglas, & Tucker, *The Anglo-Saxon Chronicle: A Revised Translation*, pp. 120–1.

105. Lewis, C.P., 'Danish Landowners in Wessex in 1066', in Lavelle, R. and Roffey, S. (eds), *Danes in Wessex: the Scandinavian impact on southern England c.800–c.1100* (Oxbow Books, 2016), pp. 172–211.

106. Stenton, F., *Anglo Saxon England* (1971).

107. Campbell, J., 'Agents and Agencies of the Late Anglo-Saxon State', in Campbell, J., *The Anglo-Saxon State*, p. 205.

108. Lavelle, R., *Alfred's Wars* (Boydell Press, 2012), p. 92.

109. Pierce, I., 'Arms, Armour and Warfare in the Eleventh Century', *Anglo-Norman Studies* 11 (1988), pp. 237–57.

110. Poyntz Wright, *Hastings*, p. 73.

111. van Houts, E.M.C., 'The Ship List of William the Conqueror', *Anglo-Norman Studies* 10 (1987), pp. 159–83.

112. France, J., *Victory in the East: a military history of the First Crusade* (Cambridge University Press, 1994), p. 71.

113. Glover, R., 'English Warfare in 1066', *English Historical Review* 67 (1952), pp. 1–18.

114. Brown, R.A., 'The Battle of Hastings', *Proceedings of the Battle Conference on Anglo-Norman Studies* 3 (1980), pp. 1–21.

115. Halsall, G., *Warfare and Society in the Barbarian West c.450–c.900* (Routledge, 2003), pp. 180–8.

116. Gravett, C., *Hastings 1066: the fall of Saxon England* (Osprey, 2000), pp. 30–1.

117. Davis, R.H.C., 'The Warhorses of the Normans', *Anglo-Norman Studies* x (1987), pp. 67–82.

118. Graham-Campbell, J., 'Anglo-Scandinavian Equestrian Equipment in Eleventh-Century England', *Anglo-Norman Studies* XIV (1991), pp. 77–90.

119. Robinson, P., 'Some Late Saxon Mounts from Wiltshire', *Wiltshire Archaeological and Natural History Magazine* 85 (1992), pp. 63–89.

120. Hollister, *Anglo-Saxon Military Institutions*, p. 140.

CHAPTER 5: RECONSTRUCTING THE BATTLE

121. Bradbury, J., *The Battle of Hastings* (Sutton, 1998), p. 124.

122. Brown, R.A., 'The Battle of Hastings', *Proceedings of the Battle Conference on Anglo-Norman Studies* 3 (1980), pp. 1–21.

123. Dominik, M., 'Holy War in *The Song of Roland*: the "mythification" of history', *SURJ: Stanford Undergraduate Research Journal* (2003), pp. 2–7.

124. Fletcher, R., *The Quest for El Cid* (Hutchinson, 1989).

125. Chibnall, M., *The World of Orderic Vitalis: Norman monks and Norman knights* (Boydell Press, 1984), pp. 204–5.

126. van Houts, E.M.C., *The Gesta Normannorum Ducum of William of Jumièges, Orderic Vitalis, and Robert of Torigni*, Vol. II (Clarendon Press, 1995).

127. Morillo, S., 'Hastings, an unusual battle', *The Haskins Society Journal* (1990), pp. 95–104.

128. Abels, R. & Morillo, S., 'A Lying Legacy? A preliminary discussion of images of antiquity and altered reality in medieval military history', *Journal of Medieval Military History* 3 (2005), pp. 1–13.

129. Lemmon, C.H., *The Field of Hastings* (Budd & Gillatt, 1956).

130. Bachrach, B., 'The Feigned Retreat at Hastings', *Medieval Studies* 33 (1971), pp. 344–7.

CHAPTER 6: THE ARROW IN THE EYE

131. Stenton, *Anglo-Saxon England*, p. 587.

132. Gibbs-Smith, C.H., 'Notes on the Plates', in Stenton, F. (ed.), *The Bayeux Tapestry: a comprehensive survey* (1957), pp. 162–76.

133. A random survey of some recent writing on Hastings shows that M.K. Lawson refuses to say one way or the other; Peter Pointz Wright does not credit

the arrow story at all; Jim Bradbury says in most likelihood he was, and that both figures are Harold; Chris Gravett says he was and both figures represent Harold. David Bernstein and Andrew Bridgeford both say that Harold was most definitely struck by an arrow. Martin Foys says that this was not the case. Eric John says that it is probable that Harold was struck in the eye.

134. The last scene of the tapestry was removed at some point, and the final current scene showing the English fleeing is largely a reconstruction.

135. Gibbs-Smith, C.H., 'The Death of Harold at the Battle of Hastings', *History Today* (1960) pp. 88–91.

136. Brooks, N. P. & Walker, H.E., 'The Authority and Interpretation of the Bayeux Tapestry', *Anglo-Norman Studies* I (1978), pp. 1–34.

137. Burgess, G.S. & van Houts, E.M.C., *The History of the Norman People: Wace's Roman de Rou* (Boydell Press, 2004), III.6985 p. 170.

138. 'HIC WILLELM DVX ALLOQVITVR SVIS MILITIBVS VT PREPARARENT SE VIRILITER ET SAPIENTER AD PRELIVM CONTRA ANGLORVM EXERCITV.' Note that in Latin inscriptions, it was traditional for 'U' to be rendered as a 'V'.

139. Orderic Vitalis *Ecclesiastical History* iv. 118: 'He was continually chided by many people, and was driven to embark on another crusade as much by fear as by shame. His wife Adela also frequently urged him to it, and between conjugal caresses (*amicabilis coniugii*) used to say, 'Far be it from you, my Lord, to lower yourself by enduring the scorn of such men as these for long. Remember the courage for which you were famous in your youth, and take up the arms of the glorious crusade for the sake of saving thousands, so that Christians may raise great thanksgiving all over the world, and the lot of the heathen may be terror and the public overthrow of their unholy law.'

140. Translation from van Houts, E.M.C., *The Normans in Europe* (Manchester University Press, 2000), pp. 125–8.

141. Shirely Ann Brown and Michael Herren argue strongly that Baudri had seen the tapestry: see Brown, S.A. & Herren, M.W., 'The Adelae Comitissae of Baudri of Bourgeoil', *Anglo-Norman Studies* 16 (1994), pp. 55–74.

142. Virgil *Aeneid*, 4.67–73. This is in the description of Dido's falling in love, where she flees like a wounded faun with a deadly shaft piercing her flank (*haeret lateri letalis harundo*), which parallels Baudri's comment on Harold (*Perforat Hairaldum casu latalis arundo*).

143. Brooks, N.P. & Walker, H.E., 'The Authority and Interpretation of the Bayeux Tapestry', *Anglo-Norman Studies* I (1978), pp. 1–34.

144. Richard Gameson, 'The Origin, Art and Message of the Bayeux Tapestry', in R. Gameson (ed.), *The Study of the Bayeux Tapestry* (Boydell Press, 1997), pp. 157–211.

145. Brooks & Walker, 'The Authority and Interpretation of the Bayeux Tapestry,' note 96.

146. Foys, M.K., 'Pulling the Arrow Out', in Foys, Overby & Terkla, *The Bayeux Tapestry: new intepretations*, pp. 166–7.

147. Dating evidence and discussion on Amatus' history comes from Dunbar, P. & Loud, G.A. (ed. & tr.), *Amatus of Montecassino: the history of the Normans* (Boydell Press, 2004), pp. 1–42.

148. Dunbar & Loud, p. 46.

149. Fouracre, P., *The Age of Charles Martel* (Longman, 2000), p. 85.

150. Davis, R.H.C., 'The *Carmen de Hastingae Proelio*', *English Historical Review* 93 (1978), pp. 241–61.

151. Barlow, F., *The Carmen de Hastingae Proelio of Guy, Bishop of Amiens* (Clarendon Press, 1999).

152. A full account of the history of the tapestry can be found in Brown, S.A. & Herren, M.W., *The Bayeux Tapestry, History and Bibliography* (1988).

153. Lawson, M.K., *The Battle of Hastings* (Tempus, 2002), pp. 228–9.

154. Bernstein, D., *The Mystery of the Bayeux Tapestry* (Weidenfeld & Nicolson, 1986), pp. 148–9.

155. David Bernstein, *The Mystery of the Bayeux Tapestry*, pp. 149–51.

156. Martin K. Foys, 'Pulling the Arrow Out', in Martin K. Foys, Karen Eileen Overby & Dan Terkla (eds), *The Bayeux Tapestry: New Intepretations* (2009), p. 169.

157. Andrew Bridgeford, 'Was Count Eustace II of Boulogne the patron of the Bayeux Tapestry?' *Journal of Medieval History* 25, Issue 3, September (1999), pp. 155–85.

158. Andrew Bridgeford, *1066: The Hidden History in the Bayeux Tapestry* (2004), pp. 191–9.

159. Bernstein, D., *The Mystery of the Bayeux Tapestry* (1986).

160. Bertelli, S., *The King's Body: sacred rituals of power in medieval and early Modern Europe* (Pennsylvania State University Press, 2001).

161. Marafioti, N., *The King's Body: burial and succession in late Anglo-Saxon England* (University of Toronto Press, 2014), pp. 233–4.

162. Marafioti. N., *op. cit.*

163. Garnett, G., *Conquered England: Kingship, Succession and Tenure 1066–1166* (Oxford University Press, 2007).

CHAPTER 7: THE LOST BATTLEFIELD

164. A good example is the Battle of Halidon Hill, which was fought to the north of Berwick-upon-Tweed in 1333 between the Scots army, under Sir Archibald Douglas, and the forces of King Edward III of England. There is an explanatory panel describing the outline of the battle at the roadside next to a hill, but there is no evidence that the battle was actually fought at that site, and there are several other possible locations.

165. 'Our target is to become completely self-funding by 2023. Our confidence in achieving this is based on our track record. During the past 10 years, our commercial income has doubled and we have raised nearly £60m in donated income.' http://www.english-heritage.org.uk/visit/places/1066-battle-of-hastings-abbey-and-battlefield/

166. Searle, D., *The Chronicle of Battle Abbey* (Clarendon Press, 1980).

167. Van Engen, J., 'The Christian Middle Ages as an Historiographical Problem', *The American Historical Review* 91, No. 3 (June, 1986), pp. 519–52.

168. Thomas, K., *Religion and the Decline of Magic* (New York, 1971), p. 50.

169. In Hobsbawm, E. & Ranger, T. (eds), *The Invention of Tradition* (Cambridge University Press, 1983), the authors explore the idea of traditions that 'appear or claim to be old [yet] are often quite recent in origin and sometimes invented',

(p. 1). Hobsbawm and Ranger argue that, as with the term 'propaganda', this concept is a phenomenon restricted to the modern world where social change was so rapid that traditions were invented that not only legitimized elite control, but provided a sense of stability for communities disoriented by what they were experiencing. As with propaganda, this stark contrast with the Middle Ages is actually based on a simplistic view of the period and thus it can, with care, be applied.

170. Bachrach, D.S., *Religion and the Conduct of War, c. 300–1215* (Boydell Press, 2003).

171. This view was expressed by Bonizo of Sutri in his *Ad Liber Amici*, Book IX, written *c.* 1085–6 in the context of Pope Gregory VII's feud with the Holy Roman Emperor Henry IV. Bonizo was seeking to support the actions of Gregory's most loyal secular supporter Margrave Matilda of Tuscany, who was a remarkable military leader operating in northern Italy during the late eleventh and early twelfth centuries.

172. Meens, R., *Penance in Medieval Europe 600–1200* (Cambridge University Press, 2014), pp. 140–89.

173. Douglas, D.C. & Greenaway, G.W., *English Historical Documents 1042–1189* II, no. 81 (Eyre & Spottiswoode, 1953), p. 606.

174. Austin, N., *Secrets of the Norman Invasion: discovery of the new Norman invasion and Battle of Hastings Site* (Ogmium Press, 2012).

175. 'Battle Abbey found in Crowhurst', *Bexhill on Sea Observer* (2 August 2013).

176. Porter, R., '"On the very spot": in defence of Battle', *English Heritage Historical Review* 7, Issue 1 (2012), pp. 4–17.

177. Hare, J.N., *Battle Abbey, the Eastern Range and the Excavations of 1978–80* (Historic Buildings and Monuments Commission for England, 1985).

178. For example, Mount Sinai: *see* Helms, M.W., 'Sacred Landscape and the Early Medieval European Cloister: unity, paradise, and the cosmic mountain', *Anthropos*, Bd. 97, H. 2. (2002), pp. 435–53.

179. Wightman, W. E., 'The Significance of "Waste" in the Yorkshire Domesday', *Northern History* 10 (1975), pp. 55–71.

180. *See* dispute between the northerners and Edward over the 1065 revolt against Tostig discussed in Chapter 3.

181. Baring, F.H., 'The Conqueror's Footprints in Domesday', *English Historical Review* 13 (1898), pp. 17–25.

182. Palmer, J.J.N., 'The Conqueror's Footprints in Domesday Book', in Ayton, A. and Price, J.L. (eds), *The Medieval Military Revolution* (St Martin's Press, 1998), pp. 23–4.

183. Bradbury, *The Battle of Hastings*, pp. 131–4.

184. Grehan, J. & Mace, M., *The Battle of Hastings 1066: the uncomfortable truth* (2012).

185. van Houts, E.M.C., *The Brevis Relatio de Guillelmo Nobilissimo Comite Normannorum, written by a monk of Battle Abbey*, Camden Fifth Series, 1997, Vol. 10, pp. 5–48.

186. Fagan, G.G., 'Far-Out Television', *Archaeology* 56, No. 3 (May/June 2003), pp. 45–50.

CHAPTER 8: LOCATING THE BATTLEFIELD

187. Hare, J.N., *Battle Abbey: the eastern range and the excavations of 1978–1980* (1985).

188. 'Battle of Lewes skeleton "dates from Norman Conquest"', press release by *Sussex Past* (14 May 2013).

189. 'Does this skull belong to a soldier of the Battle of Hastings?' *The Daily Mail* (22 May 2014).

190. *See* Cavill, P., 'The Place Name Debate', in Livingston, M. (ed.), *The Battle of Brunanburh: a casebook* (University of Exeter Press, 2011), pp. 327–50.

191. Foard, G. & Morris, R., *The Archaeology of English Battlefields: conflict in the pre-industrial landscape* (Council for British Archaeology, 2012), pp. 46–7.

192. Foard, G. & Partida, T., *Scotland's Historic Fields of Conflict: an assessment* (2005). The tone of the description is in no way influenced by the author's failure to win on the two occasions he has taken part.

193. Sutherland, T., 'Killing Time: Challenging the Common Perception of Three Medieval Conflicts: Ferrybridge, Dintingdale and Towton – "The Largest Battle on British Soil"', *Journal of Conflict Archaeology* 5 (2009), pp. 1–25.

194. Foard & Morris, *The Archaeology of English Battlefields: Conflict in the Pre-Industrial Landscape*, p. 109.

195. Fiorato, V., Boylston, A. & Knüsel, C., *Blood Red Roses: the archaeology of a mass grave from the Battle of Towton AD 1461* (Oxbow Books, 2000).

196. Foard & Morris, *The Archaeology of English Battlefields: Conflict in the Pre-Industrial Landscape*, pp. 7–36.

197. Sutherland, T., 'Battling for History: Topsoil – key battlefield layer', *British Archaeology Magazine*, Issue 79 (November 2004), p. 15.

198. Scott, D.D., Fox, R.A., Connor, M.A. & Harmon, D., *Archaeological Perspectives on the Battle of the Little Bighorn* (University of Oklahoma Press, 1989).

199. Scott, D.D., *Uncovering History: archaeological investigations at the Little Bighorn* (University of Oklahoma Press, 2013).

200. Wells, P., *The Battle that Stopped Rome: Emperor Augustus, Arminius, and the slaughter of the legions in the Teutoburg Forest* (2003).

201. Reddé, M. & von Schnurbein, S., *Alésia et la bataille du Teutoburg* (Thorbeck, 2008), pp. 175–6.

202. Clunn, T., *The Quest for the Lost Roman Legions: discovering the Varus battlefield* (Spellmount, 2005).

203. Rost, A., 'Characteristics of Ancient Battlefields: Battle of Varus (9 AD)', in Scott, D., Babits, L. and Haecker, Ch. (eds), *Fields of Conflict: battlefield archaeology from the Roman Empire to the Korean War. 1. Searching for war in the ancient and early modern world* (Potomac, 2006), pp. 50–7.

204. Sutherland, T. & Richardson, S., 'Arrows point to mass graves: the location of the dead from the Battle of Towton AD 1461', in Scott, D., Babits, L. & Haecker, Ch. (eds), *Fields of Conflict: battlefield archaeology from the Roman Empire to the Korean War. 1. Searching for war in the ancient and early modern world* (Potomac, 2006), pp. 160–73.

205. Fiorato, V., Boylston, A. & Knüsel, C., *Blood Red Roses: the archaeology of a mass grave from the Battle of Towton AD 1461* (2000).

206. Foard, G. & Morris, R., *The Archaeology of English Battlefields: conflict in the pre-industrial landscape* (2012).

207. Foard, G. & Curry, A., *Bosworth 1485: A Battlefield Rediscovered* (Oxbow Books, 2013).

208. Personal communication with Bosworth Heritage Centre.

209. 'Battle of Hastings "sequel" site found in North Devon', BBC News website (23 February 2016): http://www.bbc.co.uk/news/uk-england-devon-35633783.

210. Table adapted from Sutherland, T. & Holst, M., 'Battlefield Archaeology: a guide to the archaeology of conflict', 8 (2005), *BAJR Practical Guides*.

211. Reported by Glenn Foard in February 2017.

CHAPTER 9: MYTHOLOGIZING THE BATTLE

212. Keegan, J., *The Face of Battle* (1978), pp. 38–45.

213. Keegan, *op. cit.*, p. 45.

214. Brownlie, S., *Memory and Myths of the Norman Conquest* (2013), p. 132.

215. Samuel, R., *Theatres of Memory*, Vol. I (1994), p. 8.

216. Ben-Yehuda, N., *Sacrificing the Truth: Archaeology and the Myth of Masada* (2002).

217. Bieber, F., 'Nationalist Mobilization and Stories of Serb Suffering: the Kosovo myth from 600th anniversary to the present', *Rethinking History* 6 (1), April 2002, pp. 95–110.

218. Margalit, A., *The Ethics of Memory* (Harvard University Press, 2002), p. 97.

219. Margalit, *op. cit.*, p. 97.

220. Hardin, R., 'Social Identity', in Smelser, N. & Baltes, P. (eds), *International Encyclopedia of the Social & Behavioral Sciences*, Vol. 1 (University of Michigan Press, 2001), pp. 7166–170.

221. West, E., 'The Normans were the original liberal metropolitan elite "Remainers"', *The Spectator* (14 October 2016).

222. Hannan, D., 'The Norman Conquest was a disaster for England. We should celebrate Naseby, not Hastings', *Daily Telegraph* (14 October 2016).

223. Lee, S., 'Brexit Britain is desperate for a decent genesis myth', *The Guardian* (30 October 2016).

224. Phillips, R., *History Teaching, Nationhood and the National Curriculum* (1998).

225. Chibnall, M., *The Debate on the Norman Conquest* (1999), pp. 54–55.

226. Freeman, E.A., *The History of the Norman Conquest, its Causes and Results*, Vol. III, pp. 301–7.

227. Round, J.H., 'Mr. Freeman and the Battle of Hastings', in Round, J.H., *Feudal England* (Sonnenschein & Co., 1895), p. 394.

228. Gardiner, M., 'A review of the '"Secrets of the Norman Invasion"', A report on behalf of the Highways Agency (South-East region) (1994).

229. Garnett, *Conquered England: kingship, succession and tenure 1066–1166*, pp. 1–44.

230. van Houts, E.M.C., 'The Memory of 1066 in Written and Oral Traditions', *ANS* xix (1997), pp. 167–79.

231. van Houts, *op. cit.*, pp. 167–79.

232. de Gray Birch, W. (ed. & tr.), *Vita Haroldi: the romance of the life of Harold, king of England: from the unique manuscript in the British Museum* (1885).

233. Ashe, L., 'Mutatio dexteræ Excelsi: Narratives of Transformation after the Conquest' *The Journal of English and Germanic Philology* 110, No. 2 (April 2011), pp. 141–172.

234. 'King Harold "may have survived Battle of Hastings" claim', BBC News website (14th October 2014): http://www.bbc.co.uk/news/uk-england-sussex-29612656.

Bibliography

PRIMARY SOURCES
English Historical Documents
Douglas, D.C. & Greenaway, G.W., *English Historical Documents 1042–1189*, Vol. II (Eyre & Spottiswoode, 1953)

Anglo-Saxon Chronicle
Whitelock, D., Douglas, D.C., Tucker, S. (eds), *The Anglo-Saxon Chronicle: A Revised Translation* (Eyre and Spottiswoode, 1961)

Battle Abbey Chronicle
Searle, D. (ed. & tr.), *The Chronicle of Battle Abbey* (Clarendon Press, 1980)

Bayeux Tapestry
Foys, M.K., The Bayeux Tapestry Digital Edition (Scholarly Digital Editions, 2003)

Brevis Relatio
van Houts, E.M.C. (tr.), *The Brevis Relatio de Guillelmo Nobilissimo Comite Normannorum, written by a monk of Battle Abbey*, Camden Fifth Series, 1997, Vol. 10, pp. 5–48

Carmen de Hastingae Proelio
Morton, C. & Muntz, H., *The Carmen de Hastingae Proelio of Guy, Bishop of Amiens* (Clarendon Press, 1972)
Barlow, F., *The Carmen de Hastingae Proelio of Guy, Bishop of Amiens* (Clarendon Press, 1999)

Eadmer
Bosanquet, G. (tr.), *Eadmer's History of Recent Events in England* (Cresset Press, 1964)

Henry of Huntingdon
Greenway, D.E. (tr.), *The History of the English People, 1000–1154* (Oxford University Press, 2002)

John of Worcester
Darlington, R.R. & McGurk, P. (eds), Bray, J. & McGurk, P. (tr.), *The Chronicle of John of Worcester* (Clarendon Press, 1995)

Orderic Vitalis
Chibnall, M., *The Ecclesiastical History of Orderic Vitalis*, 6 vols (Clarendon Press, 1969–80)

Symeon of Durham
Rollason, D.W. (tr.) *A Tract on the origins and progress of this the Church of Durham* (Clarendon Press, 2000)

Vita Ædwardi
Barlow, F. (tr.), *The Life of King Edward who rests at Westminster*, 2nd edn (Clarendon Press, 1992)

Wace
Burgess, G. S. & van Houts, E.M.C., *The History of the Norman People: Wace's Roman de Rou* (Boydell Press, 2004)

William of Jumièges
van Houts, E.M.C. (tr.), *The Gesta Normannorum Ducum of William of Jumièges, Orderic Vitalis, and Robert of Torigni*, Vol. II (Clarendon Press, 1995)

William of Malmesbury
Mynors, R.A.B. (tr.), *Gesta regum anglorum* (Clarendon Press, 1999)
Winterbottom, M. & K.M. Thomson, (tr.), *Vita Wulfstani: Saints Lives* (Clarendon Press, 2002)

William of Poitiers
Davis, R.H.C. (tr.), *Gesta Guillelmi of William of Poitiers* (Clarendon Press: Oxford, 1998)

SECONDARY WORKS
Abels, R., 'Bookland and Fyrd Service in Late Anglo-Saxon England', *Anglo-Norman Studies* 7 (1984), pp. 1–25
Abels, R. & Morillo, S., 'A Lying Legacy? A preliminary discussion of images of antiquity and altered reality in medieval military history', *Journal of Medieval Military History* (2005), pp. 1–13
Aird, W., 'St Cuthbert, the Scots and the Normans', *Anglo-Norman Studies XVI; Proceedings of the XVI Battle Conference on Anglo-Norman Studies* (1994), pp. 1–20
Anderson, B., *Imagined Communities*, rev. edn (Verso, 2003)
Austin, N., *Secrets of the Norman Invasion: discovery of the new Norman invasion and Battle of Hastings site*, 2nd rev. edn (Ogmium Press, 2012)
Bachrach, B., 'The Feigned Retreat at Hastings', *Medieval Studies* 33 (1971), pp. 344–7
Bachrach, B., 'Some aspects of the military administration of the Norman Conquest', *Anglo-Norman Studies* 8 (1986), pp. 1–26
Bachrach, D.S., *Religion and the Conduct of War, c. 300–1215* (Boydell Press, 2003)

Baring, F.H., 'The Conqueror's Footprints in Domesday', *English Historical Review* 13 (1898), pp. 17–25

Barlow, F., *Edward the Confessor*, new edn (Yale University Press, 1997)

Bartlett, R., *The Making of Europe: conquest, colonization and cultural change, 950–1350* (Allen Lane, 1993)

Baxter, S., *The Earls of Mercia* (Oxford University Press, 2007)

Baxter, S., 'Edward the Confessor and the Succession Question', in Mortimer, R. (ed.), *Edward the Confessor, The Man and the Legend* (Boydell Press, 2009)

Baylé, M., 'Norman Architecture around the year 1000: its place in the art of Western Europe', *Anglo-Norman Studies* XXII (1999), pp. 1–28

Bennett, M., 'Poetry as history? The Roman de Rou of Wace as a source for the Norman Conquest', *Anglo-Norman Studies* 5 (1983)

Beresford, G., *Goltho: development of a medieval manor c.850–1150* (English Heritage, 1987)

Bernstein, D., *The Mystery of the Bayeux Tapestry* (Weidenfeld & Nicolson, 1986)

Bertelli, Sergio, *The King's Body: sacred rituals of power in medieval and early Modern Europe*, rev. & enlarged edn (Pennsylvania State University Press, 2001)

Bradbury, J., *The Battle of Hastings*, new edn (Sutton, 2005)

Breuilly, J., 'Dating the Nation: How Old is an Old Nation?', in Ichijo, A. & Uzelac, G. (eds), *When is the Nation: Towards an Understanding of Theories of Nationalism* (Routledge, 2005)

Bridgeford, A., 'Was Count Eustace II of Boulogne the Patron of the Bayeux Tapestry?' *Journal of Medieval History* 25, Issue 3, September (1999), pp. 155–85

Bridgeford, A., *1066: The Hidden History in the Bayeux Tapestry* (Walker, 2004)

Brooks, N.P. & Walker, H.E., 'The Authority and Interpretation of the Bayeux Tapestry', *Anglo-Norman Studies* I (1978), pp. 1–34

Brown, R.A., *English Castles*, 3rd rev. edn (Batsford, 1976)

Brown, R.A., 'The Battle of Hastings', *Proceedings of the Battle Conference on Anglo-Norman Studies*, 3 (1980), pp. 1–21

Brown, S.A. & Herren, M.W., *The Bayeux Tapestry, History and Bibliography* (Boydell, 1988)

Brown, S.A. & Herren, M.W., 'The *Adelae Comitissae* of Baudri of Bourgeoil', *Anglo-Norman Studies* 16 (1994), pp. 55–74

Brownlie, S., *Memory and Myths of the Norman Conquest* (Boydell Press, 2013)

Campbell, J., *The Anglo-Saxon State* (Hambledon, 2000)

Carlson, D.R., *John Gower: poetry and propaganda in fourteenth-century England* (Boydell & Brewer, 2012)

Cavill, P., 'The Place Name Debate', in Livingston, M. (ed.), *The Battle of Brunanburh: a casebook* (University of Exeter Press, 2011)

Chibnall, M., 'Military Service in Normandy before 1066', *Anglo-Norman Studies* 5 (1982)

Chibnall, M., *The World of Orderic Vitalis: Norman monks and Norman knights* (Boydell Press, 1996)

Chibnall, M., *The Debate on the Norman Conquest* (Manchester University Press, 1999)

Clark, M.D.H., *Augustus, First Roman Emperor: Power, Propaganda and the Politics of Survival: Power and Propaganda in Augustan Rome* (Bristol Phoenix Press, 2010)

Clunn, T., *The Quest for the Lost Roman Legions: discovering the Varus battlefield* (Spellmount, 2005)

Cowdrey, H.E.J., *Pope Gregory VII* (Clarendon Press, 1998)

Crisp, C., 'Hastings and Jerusalem', *The Coat of Arms* 1 (1975)

Crouch, D., *The Image of the Aristocracy in Britain 1000–1300* (Routledge, 1992)

Daniell, C., *From Norman Conquest to Magna Carta: England 1066–1215* (Routledge, 2003)

Davidson, B.K., 'Excavations at Sulgrave, Northamptonshire', *Archaeological Journal* CXXXIV (1977), pp. 105–14

Davis, R.H.C., 'The *Carmen* de *Hastingae* Proelio', *English Historical Review* 93 (1978), pp. 241–61

Davis, R.H.C., 'The Warhorses of the Normans', *Anglo-Norman Studies* x (1987), pp. 67–82

Dominik, M., 'Holy War in The Song of Roland: the "mythification" of history,' SURJ: *Stanford Undergraduate Research Journal* (2003), pp. 2–7

Douglas, D.C., 'Companions of the Conqueror', *History* 28, No. 108 (1943), pp. 129–47

Douglas, D.C., *William the Conqueror* (Yale University Press, 1964)

Douglas, D.C., *William the Conqueror: the Norman impact upon England* (Yale University Press, 1999)

Driscoll, S.T., *Alba: the Gaelic Kingdom of Scotland AD800–1124* (Historic Scotland, 2002)

Dudley, L., *Information Revolutions in the History of the West* (Edward Elgar, 2008)

Dunbar, P. & Loud, G.A. (ed. & tr.), *Amatus of Montecassino: the history of the Normans* (Boydell Press, 2004)

Van Engen, J., 'The Christian Middle Ages as an Historiographical Problem', *The American Historical Review* 91, No. 3 (June, 1986), pp. 519–52

Fagan, G.G., 'Far-Out Television', *Archaeology* 56, No. 3 (May/June 2003), pp. 45–50

Fiorato, V., Boylston, A. & Knüsel, C. (eds), *Blood Red Roses: the archaeology of a mass grave from the Battle of Towton AD 1461*, 2nd rev. edn (Oxbow Books, 2007)

Fleming, R., *Kings and Lords in Conquest England* (Cambridge University Press, 1991)

Fletcher, R., *The Quest for El Cid* (Hutchinson, 1989)

Fletcher, R., *Bloodfeud: murder and revenge in Anglo-Saxon England* (Allen Lane, 2002)

Foard, G. & Partida, T., *Scotland's Historic Fields of Conflict: an assessment* (Historic Scotland, 2005)

Foard, G. & Morris, R., *The Archaeology of English Battlefields: conflict in the pre-industrial landscape* (Council for British Archaeology, 2012)

Foard, G. & Curry, A., *Bosworth 1485: a battlefield rediscovered* (Oxbow Books, 2013)

France, J., *Victory in the East: a military history of the First Crusade* (Cambridge University Press, 1994)

Foot, S., 'The Making of *Angelcynn*: English identity before the Norman Conquest', *Transactions of the Royal Historical Society* 6 (1996), pp. 25–49

Fouracre, P., *The Age of Charles Martel* (Longman, 2000)

Foys, M.K., Overbey, K.E. & Terkla, D. (eds), *The Bayeux Tapestry: new interpretations* (Boydell Press, 2009)

Freeman, E.A., *The History of the Norman Conquest of England: its causes and results*, Vol. III (Clarendon Press, 1873)

Fuller, J.F.C., *The Decisive Battles of the Western World, and their Influence upon History*, Vol. 1 (Eyre & Spottiswoode, 1954)

Gameson, R. (ed.), *The Study of the Bayeux Tapestry* (Boydell Press, 1997)

Gardiner, M., 'A review of the Secrets of the Norman Invasion', A Report on behalf of the Highways Agency (South-East Region) (1994)

Garnett, G., *Conquered England: kingship, succession and tenure 1066–1166* (Oxford University Press, 2007)

Gat, A., *Nations: the long history and deep roots of political ethnicity and nationalism* (Cambridge University Press, 2013)

Gellner, E., *Nations and Nationalism* (Blackwell, 1983)

Gibbs-Smith, C.H., 'The Death of Harold at the Battle of Hastings', *History Today* X (1960), pp. 88–91

Gillingham, J., 'William the Bastard at War', in Harper-Bill, C., *et al.* (eds.) *Studies in Medieval History Presented to R. Allen Brown* (Boydell Press, 1989), pp. 141–58

Gillingham, John; 'Thegns and Knights in Eleventh Century England: who then was the gentleman?' *Transactions of the Royal Historical Society* 5 (1995), pp. 129–53

Glassner, J.-J., *Mesopotamian Chronicles* (Society of Biblical Literature, 2004)

Glover, R., 'English Warfare in 1066', *English Historical Review* 67 (1952), pp. 1–18

Graham-Campbell, J., 'Anglo-Scandinavian Equestrian Equipment in Eleventh-Century England', *Anglo-Norman Studies* XIV (1991), pp. 77–90

Gravett, C., *Hastings 1066: the fall of Saxon England* (Osprey, 2000)

Grehan, J. & Mace, M., *The Battle of Hastings 1066: the uncomfortable truth* (Pen & Sword, 2012)

Grierson, P., 'A visit of Earl Harold to Flanders in 1056', *English Historical Review*, LI (1936), pp. 90–7

Habermas, J., *The Structural Transformation of the Public Sphere: an inquiry into a category of bourgeois society* (Polity Press, 1989)

Halsall, G., *Warfare and Society in the Barbarian West c.450 – c.900* (Routledge, 2003)

Hardin, R., 'Social Identity', in Smelser, N. & Baltes, P. (eds), *International Encyclopedia of the Social & Behavioral Sciences*, Vol. 1 (University of Michigan Press, 2001), pp. 7166–170

Hare, J.N., *Battle Abbey, the Eastern Range and the Excavations of 1978–80* (Historic Buildings and Monuments Commission for England, 1985)

Haskins, C.H., *Norman Institutions* (Harvard University Press, 1918)

Helms, M.W., 'Sacred Landscape and the Early Medieval European Cloister: unity, paradise, and the cosmic mountain', *Anthropos*, Bd. 97, H. 2. (2002), pp. 435–53

Higham, N.J., 'Harold Godwinson: the construction of kingship', in Owen-Crocker, G.R. (ed.), *King Harold II and the Bayeux Tapestry* (Boydell Press, 2005)

Higham, N.J. & Ryan, M., *The Anglo-Saxon World* (Yale University Press, 2015)

Hobsbawm, E. & Ranger, T. (eds), *The Invention of Tradition* (Cambridge University Press, 1983)

Hollister, C.W., *Anglo-Norman Military Institutions* (Clarendon Press, 1962)

van Houts, E.M.C., 'The Ship List of William the Conqueror', *Anglo-Norman Studies* 10 (1987), pp. 159–83

van Houts, E.M.C., 'The Memory of 1066 in Written and Oral Traditions', *Anglo-Norman Studies* 19 (1997), pp. 167–79

van Houts, E.M.C., *The Normans in Europe* (Manchester University Press, 2000)

Howarth, D., *1066: The Year of Conquest* (Penguin, 1981)

John, E., 'Edward the Confessor and the Norman Succession', *The English Historical Review* 94, No. 371 (Apr., 1979), pp. 241–67

John, E., *Reassessing Anglo-Saxon England* (Manchester University Press, 1996)

Jowett, G. & O'Donnell, V., *Propaganda and Persuasion*, 4th edn (Sage, 2006)

Kapelle, W., *Norman Conquest of the North* (Croom Helm, 1979)

Körner, S., *The Battle of Hastings, England and Europe, 1035–1066* (CWK Gleerup, 1964)

Lang, J.T.; 'The Hogback: a Viking colonial monument', *Anglo-Saxon Studies* 3 (1984), pp. 85–176

Larson, L.M., *The King's Household in England before the Norman Conquest* (Madison, 1904)

Lavelle, R., *Alfred's Wars* (Boydell Press, 2012)

Lawson, M.K., *The Battle of Hastings* (Tempus, 2002)

Lemmon, C.H., *The Field of Hastings* (Budd & Gillatt, 1956)

Lewis, C.P., 'Danish Landowners in Wessex in 1066', in Lavelle, R. & Roffey S. (eds), *Danes in Wessex: the Scandinavian impact on southern England c.800–c.1100* (Oxbow Books, 2016), pp. 172–211

Lewis, M.J., Owen-Crocker, G.R. & Terkla, D. (eds), *The Bayeux Tapestry: new approaches: proceedings of a conference at the British Museum* (Oxbow Books, 2011)

Leyser, K., *Medieval Germany and its Neighbours 900–1250* (Hambledon Press, 1982)

Lifshitz, F., 'The *Encomium Emmae Reginae*: A Political Pamphlet of the Eleventh Century?' *Haskins Society Journal* 1 (1989), pp. 39–50

Marafioti, N., *The King's Body: burial and succession in late Anglo-Saxon England* (University of Toronto Press, 2014)

Margalit, A., *The Ethics of Memory* (Harvard University Press, 2002)

Marten, L., 'The Shiring of East Anglia', *Historical Research* (2008), 81

Meens, R., *Penance in Medieval Europe 600–1200* (Cambridge University Press, 2014)

Molyneux, G., *The Formation of the English Kingdom in the Tenth Century* (Oxford University Press, 2015)

Moore, R.I., *The First European Revolution c.975–1215* (Blackwell, 2000)

Morillo, S., 'Hastings: An Unusual Battle', *The Haskins Society Journal* 2 (1990), pp. 95–104.

Morillo, S., *The Battle of Hastings* (Boydell Press, 1996)

Morillo, S., 'Contrary Winds: Theories of History and the Limits of Sachkritik,' in Ragnow M., (ed.), *The Medieval Way of War Festschrift for Bernard Bachrach* (Ashgate, 2015)

Morton, C., 'Pope Alexander II and the Norman Conquest', *Latomus* xxxiv (1975)

Oman, C., *A History of the Art of War in the Middle Ages*, 2nd edn (Methuen, 1924)

Palmer, J.J.N., 'The Conqueror's Footprints in Domesday Book', in Ayton, A. & Price, J.L. (eds), *The Medieval Military Revolution* (St Martin's Press, 1998), pp. 23–44

Pastan, E.C., White, S.D. & Gilbert, K. (eds), *The Bayeux Tapestry and its Contexts: a reassessment* (Boydell Press, 2014)

Pierce, I., 'Arms, Armour and Warfare in the Eleventh Century', *Anglo-Norman Studies* 11 (1988), pp. 237–57

Porter, R., '"On the very spot": in defence of Battle', *English Heritage Historical Review* 7, Issue 1 (2012), pp. 4–17

Poyntz Wright, P., *Hastings* (Windrush, 1996)

Reddé, M. & von Schnurbein, S., *Alésia et la bataille du Teutoburg* (Thorbecke, 2008)

Rees Davies, R., *The First English Empire: power and identities in the British Isles, 1093–1343* (Oxford University Press, 2000)

Rees Davies, R., 'The Medieval State: The Tyranny of a Concept', *Journal of Historical Sociology* 16 (2003), pp. 280–300

Richards, J., *The Blood of the Vikings* (Hodder and Stoughton, 2001)

Ritchie, R.L.G., *The Normans in Scotland* (Edinburgh University Press, 1954)

Robinson, P., 'Some Late Saxon Mounts from Wiltshire', *Wiltshire Archaeological and Natural History Magazine* 85 (1992), pp. 63–89

Rost, A.,'Characteristics of Ancient Battlefields: Battle of Varus (9 AD)', in Scott, D., Babits, L. & Haecker, Ch. (eds), *Fields of Conflict: battlefield archaeology from the Roman Empire to the Korean War. 1. Searching for war in the ancient and early modern world* (Potomac, 2006), pp. 50–7

Round, J.H., 'Mr. Freeman and the Battle of Hastings', in Round, J.H., *Feudal England Swan* (Sonnenschein & Co., 1895), pp. 258–305

Rumble, A. (ed.), *The Reign of Cnut: King of England, Denmark and Norway* (Leicester University Press, 1994)

Sawyer, P., *The Age of the Vikings* (Edward Arnold, 1962)

Sawyer, P., *The Wealth of Anglo-Saxon England* (Oxford University Press, 2013)

Scott, D.D., Fox, R.A., Connor, M.A. & Harmon, D., *Archaeological Perspectives on the Battle of the Little Bighorn* (University of Oklahoma Press, 1989)

Scott, D.D., *Uncovering History: archaeological investigations at the Little Bighorn* (University of Oklahoma Press, 2013)

Sharman, Ian, *News, Propaganda and Spin in Medieval England*, Vol. 1 (Dovecote Renaissance, 2000)

Smith, M.F., 'Archbishop Stigand and the Eye of the Needle', *Anglo Norman Studies* XVI (1993), pp. 199–220

Southern, R.W., *Western Society and the Church in the Middle Ages* (Penguin, 1970)

Stafford, P., *Unification & Conquest: a political & social history of England in the tenth & eleventh centuries* (Edward Arnold, 1989)

Stenton, F. (ed.), *The Bayeux Tapestry: a comprehensive survey* (Phaidon, 1957)

Stenton, F., 'The Danes in England', *Proceedings of the British Academy*, 13 (Oxford University Press, 1927)

Stenton, F., *Anglo-Saxon England*, 3rd edn (Clarendon Press, 1971)

Strickland, M., *War and Chivalry: the conduct and perception of war in England and Normandy 1066–1217* (Cambridge University Press, 1996)

Stroll, M., *Popes and Antipopes: the politics of eleventh-century Church reform* (Brill, 2011)

Sutherland, T., 'Battling for History: Topsoil – key battlefield layer', *British Archaeology Magazine*, Issue 79 (November 2004), p. 15

Sutherland, T. & Richardson, S., 'Arrows Point to Mass Graves: the location of the dead from the Battle of Towton AD 1461', in Scott, D.D., Babits, L. & Haecker, C. (eds), *Fields of Conflict: Battlefield Archaeology from the Roman Empire to the Korean War*, 1 (Potomac, 2006), pp. 160–73

Sutherland, T., 'Killing Time: Challenging the Common Perception of Three Medieval Conflicts: Ferrybridge, Dintingdale Towton – "The Largest Battle on British Soil"', *Journal of Conflict Archaeology* 5, (2009), pp. 1–25

Sutherland, T. & Holst, M., 'Battlefield Archaeology: a guide to the archaeology of conflict', 8 (2005), *BAJR Practical Guides*

Tetlow, E., *The Enigma of Hastings* (Westholme, 2008)

Thomas, K., *Religion and the Decline of Magic* (Scribner, 1971)

Tyerman, C., *God's War: A New History of the Crusades* (Penguin, 2007)

Verbruggen, J.F., 'The Role of Cavalry in Medieval Warfare', *Journal of Medieval History* 3 (2005), pp. 49–71

Vincent, N., *Belief and Culture in the Middle Ages: studies presented to Henry Mayr-Harting* (Oxford University Press, 2001)

Wells, P., *The Battle that Stopped Rome: Emperor Augustus, Arminius, and the slaughter of the legions in the Teutoburg Forest* (Norton, 2003)

White, L., *Medieval Technology and Social Change* (Clarendon Press, 1964)

Wightman, W.E., 'The Significance of "Waste" in the Yorkshire Domesday', *Northern History* 10 (1975), pp. 55–71

Williams, A., 'A bell-house and a *burh-geat*: lordly residences in England before the Conquest', *Medieval Knighthood IV: papers from the fifth Strawberry Hill conference*, Harper-Bill, C. and Harvey, R. (eds) (Boydell & Brewer, 1992), pp. 221–40

Wormald, P., 'Bede, the Bretwaldas and the origins of the *gens anglorum*', in Wormald, P. (ed.), *Ideal and Reality in the Frankish World* (Blackwell, 1983)

Wormald, P., '*Engla Land*: The Making of an Allegiance', *Journal of Historical Sociology*, 7 (1994)

Index